Recom...
COUNT...
West Coast

"Recommended Country Inns" Series

"The guidebooks in this new series of recommended country inns are sure winners. Personal visits have ensured accurate and scene-setting descriptions. These beckon the discriminating traveler to a variety of interesting lodgings."
—*Norman Strasma, publisher of* Inn Review *newsletter*

The "Recommended Country Inns" series is designed for the discriminating traveler who seeks the best in unique accommodations away from home.

From hundreds of inns personally visited and evaluated by the author, only the finest are described here. The inclusion of an inn is purely a personal decision on the part of the author; no one can pay or be paid to be in a Globe Pequot inn guide.

Organized for easy reference, these guides point you to just the kind of accommodations you are looking for: Comprehensive indexes by category provide listings of inns for romantic getaways, inns for the sports-minded, inns that serve gourmet meals . . . and more. State maps help you pinpoint the location of each inn, and detailed driving directions tell you how to get there.

Use these guidebooks with confidence. Allow each author to share his or her selections with you and then discover for yourself the country inn experience.

Editions available:
Recommended Country Inns
New England ● Mid-Atlantic and Chesapeake Region
The South ● The Midwest ● West Coast
Rocky Mountain Region ● Arizona, New Mexico, and Texas

Recommended
COUNTRY INNS
West Coast

California • Oregon • Washington

Second Edition

by Julianne Belote
illustrated by Olive Metcalf

A Voyager Book

The Globe Pequot Press

Chester, Connecticut

Library of Congress Cataloging-in-Publication Data

Belote, Julianne.
    Recommended country inns. West Coast : California, Oregon. Washington / by Julianne Belote : illustrated by Oliver Metcalf.— 2nd ed.
       p.   cm.—(The "Recommended country inns" series)
    Rev. ed. of: Guide to the recommended country inns of the West Coast. 1st ed. c1986.
     "A Voyager book."
     Includes index.
     ISBN 0–87106–629–7
       1. Hotels, taverns, etc.—California—Guide-books. 2. Hotels, taverns, etc.—Oregon—Guide-books. 3. Hotels, taverns, etc.— Washington (State)—Guide-books. I. Belote, Julianne. Guide to the recommended country inns of the West Coast. II. Title. III. Series.
TX907.3.C2B45   1989
647'.947901—dc 19   88-38126
                                                    CIP

Manufactured in the United States of America
Second Edition/Second Printing

Contents

Indexes

How This Guide Is Arranged

The inns are arranged by states in the following order: California, Oregon, and Washington. California inns are subdivided into six areas: Southern California, The Central Coast, The San Francisco Bay Area, The North Coast, The Wine Country, and The Mother Lode and Sierras.

Before each state and area is a map and index to the inns in that section, listed alphabetically by town. At the back of the guide is a complete index to all the inns in the book listed alphabetically by name. Additional indexes list inns by category.

The Abbreviations

EP: European Plan. Room without meals.

AP: American Plan. Room with all meals.

MAP: Modified American Plan. Room with breakfast and dinner.

J: means a personal comment from Julianne.

The ☞ inserted here and there is *not* a rating. It is merely a way of pointing out something outstanding, unusual, or most memorable about an inn.

No inn was charged to be in this guide. I visited all the inns included, as well as more than a hundred others that I did not choose. Obviously, things can change between my visit and the time you use the guide. But if you feel that I have steered you wrong, or if you have a comment, please write to Julianne Belote, The Globe Pequot Press, 138 West Main Street, Chester, Connecticut 06412.

Wayfaring at Country Inns:
Caveats and Considerations

You may not need a passport or shots, but inns can be foreign territory if you've not tried them, and a few ground rules are in order.

Caveats

Rates: They can change almost as fast as the sheets. I list the high–low range for two people *at the time I visited*. Many innkeepers have unadvertised off-season and mid-week rates, but you sometimes have to ask.

Reservations/Deposits: These are almost always a necessity. But even the most popular places have cancellations, and a last-minute telephone call or your name on a backup list can bring results. Policies vary, but you will likely be charged if you're a no-show or a last-minute cancellation.

Minimum Stay: A two- or three-night stay is commonly required over weekends and holidays. *Sometimes* you can negotiate this, if the traffic is slow.

Children/Pets: Most inns are not set up to deal with either. I specifically note it when the little nippers are welcome.

Credit Cards: Unless otherwise specified, most inns accept MasterCard and Visa.

Television/Air Conditioning/Telephone: Most inns do not have these facilities in the bedrooms, but I have noted when they do. You're supposed to be getting away from it all—remember?

Food: Small inns that serve meals usually have a limited menu. If you have a dietary request, inquire when you reserve.

Smoking: A majority of West Coast innkeepers prefer that their guests not smoke. I mention it when they are adamant.

Space: Pack lightly. The inn room with a place for long garment bags or a matched luggage set has eluded me.

Manners: At an inn, you're often a paying guest at someone's home. It is frowned upon to plop your bag down on Grandmother's prize quilt, monopolize the shared bathroom while you leisurely floss between your teeth, inhale all the sherry, or act silently superior at a common breakfast table.

Considerations

On the West Coast, at least, no one is certain what you mean when you talk about an inn. Inns snuggle uncertainly in a lodging land bordered by small hotels, motels, cabins, resorts, and homestays. We have only a few that serve meals beyond breakfast, and the emergence of urban inns rules out the strictly "country" definition. There are Old Guard innkeepers who insist that their profession is nothing less than the full-service nurturing of the wayfaring stranger and who scoff at the explosion of bed and breakfast establishments offering little more than a bed and a croissant but nevertheless calling themselves inns.

Let the innkeepers sort out the labels. My task is to acquaint you with a variety of hostelries up and down the West Coast that offer a level of individual decor not found at motels, an ambience cozier and more intimate than that found at a resort, innkeepers who treat you like their very special house guest, and homemade meals or knowledgeable pointers to the best food nearby.

These choices differ vastly from one another, from sleek urban digs to solitary island retreats. Each one has its own individual flavor. None is stamped out of a corporate room plan. There probably won't be a paper strip across the toilet or a chain lock for the door. You're likely to find a basket of fruit, a bouquet, a plate of freshly baked cookies, or a carafe of wine to greet you.

Not all of these lodgings will be your cup of tea. Even the best can disappoint, but keep a sour note in perspective. It does not signal the decline of civilization as we know it; it is the risk we take when we search for the noncommercial.

Unique lodgings are one of the last frontiers to explore. Dare a little! It can be exciting to check into a place where you don't know the floor plan and where someone may actually talk to you at breakfast!

At the best inns, when you bid an innkeeper goodbye, you leave feeling that you've made a friend whom you really must have to *your* place.

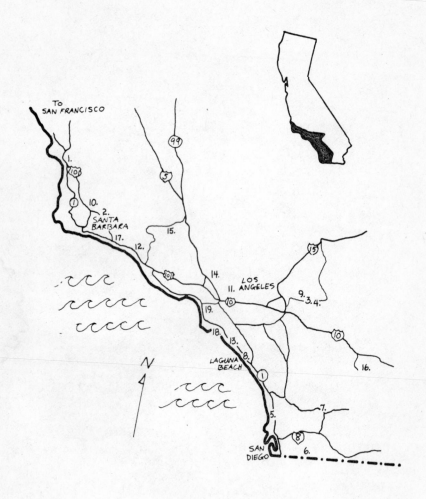

Southern California

Numbers on map refer to towns numbered below.

Olive Metcalf

Rose Victorian Inn
Arroyo Grande, California
93420

Innkeepers: Diana and Ross Cox
Address/Telephone: 789 Valley Road; (805) 481–5566.
Rooms: 8; 3 with private bath; 5 share 2 bathrooms.
Rates: $125 to $135, double occupancy; MAP. No smoking.
Open: All year, Thursday, Friday, Saturday, Sunday. Restaurant, wine bar.
Facilities and local attractions: Wedding, banquet facilities. Drive winding
back roads to wineries; 55 miles to Hearst Castle. San Luis Obispo
Mission, Mozart Festival in winter, Spring Fiesta.

When a four-story gingerbread Victorian house sits alone,
surrounded by acres of flat farmland, you notice it. When it's
painted four shades of pink—you can't miss it. The Rose Victorian
is that rare California phenomenon, a country inn with breakfast
and dinner included in the rate. It's a pleasant break in the long
drive on Highway 101 between Los Angeles and San Francisco: a
beautiful ☞ 1885 house surrounded by 200 rose bushes, with
authentic period furniture, good beds, and a first-rate restaurant.

The intensely pink exterior tended to have me guessing that
the inside would be doilies and kitsch. Wrong. The rooms are
tastefully decorated, blending some outstanding antique pieces
with comfortable, traditional sofas and chairs. Bouquets of fresh
roses, as well as good reading lights, are in every room.

At dinner we had two view choices: one to the green lawn with rose arbor and white gazebo (it's ☞ a wedding setting about as romantic as one could ask); the other to a large window looking into the kitchen where you can watch a ☞ talented kitchen staff do their thing. We chose the kitchen view. (Tell me, Dr. Ruth, is this an indication of complacency, or merely hunger?)

Smug San Franciscans and Angelinos who think only *their* cities have sophisticated cooking have a surprise in store. It was fun to watch the cooks in full-speed–dinner-hour action . . . and the results were outstanding. My baked halibut was moist and dressed with zippy, fresh salsa and sliced avocado. The traveler's companion had fork-tender veal, sautéed with wine, fresh thyme, and finished with cream. They also do fresh local salmon and an elegant albacore-scallop combination sautéed and finished with lemon, wine, and almonds. A mostly California wine list, much of it from the surrounding Central Coast wineries, was very fairly priced. A house specialty, ☞ peanut butter pie in a chocolate crumb crust, is so good, I regretted our decision to order one piece, two forks.

Breakfast is done elegantly. Inn guests gather around the dining room table for orange juice with champagne, sliced melons, hot orange muffins, and superior eggs Benedict, all served on delicate china.

How to get there: 200 miles north of Los Angeles, exit Highway 101 at Arroyo Grande. Turn left at stop sign (Fair Oaks). Go ¼ mile and turn left on Valley Road. Drive ¼ mile to the inn on your left.

J: *A splendidly ornate piano that belonged to General John Fremont sits in one of the parlors.*

Olive Metcalf

The Ballard Inn
Ballard, California
93463

Innkeeper: Beth Bryan, resident manager
Address/Telephone: 2436 Baseline; (805) 688–7770
Rooms: 15; all with private bath, some with fireplace.
Rates: $130 to $170, including full breakfast and afternnon tea.
Open: All year.
Facilities and local attractions: Accommodates business meetings, private
    parties. Groups reserving entire inn can arrange for other meals to be
    catered. Tour the many horse ranches and wineries in the valley.
    Good area for biking and hiking excursions. Picnic baskets available.
    Visit small towns in the valley: Buelton, Los Olivos, Santa Ynez,
    Solvang have shops, restaurants, galleries, and little theater. Nearby
    Lake Cachuma offers fishing, boating, and horseback riding. Gaviota
    State Park.

Beautiful Santa Ynez Valley is one of those treasured places
you don't just happen by; you have to want to get there. Its history
goes back to the Chumash Indians. The Ballard Inn's nineteenth-
century decor fits right in, but it is actually sparkling new with all
contemporary comforts. When you drive into Ballard, don't think
you've missed downtown—this is it. Eighty-one families comprise
the township, and the two-story gray-and-white inn is city center.

Rocking chairs and white wicker furniture decorate a broad porch that wraps around the inn. Roses and a white picket fence encircle it further.

The 🖝 generous size and elegance of the common rooms tell you this is an inn prepared for big parties and important business to take place. In this sleepy valley? Oh, yes. Wine makers, country-estate owners, farmers, and horse breeders have made this seemingly quiet countryside a productive (and wealthy) part of California. Resident Manager Beth Bryan would have you know that a very classy guest list of business people and celebrities have found their way to Ballard—but she's much to discreet to give any names.

Guest rooms are large, band-box neat, and mint fresh. (That's the payoff when you have a new inn that merely pretends to look old.) The appointments are all one could ask: soundprooof walls, individually controlled heating and air conditioning, and a large bath stocked with a basket of unique goodies like wine soap, wine hand lotion, and champagne shampoo. A welcoming basket of chocolate, cheese, fruit, and crackers is another treat.

Each room celebrates a person or quality in the valley's history. There's not a dreary one among them, but I was particularly taken with the Mountain Room decorated in rich dark green and earth tones. There is a brass-and-iron headboard, comfortable chairs before a fireplace, and a private balcony providing you a closer look at the magnificent mountains.

Not surprisingly, the inn is often used for business meetings and seminars. Ms. Bryan has lots of experience in covering the details of such events, from catering special lunches and dinners (when the entire inn has been reserved) to seeing that spouses are entertained. Any guests with the time have a good opportunity to explore some unique valley towns just minutes away. Solvang, the pseudo-Danish village, is quite a tourist lure, but Los Olivos is still in the early adolescence of cuteness. Its small shops and art galleries are fun to explore, and there are some delightful places to eat.

How to get there: For a beautiful winding drive from Santa Barbara, take Highway 154 north about 25 miles to Base Line Avenue and turn left. Proceed to the inn. Driving south on Highway 101, exit at Highway 154, proceed to Base Line Avenue, and turn right.

Olive Metcalf

Gold Mountain Manor
Big Bear City, California
92314

Innkeepers: Lynn Montgomery and Richard Kriegler; Trish Hastings, manager

Address/Telephone: 1117 Anita (mailing address: P.O. Box 2027); (714) 585–6997

Rooms: 7; 2 with private bath, 2 with half-bath, 2 large baths to be shared. All have wood-burning fireplace.

Rates: $65 to $150, including full breakfast. Two-night minimum on weekends. Ask about ski packages. No smoking; no pets; cannot accommodate children.

Facilities and local attractions: Pool table; computerized player piano. Woodsy setting to walk. Guest privileges for Big Bear Athletic Club. Skiing, fishing, boating, riding stables nearby. Mystery weekends arranged. Will cater small weddings, business seminars.

In the 1930s and 1940s, the kind of good-time players that are in *People* magazine today used to journey up the twisting mountain roads to this log mansion. Set 6,750 feet high in a grove of tall pine trees, rustic but comfortable, it was a favorite hideaway for the pre–jet set crowd from L.A.

World War Two gas rationing, waning popularity, and neglect inevitably took a toll, but new young owners with a creative flair began a restoration in 1985. I liked the looks of it as soon as I saw the broad green lawn in front dotted with Adirondack-style chairs and tubs of flowers. Emmy award–winning screen writer Montgomery and artist Kriegler appreciated the 1930s atmosphere and enhanced it with their decor and furniture choices. They may or may not be period pieces, but it all *looks* right for the house. There are big sofas and wingback chairs around a huge rock fireplace in the parlor. A wonderful looking 🖝 red-pine stairway goes from the parlor up to most of the bedrooms. A large playroom has a pool table, more comfortable seating, and a great selection of magazines.

There are nostalgic touches, too, like the Franklin stove that kept Clark Gable and his bride Carol Lombard cozy when they honeymooned at Big Bear. These are snuggly, colorful bedrooms, each with a wood-burning fireplace, puffy down comforter, a hodge-podge of antiques, lacy curtains, and Kriegler's painted stencil designs on ceilings and walls. One room is named for Clark Gable and one for that scamp, con-man, and mining baron, Lucky Baldwin. The Ted Ducey Room, named for one of the mountain's earliest settlers and a friend of the innkeepers, has its own Jacuzzi.

Breakfast began with juice and that European cereal favorite, muesli—only here it was cooked with brown sugar, chopped apples, and raisins. Pour a little cream on top and that's cereal! Then came blueberry muffins and an excellent crab quiche.

After all that it was time to move, and there are plenty of things to do around Big Bear. My breakfast companions were off to the stables for a ride in the woods. Winter skiing is a big attraction. Montgomery's writing talent makes her mystery weekends very special events.

How to get there: From San Bernardino take Highway 215 north to 30 east until it ends. Follow "Big Bear" signs to Highway 330 and continue 33 miles to Big Bear Dam. Stay left around dam 7 miles past Fawnskin. Turn left at Anita. Inn is on the left. Fly-in: Big Bear Airport.

Olive Metcalf

The Knickerbocker Mansion
Big Bear Lake, California
92315

Innkeeper: Phyllis Knight
Address/Telephone: 869 South Knickerbocker Road (mailing address: P.O. Box 3661); (714) 866–8221
Rooms: 4 in main house share 2 full baths. Large top-floor suite available for special occasions with lake view, Jacuzzi, television, VCR. Carriage House has 4 upstairs rooms with private bath; full suite downstairs sleeps 6 to 8. Some balcony rooms; all have television.
Rates: $75 to $110 including breakfast, afternoon refreshments, and Gramdma's Kitchen privileges. $20 each additional person. Two-night minimum on weekends. No smoking; no pets. Children by special arrangement.
Facilities and local attractions: Woodsy grounds; outdoor Jacuzzi. Nearby cross-country and downhill skiing; boating; fishing; riding stables. Facilities for weddings, small business seminars.

This is my idea of a perfect mountain retreat—a wonderful-looking log mansion sitting on two and a half acres of fir trees. It is a comfortable house for unwinding, where you can always find a quiet spot to be alone: in the large sitting room with upholstered

8

chairs and sofas, a fireplace, music, books . . . on one of the long covered porches extending from each floor of the house . . . in Grandma's Kitchen, where you're invited to help yourself to tea, coffee, and some baked treat . . . in the sunny old-fashioned dining room with individual tables and morning newspapers . . . on the back deck with a Jacuzzi . . . to the lawn and wooded area surrounding the house.

The bedrooms are cozy retreats, too, with patchwork quilts and comforters, thick towels, guest toiletries, and a television. From my Calico Room in the main house I sat out on the second-floor porch to watch a spectacular sunset. The Carriage House above the back lawn has a higher vantage over the lake. The rooms are slightly smaller here—but they all have private baths and a little balcony.

The rambling three-story house is only a quarter of a mile from the village of Big Bear Lake, so you can stroll down for the usual resort-community restaurants and shops or stay here quietly in the trees above it all. Jacuzzis work a therapeutic magic, it's true, but try a few hours in a ☞ big hammock looking out at the woods and breathing the scent of pine trees. I did, and it has my unqualified recommendation.

Owner Phyllis Knight can use her life experiences in real estate, family counseling, mothering, and entertaining to offer unusually ☞ interesting inn events. The "Lovers Only" weekends may sound terribly "California," but people love them. A certified body therapist instructs couples in how to help each other reduce stress. With the advantage of a 7,000-foot altitude and clean skies, the Knickerbocker's star parties are always booked ahead. An astronomer shows guests how to track the heavens with several telescopes set up outside. Mystery weekends, too, are popular but held irregularly, so ask to be on the list.

An excellent breakfast with a variety of fresh fruits, hot muffins, and an egg dish is served buffet style. You can eat in the dining room or take it to a sunny spot outdoors.

How to get there: Going east on Highway 210, pass San Bernardino Freeway to the Alabama cutoff and turn left. Continue to Highland and turn right; it becomes Highway 330. Proceed to Running Springs, where it becomes Highway 18. Continue into Big Bear Lake Village. When Highway 18 turns left, continue straight for 2 blocks to Knickerbocker. Turn right and proceed to the inn on the left.

Olive Metcalf

Rock Haus
Del Mar, California
92014

Innkeepers: Carol and Tom Hauser
Address/Telephone: 410 15th Street; (619) 481–3764.
Rooms: 10; 4 with private bath; 6 share 3 baths.
Rates: $75 to $135, including continental breakfast and late afternoon refreshment. Cannot accept children or pets; no smoking.
Open: All year.
Facilities and local attractions: Short walk to Del Mar shops, restaurants, beach; near Del Mar Race Track, Torrey Pines Golf Course/State Reserve.

This is one of those absolutely captivating inns you visit with enormous pleasure and contentment, then grumble on the way home, "Why can't we make *our* house look like that?"

You can, of course. Just start with an early California bungalow that's an historical landmark and ☞ overlooks the Pacific Ocean. Make sure it has a colorful past, as this one has: stately home of a land company executive; a dining room used for Catholic Mass by beach parishioners in 1911; gambling house in the roaring '20s; a boarding house, and hippie pad. Then do the extensive renovation houses with "colorful pasts" always require, and you'll be close, but not there.

You'll still need a Carol Hauser to do the decorating, because she does have a touch. Today, her sprawling house on a hill looks just the way a 1910 summer house should look. There's wicker and rattan, floral cotton comforters, and fresh flowers everywhere. It all looks light, cheerful, and clean.

First-floor bedrooms are especially comfortable with private baths and ☞ private entrances, and one has a fireplace. But upstairs you get the splendid ocean views.

We gave our room the tough Mother–Daughter Bunk-Together Test: Choose the smallest, least expensive room in the house to share, and see if somebody is snapping at somebody by morning. The Wren's Nest room was a total success—as serene to stay in as it is to look at. Its twin beds are dressed in crisp, pastel linens and big fluffy pillows; there's a *bright* reading light over each bed, and a wall of windows looking out at the ocean. Bathrooms are modern and so conveniently appointed that sharing was never a problem.

The broad, glassed-in sun porch is an inviting place to start your day with its clear view of the Pacific. Individual tables are set with teapots of fresh flowers, and newspapers, coffee, and tea wait on a sideboard. Carol or a helper brings in fresh fruit, juice, and just-made muffins. The staff enhances an already appealing breakfast atmosphere by scorning the easy jeans routine and wearing fresh, pretty outfits. It adds to a very pleasant breakfast. Just a block from the inn is a street of colorful restaurants, from small bistros and outdoor cafes to elegant eateries with ocean views.

How to get there: From Los Angeles on the San Diego Freeway, take Via de la Valle exit and head southwest along Jimmy Durante Boulevard to Del Mar Village. Turn left on Fifteenth Street to inn on the left at number 410. From San Diego, take Del Mar Heights exit off San Diego Freeway and go west to Camino Del Mar. Turn right, and at Fifteenth Street, turn right again.

Olive Metcalf

Brookside Farm
Dulzura, California
92017

Innkeepers: Judy and Edd Guishard
Address/Telephone: 1373 Marron Valley Road; (619) 468–3043.
Rooms: 7; 2 with private bath; 2 cottages with private bath.
Rates: $45 to $65, double occupancy, includes full breakfast. Weekend
   rates available with dinners. No children, pets, or cigars.
Open: All year.
Facilities and local attractions: Eat, sleep, sit by the stream. Hot tub under
   grape arbor, for the hyperactive.

Leading us into the old barn, Judy Guishard indicated a large,
unfinished room they use as a game room and where local
meetings are sometimes held. "And this," she said, "is the Dulzura
Convention Center."

Happily, both the Guishards possess a sense of humor plus
vision, and they have guests laughing with them over the tribu-
lations of renovation. But do look at their album of "before-
and-after" shots to appreciate the hard work it takes to renovate a
dilapidated building into the charming country inn so many of us
think we'd love to have. Even the real estate broker was doubtful
about selling them this 1928 farmhouse, fearing it might ruin their
friendship.

Judy and Edd's hard work has resulted in an unpretentious, rambling house where it's easy to feel utterly at home. A dining room and sunny living room have oversized Mexican bricks as flooring, covered with oriental rugs. A comfortable sofa and chairs, taped music, books, and a fireplace are inviting. Guest rooms are simply done in a fresh country style using quilts Judy has made.

Dulzura is a mountain community about ten miles from the Mexican border and thirty miles southeast of San Diego. Things got pretty exciting once about fifty years ago when big-gun Adolph Spreckles considered running his railroad through the town. But after his engineers decided it was too mountainous, the town returned to its natural pace.

When you have an urge to "get away from it all" and do nothing, this is the place: four rolling acres to stroll, fresh country air, a tree-shaded patio, and the only sound a bubbling stream. Tell your troubles to Emily, the current resident goat, or one of the pigs; they'll never disagree with you.

But my kind of quiet contemplation goes better with food, so it was good to learn that your stomach is not stranded in Dulzura. Edd is a chef, and besides serving a full breakfast, he'll do 🖙 dinners for guests on weekends by request. A succulently sauced loin of pork is typical, accompanied by a selection of Southern California's abundant fresh vegetables and fruits. The Guisards do not have a wine license, but guests are welcome to bring their own. The rest of the house is country charm, but Edd's new kitchen is strictly high-tech. There's first-rate equipment and space for the hands-on 🖙 cooking-class weekends Edd likes to host. Given his talent and easy humor, it sounds like fun.

How to get there: From San Diego, take Highway 94 1½ miles past the Dulzura Café. Turn right on Marron Valley Road. Inn is on the left.

☀

J: *Prices here aren't in the range of other inns with comparable pleasures simply because the world has not yet discovered Dulzura. Meanwhile, enjoy.*

olive Metcalf

Julian Gold Rush Hotel
Julian, California
92036

Innkeepers: Steve and Gig Ballinger
Address/Telephone: Box 856; (619) 765–0201.
Rooms: 18; 5 with private bath, 13 share 4 baths.
Rates: $55 to $135, including full breakfast. No pets. Children welcome
    weeknights.
Open: All year.
Facilities and local attractions: Walking, shopping, restaurants in historic
    Julian. Tour still-producing Eagle Mine. September Banjo and Fiddle
    Festival, fall Apple Festival, spring Wildflower Festival. Anza-Borrego
    Desert State Park; ☞ unique day trips arranged by innkeepers.

    Come to Julian for a scenic drive, the flavor of a gold rush
town, and for a stay in the ☞ oldest continuously operating hotel
in Southern California. You're 4,000 feet high in this back country
east of San Diego, and the ☞ air is pure and clear. In the fall
there's brisk weather that brings changing colors and an abundant
apple harvest.
    The entire town is an historic California landmark, but the
Julian Gold Rush Hotel is the sole survivor of the fifteen hotels it
had in its heyday at the turn of the century. It was known then as
"Queen of the Back Country," a luxury hotel boasting two
bathtubs and the "most modern mountain accommodations."

It was the remarkable achievement of a former slave, Albert Robinson, and his wife, Margaret, who built it in 1897. Albert planted the cedar and locust trees that encircle the hotel today. When the Butterfield Stage stopped here after its two-day journey from San Diego, Mrs. Robinson's cooking, especially her hot apple pie and bread, welcomed miners and travelers to the Southern Mother Lode.

The Ballingers are carrying on the Robinson tradition of hospitality and adding their personal country inn touches. They've decorated the lobby sitting room with big chairs, games and books, and an old Silvertone radio (masking a stereo) that will look familiar to anyone over the age of forty-five or fifty. Some evenings they play tapes of old-time radio shows.

The rooms all have a genuine American West feeling, simple and airy. If you arrive early enough in the afternoon, you're encouraged to peek into unoccupied rooms and choose the one that appeals to you most. Plaques on the doors bear the names of entries in the old guest register; U. S. Grant for one. Each room is decorated with authentic American antique pieces, without gimmicks or reproductions (except for a few light fixtures). Separate from the hotel are the Honeymoon Cottage, with a dressing room and fireplace, and a recently renovated Patio Cottage, with chairs on a veranda-style porch.

Guests are served a full, hearty breakfast on the patio in the summer: juice and fresh fruit, eggs Florentine, breads from Dudley's Bakery, and coffee and tea.

How to get there: From San Diego, take I–8 east to Highway 79. Turn north to Julian; about 1¾ hours from San Diego.

*

J: *My advice is to eat every bite of breakfast and then embark on one of Steve's well-researched day trips. This country is rich in Indian and gold rush history. Rolling hills and streams are at one turn, mountains at another, and . . . no smog, no freeways.*

Olive Metcalf

The Carriage House
Laguna Beach, California
92651

Innkeepers: Tom, Dee, and Vern Taylor
Address/Telephone: 1322 Catalina Street; (714) 494–8945.
Rooms: 6, all suites, with private bath, sitting room, and separate bedroom.
Rates: $85 to $125, double occupancy; $20 each additional person. No credit cards; no pets.
Open: All year.
Facilities and local attractions: Two blocks from the ocean, steps down to beach; walk to Pottery Shack; visit Laguna's art galleries, shops, restaurants. Bus stop on corner.

Instead of one of the large modern hotels on the waterfront, this might be just the secluded, pretty spot you're looking for from which to enjoy Laguna Beach. Cecil B. De Mille thought it was sweet enough to buy back in the '20s when Laguna was Hollywood's Riviera. It's now one of the town's designated historical landmarks, a charming old New Orleans–style house.

☞ Every room here is a suite with a sitting room and separate bedroom. Several have two bedrooms and a fully equipped kitchen. That kind of convenience and space is scarce anywhere; in a beach town it's rare; and done with antique charm and in a lush setting, it's almost unheard of.

Each room is decorated uniquely with antiques and memorabilia. There's Mandalay with a tropical, oriental theme in shades of coral and pink and with an ocean view. Primrose Lane has an English country feeling in yellow and deep blue. Green Palms is elegantly cool with white wicker furniture against emerald green carpet, and a bay window opens onto the courtyard. Whichever suite you have, you'll be welcomed with a bottle of California wine and fresh fruit.

All the rooms surround the quiet brick courtyard filled with tropical plants. There's a tiered fountain, chairs, and plenty of room to relax. If you don't take breakfast in the dining room, it's delightful to eat here beneath the hanging moss of a carrotwood tree. In addition to juice, fresh fruit, and cereals, there's always something hot from the oven—such as a coffee cake or muffins.

It's an ☞ easy walk to the beach from here, but for exploring more of Laguna Beach you'll appreciate the convenient bus stop on the corner.

How to get there: From the Pacific Coast Highway going through Laguna Beach, take Cress Street up the hill away from the ocean. Driving south, Cress is the first stoplight past the Pottery Shack. Inn is two blocks up on the corner of Catalina Street, number 1322.

Olive Metcalf

Casa Laguna Inn
Laguna Beach, California
92651

Innkeepers: Jerry and Luanne Siegel
Address/Telephone: 2510 South Coast Highway; (714) 494–2996.
Rooms: 20, including 1- and 2-bedroom suites and the Cottage; all with
    private bath and television.
Rates: $100 to $190, $15 for each additional person. Includes breakfast
    and afternoon refreshment. $15 per night discount October through
    May, Sunday through Thursday, excluding holidays. No pets.
Open: All year.
Facilities and local attractions: Pool, patios, and gardens with views of the
    Pacific; in-house library, TV. Walk to Victoria Beach; Laguna shops,
    galleries, restaurants.

Even local "Lagunatics" are reserving rooms at Casa Laguna
in order to see what's happened to their old landmark. It's always
had a ☞ Southern California Spanish glamour, but its recent
facelift has made it a more magical place than ever.

The original Mission House and Cottage were built in the
1930s as guest facilities for historic Villa Rockledge, the Frank
Miller (owner of the Riverside Mission Inn) estate across the street.
The Casitas, nineteen courtyard and balcony rooms and suites,
were added in the 1940s as the Laguna Beach art colony grew and
more visitors began coming.

18

This is a romantic inn of meandering brick paths, court-yards, and fountains. Colorful tiles, rock walls, even a bell tower, provide a fantasy retreat. In the complex of balconies and decks, plants, and flowers, there are many private little spots to relax, away from the bustle of Laguna at the height of the tourist season. There's also a cozy library for guests to use.

Every room is decorated uniquely with a blend of antiques and contemporary furnishings, and color television; and many have refrigerators. Some rooms open onto the flower-filled Spanish patio and pool; some have superb views of the ocean. Suites have well-equipped kitchens and deluxe space, especially the Cottage.

But charming facilities don't make an inn; it takes the fine old innkeeping tradition of pampering guests to do that, and you're on safe ground here. "Pleasing people is what it's all about," say the Siegels.

Attention to detail in every area keeps guests returning. The gardens are a labor of love for Luanne, while Jerry presides over the food service. Breakfast includes freshly squeezed juices, fresh fruits, cereals, a variety of nut breads and muffins, bagels and cream cheese, hard-boiled eggs, cinnamon Kona coffee, and many teas. Afternoon snacks include wine, lemonade from the inn's lemon tree, pates, and cheeses.

How to get there: On the east side of the Pacific Coast Highway, in the heart of Laguna Beach, number 2510. It's pink.

❋

J: *Sending an East Coast chum a color photograph of you in this patio some February—flowers, palms, pool, and blue Pacific in the background—would be cruelly insensitive. Do not do it.*

Olive Metcalf

Eiler's Inn
Laguna Beach, California
92651

Innkeepers: Annette and Henk Wirtz
Address/Telephone: 741 South Coast Highway; (714) 494–3004.
Rooms: 12, including 1 suite; all with private bath.
Rates: $100 to $165, double occupancy; $10 for each additional person;
$5 less for single; extended continental breakfast included.
Open: All year.
Facilities and local attractions: Swimming, sunning on Laguna Beach;
restaurants, art galleries, shops.

You can lose your heart when you walk through the cozy
entry lobby at Eiler's Inn into a central brick courtyard. It's a
beguiling, airy scene of plants and flowers around a tiered
fountain. Balcony rooms look down on round tables covered with
blue-and-white print tablecloths. At one end is a brick counter
where the breakfast buffet is set out: baskets of fresh fruit and hot
breads, juices, cereals, and boiled eggs.

Laguna Beach may be the essence of Southern California
beach towns, but Eiler's has a country French feeling. You'll notice
it at once in the two inviting parlors on either side of the entry.
One is a small library/den with books and a television. The other
is a pretty sitting room with a small blue-and-white patterned

wallpaper and a comfortable fat sofa and chairs. Afternoon wine and cheeses are served here or in the courtyard.

Some bedrooms are relatively small, but opening onto the courtyard or balcony above, as they do, gives them a pleasant openness. They're each furnished differently with antiques and especially colorful linens and comforters. You'll find fresh flowers, fruit, and candy in each room.

A suite upstairs has a fireplace. It's off a sun deck that is available to all guests. The ocean views are superb (you're right on the beach), and you can enjoy both sunning and sunsets without so much as a grain of sand between your toes.

You couldn't find a more secluded, romantic setting in Laguna Beach on a Saturday night than the courtyard. Aperitifs and classical guitar music are the perfect additions to this Southern California inn.

How to get there: On the South Coast Highway in the center of Laguna Beach, the inn is at number 741 on the ocean side.

❋

J: *I'm one who appreciates their complimentary tea and coffee available all day long, but the bottle of champagne you're presented at check-in is truly a sparkling extra.*

olive Metcalf

Bluebelle House
Lake Arrowhead, California
92352

Innkeepers: Rick and Lila Peiffer
Address/Telephone: 263 South State Highway 173 (mailing address: Box
    2177); (714) 336–3292
Rooms: 5; 3 with private bath; 2 share 1 bath.
Rates: $60 to $95, including expanded continental breakfast. Seasonal
    weekday discounts; two-night minimum weekends. No pets; no
    smoking.
Open: All year.
Facilities and local attractions: Two-tenths of a mile from mountain village
    shops, restaurants, entertainment; Lake Arrowhead beach, fishing
    and excursion boats. Winter sports within thirty minutes.

    Nestled in fir trees on the edge of a bustling mountain village,
Bluebelle House has a Swiss-Alpine feeling. Fresh air and recreation on Lake Arrowhead are attractions in summer; in winter,
skiing is less than thirty minutes away.

    Rick and Lila Peiffer's innkeeping style is to 🖝 lavish
hospitality and personal attention on their guests. The warmth of
their welcome says unmistakably that they're sincerely glad to see
you. And if you arrive after sundown, you'll be grateful for their
well-lighted parking area.

After your drive up the mountain, relax with late-afternoon refreshments on a ☞ large deck with the smell of fresh pine all around, or indoors beside a warm fire on crisp winter days. This is a good time to look at the Peiffers' menu collection from village restaurants and their "Things to Do in Lake Arrowhead" scrapbook. Rick and Lila have helpful suggestions and will make any reservations you need.

Bluebelle House reflects the talents and interests of both its innkeepers. Rick is a skilled carpenter and has redesigned or improved every corner of the chalet. Lila specializes in silk floral arrangements that she has designed for each room. Objects they've collected from their European holidays are everywhere. Some are outstanding, like a ☞ cuckoo clock in the parlor, and others are cheerful bric-a-brac. There are posters, prints, art objects, lace, and crocheted items. What is cheerful to some taste may be kitsch to others, but Lila puts it all together fetchingly, and the housekeeping is impeccable.

While two of the rooms on the main floor share one bathroom, each room has a ☞ lighted makeup vanity (More inns should think of this!). The largest room has two queen-sized beds and a spacious private bath with double sinks. Lila has decorated each room individually using patchwork quilts and ruffled spreads, chintz and lace curtains, pillows in velvet and eyelet, and romantic print wallpapers.

Breakfast appointments are as colorful as the decor: pretty china, linen, and crystal. Typical of the fare is fresh fruit and juice, homemade muffins, cinnamon rolls or bagels with cream cheese, hard-boiled eggs, and hot beverages.

How to get there: From San Bernardino, take Highway 18 to Lake Arrowhead turn-off, which is Highway 173. Follow signs to Lake Arrowhead. At the Village, turn right at the only stoplight. Continue ²/₁₀ mile to the inn on the right.

Olive Metcalf

Union Hotel
Los Alamos, California
93440

Innkeeper: Richard W. Langdon
Address/Telephone: 362 Bell Street (mailing address: Box 616); (805)
    928–3838 or (805) 344–2744
Rooms: 16; 3 with private bath, 13 with sink in room and shared bath.
Rates: $81 to $98, including full breakfast. Children discouraged.
Open: All year, Friday, Saturday, Sunday. Restaurant, saloon also available
    weekdays for private parties.
Facilities and local attractions: Swimming pool, Jacuzzi, pool table, table
    tennis, shuffleboard. Ride around Los Alamos in 1918 touring car.

Make no mistake about it, when you visit the Union Hotel you're in for a happening, not a quiet mountain reverie. Owner Dick Langdon keeps an entertaining place, particularly for special events. A wedding celebration was in preparation the morning we visited. Bridesmaids ran up and down the stairway, and the dining room was being set up for the wedding buffet. Out in the yard, the grape arbor and gazebo looked gala decorated with ribbons and flowers.

Langdon has a knack for turning every visit into an occasion. Being open only three days a week keeps it fun. Beyond that, says Langdon, it becomes work.

The hotel is his home, hobby, and occupation. Knowing this, you might feel it possibly rude to laugh when you walk in, but he's obviously decorated with just that reaction in mind. In the lobby you'll see red-flowered wallpaper, stuffed life-size fabric figures, and a copper bathtub in front of the fireplace. It's an astonishing collection of wonderful antique objects, like 200-year-old Egyptian burial urns and funky furniture. Langdon claims it's all a re-creation of the original 1880 hotel.

Upstairs is a parlor for overnight guests with pool table and an extensive library. Each bedroom is restored and furnished with brass fixtures, pedestal sinks, and a variety of china wash bowls and pitchers and handmade quilts. In Union Hotel lingo, a room with a shared bath is a dry room; a wet room has a private bath.

The saloon has a great Old West feeling. The doors came from a bordello, and the bar is about 150 years old. After 9 P.M., it's closed to everyone except hotel guests.

Family-style fare is featured in the large dining room. Platters of country-baked chicken and BBQ beef are the mainstays, along with soup, salad, corn bread and honey butter, potatoes, vegetables, and dessert.

The town of Los Alamos (it means "The Cottonwoods" in Spanish) is just a jog off Highway 101 and worth a stop for a look back at the West of the 1880s. The way to see it in style is from one of the original 1918 white touring cars that were made to replace stagecoaches for Yellowstone National Park touring.

How to get there: From Highway 101, exit at Los Alamos. Follow the road into town. Inn is on the right.

৵৹

J: *The town's telephone system is not quite as efficient as Wells Fargo was at delivering messages. Langdon hopes you'll keep trying when you call. It works . . . eventually.*

Eastlake Inn
Los Angeles, California
90026

Innkeepers: Murray Burns and Planaria Price
Address/Telephone: 1442 Kellam Avenue; (213) 250–1620
Rooms: 5 share 4 baths.
Rates: $50 to $99, including breakfast. Special packages available. No
  smoking.
Open: All year.
Facilities and local attractions: Minutes from central Los Angeles business
  district; walk to Dodger Stadium, Music Center, Olvera Street, the
  Old Plaza, Echo Park Lake. Weekend celebrations planned by
  innkeepers.

There is a Los Angeles lots of people don't know about:
gracious old neighborhoods, houses that have survived since the
1800s, and tree-shaded streets where you actually *walk* places.
Angelino Heights, the city's oldest suburb, is one of those areas
making a comeback, and the Eastlake Inn sits on a hill in this ☞
first L.A. Historic Preservation zone.

It was built in 1887 as a duplex. Both innkeepers have years
of historic preservation experience and have combined talents to
restore the Victorian. From the spacious living and dining room,
two stairways lead to the bedrooms upstairs. Two guest rooms are

large, one with white wicker and a fireplace, and one with a romantic queen canopy bed and a pink velvet "fainting couch." Two tiny rooms fine for a solo traveler are Tom Thumb and the completely redecorated Thumbelina. The latter now features an amazing trompe l'oeil painting (I love to write this phrase because I don't have the nerve to say it), creating the impression of an open door to a balcony overlooking a sea view. All of the rooms have antiques and curiosities of the period.

Amenities for the business traveler are thoughtful ones. Besides fresh flowers, fruit, and a robe in my room, I appreciated being asked how early I'd like my coffee and morning paper. When I said I'd be working at the inn a few hours before going out, Murray showed me to a small library with a desk. The sitting room would be just as quiet and pleasant for work, but you could easily be distracted with the stereopticon, jigsaw puzzles, old and new books, and the Victorian costumes from Planaria's collection.

After a day of business or touring, afternoon wine and cheese in this setting is a change that refreshes. Maybe you'll want to take in a night game at Dodger Stadium. No need to get out the car—just walk over.

The innkeepers' latest production is a landscaped garden and reception area featuring (remember, this is L.A.) a Greek Revival temple. Considering that you're right downtown, this is a wonderfully convenient and pretty wedding or party site.

Don't miss ☞ Carroll Avenue, just behind the inn. The contrast between its row of restored Victorian homes and the sight of modern downtown Los Angeles beyond is a pleasing one, especially at dusk when the lights are coming on.

How to get there: Drive north on the Hollywood Freeway; exit at Echo Park/Glendale Boulevard. Make hard right on Bellevue to first stop sign, left onto Edgeware, left at Carroll (to see the Victorian houses). Turn right on Douglas and go one block to Kellam. Turn left; inn is last house on left at 1442 Kellam.

❋

J: The ☞ *special adventures the innkeepers have devised, from hot-air ballooning to horse trail rides to a Mexican restaurant, are an easy way to have a razzle-dazzle time in Lotus Land.*

Olive Metcalf

Salisbury House
Los Angeles, California
90018

Innkeepers: Si and Alice Torvend
Address/Telephone: 2273 West 20th Street; (213) 737–7817
Rooms: 5, including an attic loft; 3 with private bath, 2 share large bath
   with tub and shower.
Rates: $60 to $75, double occupancy, includes full breakfast.
Open: All year.
Facilities and local attractions: Close to downtown Los Angeles, Convention
   Center; near freeways.

There's good news for travelers to downtown Los Angeles. Business people who never considered an inn are likely to reappraise their usual lodgings if they sample the comforts of Salisbury House. Not many hotel suites provide the ambience of leaded-glass windows, beamed ceilings, wood paneling, and a sitting room filled with antique pieces and cushy sofas and chairs.

This spacious 1909 California Craftsman house is in Arlington Heights, a quiet, residential neighborhood regaining its former elegance. It's an oasis after a day of city bustle, yet it's ☞ only minutes from the Convention Center and downtown businesses.

Since our last visit, new innkeepers are ruling the roost. Without making any drastic changes, the Torvends have been

28

gradually doing what all innkeepers must—putting their own stamp on the house. Their interests can be guessed by the remark a friend made to Alice. "All you do is put in more flowers and books!" I can't think of better additions. The cozy common room is even more relaxing now with classical music on the stereo and a collection of books on art, museums, and music.

Each of the five guest rooms has a different feeling. They're comfortable rooms, with good beds and reading lights, as well as having pretty linens, lace curtains, and ceiling fans. There's the Victorian Rose room and a sunny garden room with a collection of garden books. The paneled attic suite is 600 square feet of privacy and charm with an antique claw-foot tub, game table, king-sized bed, and pine walls and floors. On the landing at the top of the stairway is a stocked wine rack with glasses, a desk, and a telephone—all for guests to use.

In the morning, Si opens sliding wood-paneled doors and reveals the blue and white dining room with the table set for breakfast. At the sight of sparkling crystal and silver, fresh flowers, and pastel linen napkins on white lace, you're likely to wonder why you ever put up with a plastic hotel coffee shop.

Alice varies the breakfast buffet (as she does the table settings), but at our visit it held a bounty of mixed fresh fruits with praline cream, crepes Normandy, sausage, corn pudding, and boiled eggs in pretty blue-and-white egg cups.

How to get there: Take the Santa Monica Freeway (10) east to downtown. Go north on Western Avenue. Turn left onto West 20th Street; it's the first street. Inn is on your right at 2273 West 20th.

J: *Early-morning jamoca almond coffee or herb tea and the newspapers is a pretty civilized way to start the day while you await breakfast. And you said you were dreading L.A.?*

olive Metcalf

Terrace Manor
Los Angeles, California
90006

Innkeepers: Sandy and Shirley Spillman
Address/Telephone: 1353 Alvarado Terrace; (213) 381–1478
Rooms: 5; all with private bath.
Rates: $55 to $85, including full breakfast and afternoon wine. $20 for
each additional person. No children; no smoking.
Open: All year.
Facilities and local attractions: Inn is available for small parties and
meetings. Ample off-street parking. Excellent location in heart of L.A.
provides easy access to Convention Center, Sports Arena, Coliseum,
USC, Dodger Stadium, Chinatown, and the Music Center.

Alvarado Terrace is a Los Angeles surprise. Nestled between
Pico and Hoover streets, it is one curved block of splendid
turn-of-the-century houses, all registered as national historical
landmarks. This is an L.A. few visitors even know exists, surrounded as it is by typical inner city streets. But, Terrace Manor,
along with its neighbors, is a beautiful house and enjoys great
convenience to freeways and downtown.

It shakes a lot of preconceived notions about gaudy L.A. to
step into this refined 1902 mansion with its original stained- and
lead-glass windows, paneled walls, and gracious atmosphere.

Shirley Spillman has decorated each of the guest rooms in a fresh, tasteful style in deep, rich colors. She has used some antiques, brass beds, Victorian settees, and collections, but none of it is overdone. Our room was the Sun Room Suite, especially comfortable with an attached porch and a trundle bed making an airy sitting room.

The common rooms are fascinating (there's an Ionic-columned fireplace with a built-in clock that still chimes on cue) and handsomely furnished with period pieces. I was particularly drawn to ☞ an inviting paneled library off the living room with stunning windows of lead glass.

The Spillmans are thoughtful hosts who know L.A. well. They're ready to tell you what's going on in town that's new and make any reservations you may need. They can also make arrangements for business luncheons at the inn. Sandy may look familiar to you, as he did to me. I finally realized he is in a series of Pacific Bell commercials currently on television in which he and an old pal reminisce about their youth and a girl named Mary Ellen. He is also a professional magician. A very special perk he can arrange is ☞ an entree to Hollywood's famed Magic Club. This stylish private club offers both a glamorous place to dine in the Hollywood hills and an opportunity to see outstanding magic acts.

In addition to a full breakfast featuring a quiche, frittata, or French toast served in the dining room (and early enough for most business travelers)', you may, with just a little arm twisting, ☞ get Sandy to perform some of his magic. I can promise that you'll leave the table reluctantly.

How to get there: From LAX Airport take Century Boulevard east about 8 miles to Harbor Freeway (10) west. Immediately get into left-hand lane for Pico off-ramp. On Pico, turn left (west) to Alvarado Terrace; turn left to the inn.

✻

J: *Isn't it wonderfully appropriate that even a breakfast in L.A. has a little show biz?*

Olive Metcalf

San Ysidro Ranch
Montecito, California
93108

Innkeeper: Jan Martin Winn, manager
Address/Telephone: 900 San Ysidro Lane; (805) 969–5046
Rooms: 43; all with private bath, television, telephone, fireplace, porch, and stocked refrigerator.
Rates: $155 for cottage rooms to $340 for cottages with private Jacuzzi; EP. Two-night minimum on weekends. Children welcome.
Open: All year. Breakfast, lunch, dinner, Sunday brunch.
Facilities and local attractions: Horses, guided rides, swimming pool, tennis courts, golf.

Meanwhile, back at the ranch, things are changing. The San Ysidro has been around since 1893, always a premier hideaway and favorite of celebrities and writers. I admit being worried when I heard about its new corporate ownership, but the blue business suits have wisely not changed the unique feeling at this gorgeously situated inn. There are more elegant room appointments now—televisions, telephones, and fresh decor, but I was relieved to see the ranch has not gone California chic. Those infamous cheery signs announcing "I am a Catalpa Tree," or "late check-outs will be charged an arm and a leg" have disappeared, but the special low-key ambience, elegant but not slick, still prevails.

Admittedly, the San Ysidro is not inexpensive, but I think you'd have the curiosity of a turnip if you didn't want to see the place where John and Jacqueline Kennedy honeymooned, Laurence Olivier and Vivien Leigh married, and where Winston Churchill and John Galsworthy relaxed and wrote.

Privacy, in a setting of great natural beauty, was and still is the story of the ranch's appeal. The soft foothills of the Santa Ynez Mountains offer miles of riding trails with breathtaking views. You can disappear into one of the cottages and not see another soul for days, though the innkeepers claim if a guest doesn't come out for twenty-four hours, they do force-feeding.

There is no typical room in the buildings scattered around the lush grounds. Some are parlor suites with patio or deck; some are individual cottages nestled here and there. They're not all equally spiffy, it must be admitted. There's the odd piece of antique plumbing or worn upholstery, but luxury appointments aren't what has attracted people here for so long.

A kind of "we're all country gentlemen here" atmosphere is also part of the charm. Take the stocked refrigerators in every room that serve as honor bars. Mix your own and keep tabs. Very upper class, don't you think?

One other major lure is the outstanding food at the Plow and Angel restaurant. From al fresco breakfasts on the deck to candlelit continental dinners in the beautiful white-stuccoed dining room, the cuisine ranges from Western to sophisticated. Its reputation attracts even diners who aren't ranch guests.

How to get there: From Highway 101, take San Ysidro Road exit in Montecito, 4 miles south of Santa Barbara. Follow signs to San Ysidro Ranch, 2 miles toward the mountains.

$$*$$

J: *The loveliness of these evenings moves the heart; and of the mornings, shining, cool fragrant.*
 —John Galsworthy, writing of San Ysidro Ranch

Olive Metcalf

Doryman's Inn
Newport Beach, California
92663

Innkeeper: Michael D. Palitz
Address/Telephone: 2102 West Ocean Front; (714) 675–7300
Rooms: 10; all with private bath, fireplace, television.
Rates: $135 to $275, including extended continental breakfast.
Open: All year.
Facilities and local attractions: Directly across from Newport Pier; swimming,
 wind surfing, deep-sea fishing; largest pleasure craft harbor in the
 world; Newport restaurants, waterfront shops, cabarets. Bicycles and
 off-street parking available.

If you get up very early here, you'll see the commercial Dory
Fishing Fleet returning from the sea in their traditional small boats
with their catch. For nearly 100 years they've supplied fresh fish
for sale in the open-air market at McFadden Wharf, Newport Pier
area. It's now one of California's designated historical landmarks.

Such a humble basis for Newport's origins contrasts sharply
with the opulence of Doryman's Inn. The bed and breakfast is on
the second floor of a modest red brick building that dates from the
1920s. The Rex restaurant occupies the first floor (inn guests can
order meals sent to their rooms), but a private elevator whisks you
to the inn's lobby upstairs.

34

Victorian is the motif and resoundingly elegant is the atmosphere. But elegance is not surprising when you consider that it took five years and a couple of million dollars to renovate and decorate the ten rooms. There's ample use of polished oak and brass for staircases and doors, hand-stenciled trim on ceiling borders, luxurious carpets, and etched-glass light globes.

The romantically decorated bedrooms are furnished with antiques and elaborate beds. Some are brass; others have carved headboards or canopied four-posters. There are matching floral draperies and quilted bedspreads, lace curtains, ruffled pillow shams, gilt-edged beveled mirrors, and plants. Each room has a gas fireplace turned on with the flick of a wall switch, and perhaps a porcelain animal sits on the hearth.

Should this setting sound too austere for your taste, I recommend you proceed to the bathroom where you'll find a taste of extravagant luxury. ☞ Tubs are sunken Italian marble—two with Jacuzzis—highlighted by sun streaming in from fern-filled skylights.

Guests can see each other in the parlor for breakfast, but it's not hard to see why many opt for enjoying it in the privacy of their rooms. Or you might prefer the blue-tiled roof deck with its unobstructed views of the pier and the Pacific. International coffees and teas are served along with fresh pastries, seasonal fresh fruits, brown eggs, and juice.

How to get there: From Highway 405 (San Diego Freeway), take Highway 55 to Newport Boulevard. Continue to 32nd Street, and turn right. Turn left on Balboa Boulevard; bear right at signs to Newport Pier. Inn is on right at 2102 West Ocean Front.

J: *The Newmans (Paul and Joanne to those of us who feel as though we know them) and Jerry Lewis have been among the guests. Not at the same time, you understand.*

Olive Metcalf

La Maida House
North Hollywood, California
91601

Innkeeper: Megan Timothy
Address/Telephone: 11159 La Maida Street; (818) 769–3857
Rooms: 12, 4 in main house, 8 in bungalows; all with private bath and
  some spa baths.
Rates: $80 to $205, including continental breakfast and evening aperitif.
  No credit cards. No pets; no smoking on premises.
Open: All year.
Facilities and local attractions: Pool; gym ; convenient to Universal Studios,
  Beverly Hills, downtown Los Angeles, shopping, Hollywood/Burbank
  Airport, restaurants.

No matter how splendid a stay you have at La Maida
House—and I don't see how you could avoid it—you're going to
leave feeling like an underachiever after meeting Megan Timothy.
She's turned a derelict 1920s Italianate mansion into a ☞ luxury
inn that rises above the valley bungalows and exudes elegance,
inside and out. Two black swans gliding over a pond outside the
drawing room set the tone: old-style Hollywood glamor.

The formidable talents Ms. Timothy brings to innkeeping start
with her design skills. The stunning decor in every room and the
☞ ninety-seven original stained glass windows (and an exquisite
shower door) throughout the house are remarkable.

Then there are her professional-caliber cooking skills. Megan grows all the flowers and herbs and much of the fruit and vegetables she serves. Timothy standards are high, even for the continental breakfasts she serves her guests. "Every innkeeper should invest in a first-rate juice machine," she declares. Hers is one that can make juice out of everything but the *Los Angeles Times*. She makes it on the spot with fresh combinations every morning, and guests try to figure out what has been "juiced."

No other meals are served regularly, but everything is possible. Megan will prepare an intimate dinner for two to four, served in a second-floor balcony overlooking the garden or an alfresco meal on an outside patio off the main dining room. She'll do an elegant dinner for eight around a glass-topped table in a solarium dining room, or a formal affair in the candle-lit, chandeliered dining room with seating for thirty-two at round tables covered with peach linen. This is a Limoges and crystal affair, you understand, not California pottery. The food, custom planned to your wishes, is as beautiful as the surroundings, and *everything* is made from scratch.

From the entryway with its graceful staircase, to the handsome drawing room with grand piano, Carrara marble fireplace, and polished oak floors, this flower-filled house is a pleasure. Every bedroom is a knockout and has all the comforts you might need: robes, bath toiletries, even crocheted lap throws made by Megan's mother. Bungalow accommodations are as comfortable and glamorous as those in the mansion. Several suites have fireplaces and private patios with fountains, a perfect place to hide out and write your screenplay. Release the tension during creative bouts with a stroll to the pool area with its plant-filled cabana and nicely equipped gym.

How to get there: From Hollywood Freeway, exit at Magnolia. Turn east to first light, and then turn right on Tujunga. At next light, turn left on Camarillo. Go 3 blocks to Bellflower and turn left. Continue 1 block to northeast corner of La Maida.

$$*$$

J: It's no wonder the guest list includes movers and shakers; this is a class act in personalized Hollywood digs.

olive Metcalf

Ojai Manor Hotel
Ojai, California
93023

Innkeeper: Mary Nelson
Address/Telephone: 210 East Matilija Street; (805) 646–0961
Rooms: 6 share 3 baths.
Rates: $70 to $75; special weekday rates. Continental breakfast, complimentary wine included.
Open: All year.
Facilities and local attractions: Walk to Ojai shops, galleries, restaurants. Golf, tennis close by. Wheeler Hot Springs Mineral Baths. May music festivals, June Shakespeare Revels. Hiking, camping in surrounding mountains. Fishing, Lake Casitas.

Travelers on the California coast who dash between San Francisco and Los Angeles and fail to explore some of the more obscure places in between are missing copious treasures. The beautiful Ojai Valley is one of the jewels.

Imagine a small-town version of Santa Barbara's Spanish architecture, Carmel's artists and galleries, and San Francisco's smart shops. Bless it with Los Angeles weather (but with sparkling clean air), and you have the lovely little town of Ojai, population 6,325.

Comfortably settled into Mary Nelson's inn, you'll have no

need for a car to get anywhere in town. But you should take some of the scenic drives around the area: up Dennison Grade for memorable vistas of the abundant valley; up Sulphur Mountain Road for spectacular views of the Pacific Ocean on one side, the Ojai Valley on the other. Another big attraction in town are the hot mineral baths at Wheeler Hot Springs and their highly recommended restaurant.

Mary and her late partner, artist Boyd Wright, have restored the oldest building in town as a fresh, inviting inn. In 1874, it was a school in the heart of this agricultural community. Now, the polished oak floors and the pale lavender-gray-white walls are an intriguing background for Boyd's contemporary art pieces— many of them large and dramatic. Guests get to enjoy a fascinating home gallery.

The colorful living room has a beautiful oriental rug and an Art Deco–looking blue plush sofa and club chair by the fireplace. Adjoining it is a sunny dining room with a long table where Mary serves a generous continental breakfast. This day it was juice, fresh raspberries, and a variety of her freshly baked breads and muffins with preserves and cream cheese.

The six fresh bedrooms upstairs feature the best-looking beds you'll find anywhere. It must be those oversize down pillows and fine linens! What a luxury for people who like to prop up in bed and read—and there are good lights on both sides of the bed, too.

Mary cautions guests to be sure to call ahead for reservations. This is a one-person show and a drop-by during the week could miss Mary.

How to get there: About one hour north of Santa Barbara on Highway 101, take Lake Casitas exit, Highway 150, east to Ojai—a beautiful drive. At Libby Park in town center, turn left one block to East Matilija.

☀

J: *Be sure you walk to Bart's Corner, a unique outdoor meeting place, garden, and used-book store. Mary will direct you.*

Olive Metcalf

Villa Royale
Palm Springs, California
92264

Innkeepers: Bob Lee and Chuck Murawski

Address/Telephone: 1620 Indian Trail; (619) 327–2314

Rooms: 31 suites and rooms; all with private bath, television, and telephone; some with fireplace, kitchenette, and private spa.

Rates: $65 to $200, including continental breakfast; lower summer rates and for longer stays. No children; no pets.

Open: All year.

Facilities and local attractions: Restaurant serves lunch and dinner. Three swimming pools; bicycles; spas; courtyards with fountains and outdoor fireplaces. Nearby golf, tennis, and horseback riding. Palm Springs shops and restaurants. Aerial tramway ride up Mt. San Jacinto.

Only a few blocks from slick, downtown Palm Springs with glamorous big hotels lining the main drag, a heartwarming alternative lies low on the desert plain just waiting to beguile you. Everything conspires at Villa Royale to make ☞ you think you're in an old Mexican resort. Winding brick paths connect a series of courtyards with ancient-looking pillars under the red-tile roofs of surrounding rooms. Everywhere there are shade trees and pots of flowers, exotic vines and palms, small gardens and fountains. And on my March visit, the cascading bougainvillea was dazzling.

From the blazing Palm Springs sun, you step into a lobby/ sitting room with a cool tile floor and squashy sofa and chairs. Just outside the door in the courtyard are bicycles ready for guests to borrow for sightseeing around the quiet residential streets or touring the shopping plazas. The kitchen will pack you a picnic basket to take along on request. Owners Chuck and Bob, along with a well-trained staff, are always ready to help. There aren't just *two* bikes; there are lots of them. You don't get just *one* extra towel for the pool; you get big thick ones, as many as you need.

The variety of accommodations at Villa Royale is only one of its attractions. Whether you take a standard guest room or splurge on a deluxe studio with kitchenette, private patio, and spa, all the colorful ambience of flowers, fountains, and dramatic views of the San Jacinto Mountains are available to everyone. Every room, large or small, is decorated in an individual international style, the result of the owners' frequent buying trips to Europe and owner Murawski's former work as a Hollywood production designer. Each one has interesting treasures: woven hangings and table covers, wall carvings, bright pottery, sculpture, pillows, and antique furniture.

Across the first courtyard is the dining room with a glass-enclosed casual area where breakfast is served looking out at the pool. The brick floor extends into a more formal interior room with a wonderful feeling. Armchairs with rush seats and cushions surround tables skirted with dark floral cloths to the floor and topped with lighter color linen. The walls are a rosy adobe, and in the soft lighting, with beautiful china and glassware, it's an atmosphere I would like to get used to. Our dinner was an attractively presented, relaxing experience: tortellini soup, green salad, scampi, and a marvelous fresh mango sherbet with fresh peaches and raspberries.

Visually rich as days are, relaxing here in the sunshine surrounded with colorful flowers, wait 'til you see it at night! Dozens of small ornate brass lanterns hanging from trees and vines gleam with tiny lights and cast light and shadows throughout the courtyards. If you aren't enchanted, check your pulse.

How to get there: Proceed through downtown Palm Springs on its main street, North Palm Canyon. When it becomes East Palm Canyon, look for Indian Trail, just past Indian Avenue. Turn left to the inn on your right.

olive Metcalf

The Cheshire Cat
Santa Barbara, California
93101

Innkeeper: George Mari; Owner, Chris Dunstan
Address/Telephone: 36 West Valerio Street; (805) 569–1610
Rooms: 11; all with private bath.
Rates: $79 to $159, including generous continental breakfast. No credit
cards. No children or pets; no smoking.
Open: All year.
Facilities and local attractions: Spa, patio, private telephones, bicycles. Walk
to Santa Barbara restaurants, shops, theaters.

Chris Dunstan knew exactly what she wanted to accomplish
when she began restoring two elegant Victorian houses: simply to
create a ☞ showplace among Santa Barbara inns. By George, I
think she's done it! And so does the Romantik Hotels and
Restaurants, an association that links some of the finest accommodations in Europe and America. They've added The Cheshire
Cat to their list of members.

Her theme, beginning with the inn's name, is "Alice in
Wonderland." A set of porcelain figurines representing characters
from the story sits on an antique desk in the living room, and most
of the rooms are named for the characters. If all this sounds too
cute for words, let me tell you it's gorgeously done.

The finest Laura Ashley prints in fabric and wallpaper are used throughout the house as the background for beautiful English antique furniture. How can you resist an atmosphere of high ceilings and fresh flowers, where the glow of polished wood vies with the sparkle of beveled glass? How genteel.

Every room is a stunner with Ashley print bed linens and coordinated drapes and wall coverings. ☛ Color schemes have to be described as delicious: the Caterpillar Suite in rose, moss green, and stone; Mad Hatter in plum and cream; Alice's Suite in ivory and pink, which has a private patio overlooking an oak tree, gardens, and mountains.

A flower-filled brick patio with a white gazebo separates the two houses. White chairs and round tables are dressed for breakfast in pink cloths. Add blue and white Wedgwood china and you have a scene as engaging as a stage setting. A beautiful continental breakfast is set out around a palm tree in the center of the courtyard: fresh fruits, fresh croissants, homemade jams and granola, yogurt, tea, and just-ground coffee.

Take a look at the professionally equipped kitchen. It was designed for more ambitious things than mere continental breakfasts. ☛ Week-long gourmet cooking classes are planned with notable chefs from across the country invited to teach inn guests. Ask about them when you call.

How to get there: From Highway 101 going through Santa Barbara, take Valerio Street toward the mountains. Inn is on your left at number 36.

olive Metcalf

The Glenborough Inn
Santa Barbara, California
93101

Innkeepers: Jo Ann Bell, Pat Hardy, and Pat Morgan
Address/Telephone: 1327 Bath Street; (805) 966–0589
Rooms: 9; 4 upstairs in main house share 2 baths; 1 downstairs with
 private bath, fireplace, and outside entrance; 4 in cottage, each with
 private bath and separate entrance.
Rates: $60 to $150, with full breakfast; singles $5 less, $10 per extra
 person. No smoking in main house; no children or pets.
Open: All year.
Facilities and local attractions: Hot tub to be used privately in the gardens.
 Walk to Santa Barbara's museums, shops, restaurants, galleries.
 Close to beach, harbor, mountains.

Three real inn "pros" own and operate The Glenborough Inn.
They know all the right moves to give an inn flavor, and what's
more, they share their techniques in a book they've written and in
classes on innkeeping they give. If you're thinking of becoming
one of the thousands of people each year who open an inn, they
have a 🖝 bonanza of information about everything from how to
balance the budget to how to avoid inn burnout.

Their inn consists of two charming houses in a pleasant
neighborhood: the Main House, a two-story 1906 home, and the

early 1880s Cottage across the street. You can tell from the warmth of your welcome that these innkeepers aren't suffering from burnout. They obviously enjoy giving guests ☞ the kind of personal attention that defines an inn's style.

The four bedrooms in the Main House are cozy and very Victorian. Curtains of old lace, embroidered pillows, velvet coverlets, and quilts enhance the antique furniture. I'm crazy about sun porches, so I was smitten with the smallest room of all, the Garden, with old-fashioned wicker and a view of backyard flowers. A romantically private garden with a waterfall and brick patio is the entrance to the Nouveau Suite. It has a sitting room with a fireplace and a queen-sized canopy bed.

If privacy and easy access are important, you'll like the four rooms in the Cottage. Each has a separate entrance and bath, and two are suites with a sitting room and fireplace. Plants and flowers inside and out live up to Santa Barbara's reputation for lushness. Indulge yourself with breakfast in bed when it arrives in a picnic basket, or take it alfresco in the secluded backyard garden.

Ah, those ☞ breakfasts of Pat Hardy. She does everything from scratch, salt-free, with low-fat and low-cholesterol ingredients fresh from the garden or local markets. One of her menus is Spanish: juice, Huevos Rancheros, Ban Huelos (crispy flour tortilla sprinkled with cinnamon sugar), and sliced grapefruit lightly touched with brown sugar beside fresh berries. She has many such specialties, all scrumptious.

Everyone who feels like socializing is encouraged to gather in the cheerfully cluttered Main House parlor for evening wine and hors d'oeuvres. Pat and Jo Ann know all the best restaurants in a city full of them, and they'll direct you to one that's bound to please. After dinner, stroll back to the inn for ☞ a very private hot tub under the stars. Don't forget to put out the "occupied" sign.

How to get there: From Highway 101, exit at Carrillo Street. Go east toward the mountains to Bath Street. Turn left onto Bath Street; inn is 3½ blocks ahead at number 1327.

Olive Metcalf

The Old Yacht Club Inn and The Hitchcock House
Santa Barbara, California
93103

Innkeepers: Lucille Caruso, Nancy Donaldson, and Sandy Hunt
Address/Telephone: 431 Corona Del Mar; (805) 962–1277
Rooms: 5 in Old Yacht Club; 1 with private bath, 4 share 2 baths. 4 in
    Hitchcock House; all with private bath.
Rates: $60 to $90 at Old Yacht Club; $90 to $115 at Hitchcock House. All
    rates double occupancy; extra person $25. Includes full breakfast. No
    children or pets. Smoking discouraged indoors.
Open: All year. Dinner by reservation, usually weekends.
Facilities and local attractions: Bicycles provided. Walk half a block to beach.
    Swimming, fishing, sailing, tennis, golf close by.

After the first clubhouse of Santa Barbara's Yacht Club was
swept out to sea during a terrible storm in the 1920s, this house
served as the headquarters. The name seemed a perfect choice
when it became Santa Barbara's first bed and breakfast inn. It does
sit a mere ☛ half a block from the waterfront, but there's nothing
nautical about it.

It's a 1912 Craftsman-style house, which means it has the
period charm of a wide, covered front porch, and balconies and

dormers that provide charming, light-filled rooms. Two of the upstairs bedrooms at the Old Yacht Club have built-in window seats—surely one of the most appealing details a room can have. They're decorated with an old-fashioned, personal touch and accented with fresh flowers and decanters of sherry.

Hitchcock House is just next door, a good choice for privacy. Its four large rooms have the advantages of sitting areas plus private baths *and* private entrances. These are especially personal rooms, since each of the four innkeepers decorated a room to reflect her heritage. The Italian Room, for instance, has the trunks that came with the immigrants from Europe, family photographs, and other treasures.

Downstairs at the Old Yacht Club, guests of both houses are welcome to enjoy the warm atmosphere of antiques and oriental rugs and to join in sherry or tea by the fire. An ☞ exceptional breakfast is served here in the dining room or delivered in a basket to your door at Hitchcock House: freshly ground coffee, juice, fresh fruit, home-baked breads, and interesting omelets (maybe spinach or zucchini). These innkeepers maintain their Santa Barbara omelet is the best.

Check the dinner schedule with the innkeepers when booking your room. Most weekends (and for special events) Nancy Donaldson does a ☞ five-course candle-lit dinner, by reservation, that could be the highlight of your visit. She's a professional member of the American Wine and Food Institute and loves to cook. Homemade fettuccine, Artichokes Athena, Halibut Florentine, and Chocolate Decadence are some of her specialties.

How to get there: Driving north on Highway 101 to Santa Barbara, exit (left lane) on Cabrillo. Turn left, continue past Sheraton Hotel; turn right on Corona Del Mar Drive and turn right to the inn. Coming south, take second State Street exit, turn right. Turn left on Cabrillo; just before Sheraton Hotel, turn left on Corona Del Mar.

Olive Metcalf

The Parsonage
Santa Barbara, California
93101

Innkeeper: Hilde Michelmore
Address/Telephone: 1600 Olive Street; (805) 962–9336
Rooms: 6; all with private bath.
Rates: $70 to $130 for suite; includes full breakfast. Two-night minimum
on weekends. No children under 12; no pets. Smoking discouraged.
Open: All year.
Facilities and local attractions: Sun deck. Walk to Mission Santa Barbara,
shopping, theater, restaurants.

If ever the talk about splitting California into northern and
southern states is seriously considered, you can bet that the
custody battle over Santa Barbara will be ferocious. Both sides
would fight to keep this lush, distinctly Mediterranean city.

From The Parsonage, one of Santa Barbara's many notable
Victorian houses, you can explore a host of the city's attractions on
foot. The inn is nestled between the mountains and the downtown
area in a quiet residential neighborhood. This splendid Queen
Anne was built in 1892 as a parsonage for the Trinity Episcopal
Church. It's now home and business to Hilde Michelmore, who
has restored and decorated it with her impressive collection of
antiques and rugs.

The minister's library on the first floor is now the Rosebud Room in pinks and mauves and furnished with antiques. The Versailles, with Louis XIV decor, is another main-floor room. You might appreciate having immediate access to an attractive living room with a fireplace and oversize sofa. A large iron baker's rack filled with books and plants decorates one wall, and there's a small television. I wonder what the long-ago cleric would think of the ☞ unusual lilac-and-green Chinese rug that now decorates his Victorian sitting room. It's memorable!

At the top of the redwood staircase are four uniquely decorated rooms. There's the Peacock Room, with exotic blues and greens in comforter and oriental rug; the Lavender and Lace Room; and Las Flores, with a bay window looking out at the ocean. The Honeymoon Suite runs the entire length of the house. It comprises a bedroom, a solarium (old-fashioned sun porch), and an enormous bathroom with a handsome pedestal sink and footed tub. It has a king-size canopied bed and an antique armoire. The ☞ views from here of mountains, ocean, and city are quite spectacular.

A formal dining room with a graceful bay window, or a sunny deck with more outstanding views are equally pleasant spots for breakfast. Hilde serves a large one, with favorites like scrambled eggs, quiche, or French toast.

How to get there: Driving south on Highway 101, exit at Mission Street east toward The Mission. Turn right on Laguna Street, turn left to Olive Street. Driving north on 101, exit at Milpas Street; cross town to Olive Street.

olive Metcalf

Simpson House Inn
Santa Barbara, California
93101

Innkeepers: Glyn and Linda Davies; Gillean Wilson
Address/Telephone: 121 East Arrellaga Street; (805) 963–7067
Rooms: 6; all with private bath.
Rates: $75 to $130, includes full breakfast and afternoon tea or wine. Ask
about business and winter rates. No children; no smoking inside.
Open: All year.
Facilities and local attractions: Lovely grounds and gardens to enjoy.
Convenient to Santa Barbara attractions: beach, mission, shopping
plazas, restaurants, museums, theaters, and galleries. Attractive
neighborhood to walk.

Now that B&B inns have become commonplace to U.S.
travelers, Victoriana may be a style genre you've had quite enough
of, thank you. What you may not know is that "Victorian charm"
does not necessarily mean a suffocating hodge-podge of dark
furniture and knickknacks. There are also distinguished houses
like Simpson House—spacious, airy, handsomely decorated, and
meticulously maintained.

Simpson House sits in a beautiful neighborhood close to
downtown Santa Barbara on an acre of fine old trees, with an
English garden as background. It has received a Structure of Merit

award for its unique 1874 architecture (Eastlake-style Victorian) and is considered by many to be one of Southern California's finest Victorian homes. That it survived the developers and thrives as an inn today is a testament to the perseverance of Glyn and Linda Davies. "We just couldn't bear the thought of this place being torn down," Linda says.

Instead of restoring and decorating the historic home as an inn in one bold stroke, the Davieses had years of research and work ahead after buying the house in 1976. Then there was a wrenching battle over zoning restrictions. But what a difference it makes when a house is loved like one of the family rather than just a business. Every corner tells the tale of careful, well-planned work and a dedication to quality. The result is the kind of mellow look that is only achieved when treasures are acquired gradually. Much of the furniture was brought back from trips to England.

The guest rooms are all different in mood, but each is elegantly appointed with European goosedown comforters, fine linen, and fresh bouquets. Several rooms open to a large private deck overlooking the gardens. Even here, there are large tubs of blooming flowers. Downstairs, the sitting room with its fireplace and book-lined walls and the large formal dining room have French doors opening to the garden verandas. Teak floors, white wicker furniture, and the aromas of lilac and orange blossoms create a nostalgic atmosphere.

Our breakfast served out here was a pleasure we extended as long as possible. A help-yourself buffet offered big glass containers of terrific homemade granola and other cereals, plus yogurt, milk, and raisins. Then came just-squeezed juice and a fruit compote. I was halfway through the crossword puzzle and feeling quite well fed when thick French toast topped with fresh, chunky applesauce appeared, accompanied by a basket of hot blueberry-bran muffins and yet another pot of coffee.

Admittedly, it was an idyllic March morning in Santa Barbara, but it will be a long time before I'll forget breakfast on this lilac-draped veranda.

How to get there: From Highway 101 as it rounds Santa Barbara, turn right on East Arrellaga Street if heading north; turn left if heading south. Follow it 1 block past State Street to the inn on your left. Turn in the driveway and park in back or on the street.

❋

The Tiffany Inn
Santa Barbara, California
93101

Innkeepers: Carol and Larry MacDonald
Address/Telephone: 1323 De La Vina Street; (805) 963–2283
Rooms: 6; 4 with private bath.
Rates: $75 to $145 double occupancy, includes full breakfast and evening
refreshments. Reduced rates in winter season; two-night minimum
on weekends. Smoking outside only; no pets.
Open: All year.
Facilities and local attractions: Walking distance to many restaurants, shops;
close to The Mission, Stearn's Wharf. Hike mountains, walk beach,
visit museums, galleries, theaters. Tour local wineries.

Some inns are just so outlandishly pretty, it hardly matters if
they serve a good breakfast, are conveniently located, or indulge
your need to be pampered with some degree of style. The Tiffany
Inn scores high on all counts, but the truth is, it's such a beautiful,
enchantingly decorated house, the rest is lagniappe.

This stately 1898 Victorian that Carol and Larry have restored
so lovingly and authentically is a picture-perfect setting for the
collection of fine furniture and antiques that they've acquired over
the years. The ambience begins with the genuine articles—glowing

52

dark wood, colonial diamond-paned bay windows, a century-old wood staircase, and a bathroom with all the original fixtures.

What Carol MacDonald has done is make the antique background stunning by lavishly decorating with the finest colorful fabrics, artfully arranging her splendid furniture, and then maintaining it all immaculately.

I couldn't choose a favorite among the upstairs bedrooms. They each have a romantic feeling and delicious appointments: rockers placed to look out at mountains or garden, lace curtains at French windows, elegant bed linens, and a wood-burning fireplace in several.

The impeccable garden is as Victorian in atmosphere as is the house. It's a lovely place to relax, or you might enjoy the wicker chaise on the old-fashioned lattice-covered porch.

I would love to see the house when the MacDonalds and son David decorate it for Christmas. They offer a low holiday rate then to encourage guests to come and stay while doing their Christmas shopping in Santa Barbara—where there's some of the greatest shopping anywhere. The idea sounds appealing to me. Shop all day, have dinner at one of Santa Barbara's outstanding restaurants, and return to the richly decorated inn for wine or a grog in the elegant parlor around the fire. Retire for the night to your beautiful cozy room and dream of no-limit Visa Land. Next morning, after fresh fruit, croissants, and coffee, you'll be ready to hit the shops again.

How to get there: From Highway 101 through Santa Barbara, exit at Mission Street. Drive east to De La Vina Street and turn right. Inn is on the right at number 1323.

The Seal Beach Inn
Seal Beach, California
90740

Innkeeper: Marjorie Bettenhausen
Address/Telephone: 212 Fifth Street; (213) 494–2416 or 493–2416
Rooms: 23, including 14 suites; all with private bath and television, many
  with small kitchen.
Rates: $88 to $155 includes breakfast; $10 each additional guest. Ask
  about weekend package rates off season. Smoking only on patios. No
  pets; children discouraged. No air conditioning.
Open: All year.
Facilities and local attractions: Gardens, pool. Wedding, small business
  facilities. Short walk to beach. Old Town boutiques, bistros. Easy
  access to L.A. and freeways to airports, Disneyland, Convention
  Center.

If ambience could be packaged, I would like to market the
kind of feeling Seal Beach Inn exudes. Potential buyers might
doubt my claims that you can find a gentle, old-world atmosphere
of wrought-iron balconies and flower-filled patios just a jog off
several major freeways, but it's true. Not a hint of plastic or slick
California chic touches this quiet, utterly charming hideaway.

Seal Beach enjoys an enviable low profile; it's even missing
from many maps of the area. The ☞ quaint old town with its

clean beach and pier are a surprise to Southern California visitors expecting the usual commercial sprawl. I took an early morning walk past tile-roofed bungalows to the beach and shared the waves for a time with only two windsurfers and the sea gulls.

The inn was built in the 1920s. The Bettenhausens found it and began a restoration in 1977. They imported crates of antiquities from Europe—a 2,000-pound iron fountain from Paris, old murals, seventeenth-century iron gates—and put the inn together with a light touch. The look is mostly French-Mediterranean, but there is no "decorated" look, and nothing is predictable. Rooms and baths range from tiny to large. In the Azalea Room I slept in a bed from the John Barrymore estate surrounded by lace curtains, big easy chairs, and oriental carpets. Like many of the rooms, this one had a sitting area, kitchenette, and eating area.

But it's the color of brilliant flowers that you'll remember. They bloom in profusion around the brick courtyard, in pots lining the steps, and exotic vines spill over the railings and balconies. Little wonder that this romantic setting makes the inn a favorite choice for weddings. The inn does an outstanding job of catering parties and has seven lavishly decorated bridal suites.

I ate breakfast in a sunny tea room adjoining a downstairs library/sitting room. Both rooms open to a snug patio. Luscious platters of ripe fruit, cereals, breads, and pastries seemed just right with the never-ending supply of excellent coffee, but an egg casserole dish was also fresh from the oven.

How to get there: Exit the San Diego Freeway (405) at Seal Beach Boulevard going south. Turn right on Pacific Coast Highway and left on Fifth Street to the inn on the left.

*

J: *I chatted at breakfast with a couple from Texas in town for business appointments. We all felt pretty smug about how smart we were to make business travel this pleasant.*

olive Metcalf

Venice Beach House
Venice, California
90291

Innkeeper: Scott Seiffert
Address/Telephone: 15 Thirtieth Avenue; (213) 823–1966
Rooms: 9; 5 with private bath, 4 share 1 large bath.
Rates: $65 to $140, includes continental breakfast. No pets, no smoking.
    Children over 10 welcome.
Open: All year.
Facilities and local attractions: Walk to swimming beach, Venice Pier. Close
    to Los Angeles Airport, restaurants, shops.

Abbot Kinney bought this stretch of California coast at the turn of the century with a slightly wacky but grandiose vision of re-creating Venice, Italy: canals, elegant hotels, boardwalks, piers, and cultural events—and he did it. "Kinney's Folly" was a success for more than thirty years before it fell out of fashion.

This gray-shingled beach house was built a half-block from the beach in 1911, the heyday of Venice, by Warren Wilson, a wealthy newspaper publisher. Two of his eight daughters married Kinney sons, and the house was filled with family for many years. It's that kind of house still—big and friendly.

Now that the '60s hippie encampment is past, Venice is having a revival of popularity. The beach is clean for swimming, property values have skyrocketed, and the boardwalk is lively with shops, tourists, and roller skaters.

Once you're over the age of sixteen, it's probably best to dip into the exotic scenes of Los Angeles beach life from a base that is utterly sane, even conventional. This house is a ☞ quiet, tasteful retreat that will welcome you back when you've had enough "colorful sights."

The living room is restful in shades of rose and mauve with a beautiful antique oriental rug in those shades, comfortable furniture, and a fireplace. Bedrooms are romantically decorated with fabric over padded walls, and there are ☞ fine bathrooms. One has a deep, tiled shower with dueling shower heads at either side of the shower, one is a Jacuzzi tub for two, and another has two gilded, claw-foot tubs.

A sheltered veranda or the cheerful sun room adjoining the living room are the breakfast spots. Fruits, cereals, hot breads, tea, and coffee are set out to help yourself. You sit at small, round tables covered with flowered skirts. Outside the bay window are pink hibiscus and a bit of ocean view.

How to get there: From San Diego Freeway (405), go west on Washington, one street past Pacific to Speedway. Turn right, and go one block to 29th Street. Turn right; park immediately at gray board fence.

❧

J: *Among the performers on the boardwalk this summer were a one-man blues band, the "Texas Chainsaw Juggler," and a man who swallows dipsticks. Just your everyday, homespun entertainment—Venice style.*

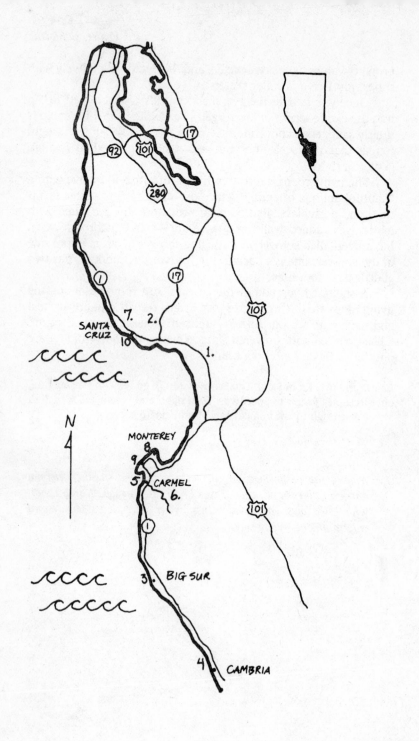

California: The Central Coast

Numbers on map refer to towns numbered below.

olive Metcalf

Apple Lane Inn
Aptos, California
95003

Innkeeper: Ann Farley
Address/Telephone: 6265 Soquel Drive; (408) 475–6868
Rooms: 5; 3 with private bath (tub and hand-held shower), 2 share 1 bath
  (have basin in room).
Rates: $65 to $95, including full country breakfast. No smoking.
Open: All year.
Facilities and local attractions: Beaches within walking distance. Visit Santa
  Cruz mountain wineries. Antiquing. Good restaurants nearby. Ca-
  brillo Music Festival in August. U.C. Santa Cruz.

Apple Lane Inn has all the ingredients that first made people
fall in love with B&Bs. It's a sweet Victorian farmhouse set amid
vineyards and apple orchards. There's an old-fashioned parlor
with comfortable old-fashioned furniture, sweetly decorated bedrooms, and a bountiful breakfast served at one big table. This is
vintage B&B stuff.

And the indispensable ingredient that makes the mixture
work is a warm-hearted, interested-in-you, helpful-about-the-
area innkeeper. In this case, Ann Farley fills the role admirably. I
watched her cheerfully answering guests' questions about the
house and local attractions as if she were hearing them for the first
time. That's talent!

This rural charmer of an inn is well off the highway on a hill that used to contain an apple orchard. Now the driveway up to the house is lined with apple trees. A ☞ brick patio at the front is sheltered by grape and wisteria vines, hanging begonias, roses, and hydrangeas.

Three bedrooms on the second floor are not large but comfortable and charmingly decorated. One has white wicker furniture, hearts-and-flowers wallpaper, and a claw-footed tub with hand-held shower; one has antique pine furniture and a four-poster queen-sized bed. A small sitting room on this floor has a view of Santa Cruz and is the kind of bonus room that makes inn lodging especially pleasant. Furnished with a wicker settee and chairs, it's a cozy place to read, help yourself to a cold drink, or do some needed pressing on the house ironing board. Ann has coffee ready here for early risers.

On the third floor are two beguiling attic rooms with exposed rafters painted white. One has two double beds; the other has a queen. They share a bath, but each has a basin in the room.

An easy atmosphere around the breakfast table brought on an exchange of traveling tales. One couple from Michigan told of a friend's reaction on hearing their plans to drive the California Coast and stay at bed-and-breakfast inns. "Why do you want to do that?" asked the friend. "Personally, I never liked breakfast in bed!"

We did have to get out of bed for breakfast, but all present were able to sit up and do justice to a fine meal: juice, fruit platter, ☞ homemade lemon bread and cinnamon rolls, and an egg casserole with Canadian bacon accompanied by pots of the inn's own coffee blend.

While nearby Santa Cruz is filled with interesting restaurants, I found a place down the road called The Farm that was well worth a visit. The five-acre complex of gardens, bakery, and shops includes the attractive Greenhouse Restaurant.

How to get there: From Highway 1, south of Santa Cruz, take Park Avenue exit east. Turn right on Soquel Drive. The inn is on the east, just before you reach Cabrillo College.

olive Metcalf

Mangels House
Aptos, California
95001

Innkeepers: Jacqueline and Ron Fisher
Address/Telephone: 570 Aptos Creek Road (mailing address: P.O. Box 302); (408) 688–7982
Rooms: 5; 3 with private bath, 2 with half-bath in room share 1 full bath.
Rates: $84 to $98, including full breakfast and afternoon refreshment. Smoking only in the sitting room. No pets; children over 12 welcome.
Open: Closed Christmas.
Facilities and local attractions: Darts and table tennis. Excellent hiking and biking in Forest of Nisene Marks. Minutes from New Brighton Beach; ¾ mile from Monterey Bay. November to March winter whale watch. Elephant seal watch. Summer Cabrillo Music Festival and theatrical events.

Driving down the lane through dense trees, your heart lifts at the sight of this handsome white house glimpsed through the gateposts. Looking somewhat like a white Southern mansion, it sits on four acres of lawn and orchard bordered by the Forest of Nisene Marks. It was built in the 1880s as the country home of Claus Mangels, who, together with his brother-in-law Claus Spreckels, founded the sugar beet industry in California.

Remarkably, the house remained in the same family until 1979 when the Fishers bought it. Perhaps its stable history accounts for the peaceful feeling the house exudes. I certainly felt contented in the long sitting room with tall ceilings, polished wood floors, and oriental rugs. Chintz-covered sofas face a large stone fireplace; a grand piano sits at one end of the room. A huge back porch is another pleasant sitting area where you can pursue the gentle sports of table tennis and darts.

Upstairs are five spacious guest rooms, airy and decorated in delicate colors, except for Nicolas's Room, which has brown walls and an African motif. (The Fishers spent two years in Zaire.) The Mauve Room has a marble fireplace, and one room has a deck with garden views.

Coffee is ready and set in the hall by 7 A.M. for the early risers. Later, Jackie serves an attractive breakfast in the big family kitchen—homey things like scones or oatmeal, fresh egg dishes, or puffed apple pancakes along with fruits and juice. And when they're in season, fresh-picked berries with yogurt are a treat.

☛ Berry picking in the area is first-rate, and Mangels would be a lovely spot to rest up from your labors. But this Northern Monterey area offers so much to do. ☛ The Forest of Nisene Marks was a new discovery for me. Not as well known as many recreation areas, its 10,000 acres of redwoods, creeks, and trails have great hiking and biking trails. A variety of summer music and drama festivals are becoming more popular every year, and Jackie will advise you about what's coming up. But the natural attractions of winter are even more seductive. This quieter, less crowded time means beach walks to see the elephant seals, monarch butterflies, and whale watching.

Plenty of good dinner options are nearby. Two Jackie recommends are Theo's (French food) and The Salmon Poacher.

How to get there: From Highway 1, exit at Seacliff-Aptos State Park Drive. Turn right on Soquel Drive to Aptos Creek Road. Turn left and continue ½ mile to the inn.

J: *If you collect inn brochures while anticipating future visits, this one is especially appealing. Black-and-white photos of some of the inn's rooms and exterior capture its quiet feeling.*

Olive Metcalf

Fairview Manor
Ben Lomond, California
95005

Innkeepers: Nancy Glasson and Frank Feely
Address/Telephone: 245 Fairview Avenue; (408) 336–3355
Rooms: 5; all with private bath.
Rates: $89 to $99, double or single. Breakfast and complimentary wine
   included.
Open: All year.
Facilities and local attractions: Fishing the San Lorenzo River; walk to Ben
   Lomond restaurants, shops; Henry Cowell Park; Roaring Camp
   Narrow-Gauge Railroad rides from Felton; 20-minute bus ride to
   Santa Cruz Boardwalk.

   If you ever want to hide out for a while but can't go far from
San Francisco, you might head for Ben Lomond. Once at this
remote little town in the Santa Cruz Mountains, follow a country
road to a tree-shaded driveway and a sign saying Fairview Manor.
   The house you see is deceptive—just a well-maintained 1920s
vintage attractive country house. But open the front door and you
look straight through a large living room/dining room to a deck,
and beyond that to a green forest of redwoods, madrone, and live
oak trees. Walk through those trees down a short path and you're
on the San Lorenzo River. Here's your hideaway.

It's the idyllic kind of shaded, sandy river bank with smooth round rocks and see-through water that some of us could spend whole days playing on. Others are much more interested in the steelhead and salmon fishing. The season is mid-December to the end of February, no nets allowed. A local fishing columnist reports not a lot of catches but big sizes when you get one.

The house sits on three acres of total privacy, but it's just a short walk to central Ben Lomond, where there are restaurants and antique shops. Landscaped grounds around the house have winding paths, a fish pond, and shady areas to sit in. The whole feeling here is of an earlier, quieter time.

Inside are five simple, immaculate guest rooms. The wood-paneled living room is cheerful, with a rich green carpet, a floral-covered sofa and comfortable chairs grouped before a rock fireplace. Magazines, books, a refrigerator stocked with cold beverages, and an electric organ make a warm, inviting atmosphere. You won't need days to unwind here—you'll feel at home right away.

Being a retired fireman, Frank is as proficient in the kitchen as Nancy. Together they turn out a full breakfast that ought to light your fire for a full day of activity: juice, fresh fruit, home-baked muffins, and a variety of hot main dishes like crab quiche or frittata with Canadian bacon.

It's all served at a long dining table in front of a big window looking out at the trees, or in good weather, out on the deck.

How to get there: From San Jose on Highway 17, turn right on Highway 9 north to Ben Lomond. Turn right on Main Street at the Bank of America, left at Central, and right on Fairview. Inn is on the left.

✷

J: *Forget the UIC (ubiquitous inn cat). Frank and Nancy have something different: a lop-eared bunny named Burt, completely house-trained and just about the cutest black-and-white bundle of fluff you can imagine.*

Olive Metcalf

Deetjen's Big Sur Inn
Big Sur, California
93920

Innkeeper: Bettie Walters; restaurant manager, Doris Solicoeur
Address/Telephone: Highway 1; (408) 667–2377
Rooms: 20; 13 with private bath, 7 share baths.
Rates: $30 to $80, EP. No credit cards; cash or traveler's checks preferred.
     One dining room smoke free. No pets; children welcome in some
     rooms.
Open: All year. Breakfast, dinner daily. Wine/beer bar.
Facilities and local attractions: Walk high meadowlands, beaches, redwood
     canyons. Several restaurants, shops along 6-mile section of Highway
     1.

"When I have to begin *explaining* Big Sur Inn to people, I
know it's probably not for them," says one of the staff. In other
words, if you like the manicured luxury of The Lodge at Pebble
Beach, Big Sur Inn may not be your style. But for many people,
Deetjen's Big Sur Inn reflects the character of the area better than
any other place.

You can't compete with the ☞ heart-stopping beauty of the
Big Sur coast stretching 80 miles from Carmel to San Simeon, and
the inn does not try. It is a rustic lodge with an add-on tumble of
cottages that simply blend into the mountains and trees. Helmuth

Deetjen, a Norwegian immigrant, built the homestead in the '30s. Today, the inn is owned by his estate and leased to a not-for-profit corporation owned by local residents.

The atmosphere is California casual, a nonpolyester, natural-fabric feeling, with a few traces of hippie life remaining. You're as likely to meet a San Francisco stock broker as you are a breakfast companion who'll discuss the meaning of Zen. Accommodations are unabashedly simple, still very much the way Grandpa Deetjen built them. Some bathrooms are shared, and heating is provided by fireplace, wood-burning stove, or heaters. Recent improvements are new beds, down comforters, and new rag rugs.

Fresh food, thoughtfully prepared, is the premise behind a menu that ranges from old counter-culture favorites like crisp vegetable stir-fry with brown rice, to duckling with fresh peach sauce, or pasta with fresh basil. A good wine list is frequently revised. A comfortable, family feeling among the staff extends over to guests, and the atmosphere is enhanced by hearth fires always burning, candles lit, and classical music playing on tape. Breakfasts are popular here, too.

Ask the innkeeper for directions to Pfeiffer Beach. A hidden one-lane road leads to a ☛ very private, special beach. And don't miss having a drink or lunch down the road at ☛ Nepenthe. Originally an adobe and redwood house that Orson Welles bought for Rita Hayworth, and at one time a refuge for Henry Miller, it's become a California equivalent of the Via Veneto: Eventually *everyone* makes the scene on its terrace perched 800 feet above a dramatic surf.

How to get there: The inn is on the east side of Highway 1.

✳

J: *If that fine word* funky *did not exist, it would have to be invented for Deetjen's Big Sur Inn.*

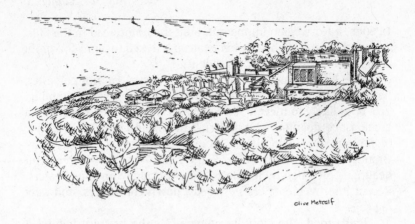

Olive Metcalf

Ventana Inn
Big Sur, California
93920

Innkeeper: Robert E. Bussinger
Address/Telephone: Big Sur; (408) 667–2331 or (408) 624–4812
Rooms: 60; all with private bath and television, most with fireplace.
Rates: $145 to $525, double occupancy; includes continental breakfast,
afternoon wine and cheese buffet.
Open: All year. Restaurant serves lunch, dinner; cocktail lounge.
Facilities and local attractions: Hot tubs, saunas, swimming pool. Hike,
picnic; the Ventana general store.

The Big Sur Coast has always welcomed the offbeat, and even
this sybaritic paradise was designed as a "different" kind of place:
no tennis, no golf, no conventions, no Muzak, no disco delights.

What it does offer is a window (*ventana* means "window" in
Spanish) toward both the Santa Lucia Mountains and the Pacific
Ocean from a redwood and cedar lodge on a magnificent slope.
This is the 👉 ultimate hideaway, a tasteful, expensive world of its
own harmonizing with the wilderness surrounding it. For activity
there are two 75-foot pools (heated all year) and two separate
bathhouses with luxurious Japanese hot tubs, one of them with
saunas. And there are walks over grassy slopes, through the
woods, or on the beach. From every point your eyes go to the 👉

spectacular Big Sur Coast, where boulders send white foam spraying into the air.

Some rooms in the cottages clustered around the lodge look down into a canyon of trees; others face the ocean. Their uncluttered blend of natural fabric and design makes each room seem to be the best one. Every detail—folk baskets holding kindling, window seats, quilts handmade in Nova Scotia, private terraces—has been carefully conceived.

A gravel path leads to the restaurant, with the opportunity of seeing native wildflowers and an occasional deer or bobcat on the way. The food is colorful California cuisine: fresh fish, veal, chicken, creative pastas, and a good wine list. The place to be at lunch is the ☞ expansive terrace with a 50-mile view of the coast. Dinner inside is a candlelight and pink linen affair. If you've walked the hills enough, indulge in a chocolate torte the *Washington Post* called "celestial."

At breakfast, a continental buffet, accompanied by baroque music, is spread in the lodge lobby by the rock fireplace: platters of melons, papayas, strawberries—whatever is fresh—pastries and breads baked in the Ventana kitchen, honey and preserves, yogurt and homemade granola. An afternoon wine and cheese buffet has an incredible array of domestic and imported cheeses.

The Store by the restaurant (books, baskets, mountain clothing, handmade knives, bird whistles) is as intriguing as its staff—all of whom seemed to be bilingual and have fascinating histories.

How to get there: On State Highway 1, Ventana is 311 miles (about a six-and-a-half-hour drive) north of Los Angeles. The inn's sign is on the right. From San Francisco, the inn is 152 miles, 28 miles south of Carmel.

✸

J: *I've heard that the best substitute for a rich father is a rich father-in-law. Short of that, a few days at Ventana will do.*

olive Metcalf

The J. Patrick House
Cambria, California
93428

Innkeeper: Molly Lynch
Address/Telephone: 2990 Burton Drive; (805) 927–3812
Rooms: 8; all with private bath. Room and bath facilities for wheelchairs.
Rates: $95, including breakfast. No smoking; no pets. Children over 16
   welcome.
Open: All year.
Facilities and local attractions: Close to Cambria beaches, shops, restaurants.
   Visit nearby Hearst Castle. Many vineyards in the area.

It wasn't too long ago that this warm early American–style inn wasn't here, only the log house in front. Guests gather there in the living room for wine and cheese in the early evening. With its rosy rug and wingback chairs flanking the fireplace, it's especially inviting on those damp, cool days that come winter and summer along the Central Coast.

The log house also has the dining room, office, and one large bedroom upstairs. It has log walls and a big brick fireplace, a spacious bath, and windows galore that look out into the garden.

Passion vine is growing up an arbor that connects the main house to a fine, two-story cedar building with seven bedrooms. I liked the feeling of the guest house the moment I walked in, partly because of the wonderful aroma. The cedar gives it a light fresh look, besides smelling good. All the bedrooms are spacious and have great tile baths. Another pleasant sitting room is on the first floor.

The early American decor is not the fussy, uncomfortable kind. It's appealing but uncluttered, with cushioned window seats framed by pretty curtains, some beautiful hand-crocheted bed coverings and a few special pieces. A huge California-willow rocker and headboard in one room are wonderful. (A smaller version of the rocker is in the living room.) They're the work of a local craftsman, says Molly.

Across the back of the log house is a sunny breakfast room that looks out on the garden. Molly's idea of continental breakfast is first-rate: coffee from freshly ground beans, freshly squeezed juice, cinnamon rolls or another baked treat just made, as well as granola, yogurt, and fresh fruit to layer and mix as you choose.

Running an inn is a business, but it's an intensely personal one for this innkeeper. It bears her father's name, and every room is named for a county in southern Ireland: Tipperary, Kerry, Kilkenny, and the like. Says Molly, "My whole point is that people are comfortable and that they feel they've been treated well. After that, this business is all fluff."

How to get there: North on Highway 1, exit at signs to Cambria; follow Main Street into town. At Burton Drive (Chevron Station on left), turn left; follow about ¾ mile. Just before reaching the inn, Burton takes a hard right turn. Inn is on left at number 2990.

✳

J: *There's not a shred of truth to the rumor that you have to be Irish to get a reservation here.*

olive Metcalf

The Cobblestone Inn
Carmel-by-the-Sea, California
93921

Innkeepers: Aileen Kelly and Janet Miller
Address/Telephone: Junipero Street between 7th and 8th (mailing address: Box 3185); (408) 625–5222; (1-800) AAA–INNS
Rooms: 24; all with private bath; fireplace, color television, small refrigerator in most rooms.
Rates: $90 to $170, double occupancy; $15 each additional person. Included are breakfast buffet, afternoon hors d'oeuvres, wine. No smoking inside.
Open: All year.
Facilities and local attractions: Short walk to Carmel Beach, shops, restaurants, art galleries. Picnics: Drive to Point Lobos State Reserve, Pebble Beach, Big Sur. Tennis, golf facilities within short drive.

The Cobblestone is one of five inns owned by the same management. Having visited all their inns, I'm ready to suggest that this group write a text on the art of personalized innkeeping. Each of their inns, from the Cobblestone here in Carmel to the Petite Auberge in San Francisco, is a classic example of exquisite decorating, first-class comforts, and exceptionally high standards of service and personal attention.

An on-duty innkeeper keeps it all working—in this case,

Aileen or Janet. They oversee all the basics thoroughly, like impeccable housekeeping and a friendly staff, but it's those ☞ deftly done little extras that are so winning: flowers, fruit, and a handwritten card in your room welcoming you by name; champagne, if they know it's a special occasion; a morning newspaper outside your door, and your shined shoes or golf clubs, too, if you put them out the night before.

Bedrooms have a French country feeling, with pretty wallpapers, fresh quilts and pillows, and handsome antiques. It's a pleasure to relax in a room with a comfortable sitting area, good reading lights, and a ☞ cobblestone fireplace.

When you cross the courtyard to the living room lounge, you'll discover still another area where the Cobblestone shines. The ☞ lavish breakfast buffet is beautifully presented and is the essence of fresh California eating. There are fresh juices and colorful platters of fresh fruit, homemade hot muffins and breads, a daily-changing hot baked egg dish, homemade granola, yogurt, cider, hot chocolate, teas, and coffee.

From 5:00 to 7:00 P.M. guests are invited to gather by the big stone fireplace and enjoy complimentary tea, sherry, wine, and a variety of hors d'oeuvres. The tempting platters of fine cheeses alone make it mandatory that you *walk* to dinner. The innkeepers are happy to make dinner suggestions and reservations for you. When you return, your bed will be turned down, and a fresh rose and a piece of candy will be on the pillow.

Given this kind of comfort and attention, it's not surprising that a weekend reservation is needed almost three months in advance. Weekdays and winter are easier.

How to get there: Exit State Highway 1 on Ocean Avenue. Proceed down Ocean to Junipero; turn left. The inn is two blocks farther on the right, at the corner of 8th Street.

Olive Metcalf

The Happy Landing
Carmel-by-the-Sea, California
93921

Innkeepers: Jeannine and Carl George
Address/Telephone: Monte Verde Street between 5th and 6th (mailing
  address: Box 2619); (408) 624–7917
Rooms: 9; including 2 suites; all with private bath and television, 3 with
  fireplace. 1 nonsmoking room.
Rates: $80 to $125 for two, $15 each additonal person; children over 12
  welcome. Breakfast delivered to your room. Some designated parking
  spaces on street.
Open: All year.
Facilities and local attractions: Wedding facilities. Short walk to Carmel
  Beach, unique shops, art galleries, restaurants.

I'm not the first to describe the architecture of this inn as pink
Hansel and Gretel. It has a picturesque, fairy tale cottage-in-
the-woods look, and Carmel is exactly the right setting. To be
perfectly accurate, however, it's really not a cottage, but rather a
cluster of accommodations all connected by rambling flagstone
paths.

Each room opens onto a ☞ colorful central courtyard with a
gazebo and a small pond. As I arrived, a young couple were
making arrangements to have their wedding there. The poor kids

74

didn't realize that a veteran mother-of-the-bride was standing right there ready to approve their choice . . . if only they'd asked. This was late November, but the abundant plants, flowers, and bright hanging baskets of fuchsias were dazzling. Ah, California.

The rooms are delightfully decorated with antiques and a romantic flair. Their steep roofs are especially inviting, and high cathedral ceilings make even the smallest room seem light and open. A television and a decanter of sherry in every room are pleasant to come back to after a day of shopping at Carmel's unusual stores or walking the beach.

A warm, attractive common room is also available for guests to use. You might enjoy afternoon coffee or a steaming cup of English tea here by the fireplace.

Breakfast is delivered to guest rooms on silver trays, but given the pleasant courtyard, many people elect to take theirs outside. A hot, baked item is always fresh every morning in addition to juice and fresh fruit. This fall day it was warm gingerbread with a lemon sauce.

The innkeepers are professionals, but better still, they have the ☛ knack of making each guest feel special and comfortable. You can't beat the personal touch.

How to get there: From State Highway 1 at Carmel, turn off at Ocean Avenue. Continue to center of town; turn right at Monte Verde Street. Inn is two blocks on the right.

❋

J: *Part of experiencing Carmel is walking everywhere! This is a good location, just off the crowded main street and only four blocks from the beach.*

olive Metcalf

Mission Ranch
Carmel-by-the-Sea, California
93923

Innkeeper: Joyce Kutchins
Address/Telephone: 26270 Dolores; (408) 624–6436
Rooms: 6 in The Farmhouse, all with private bath; a variety of other accommodations available, including cottages, The Bunkhouse (sleeps 3 couples or a family), and motel units.
Rates: $58 to $80 for The Farmhouse, including generous continental breakfast; $80 to $103 for cottages. The Bunkhouse, with kitchen, $100; motel units $44 to $66 with breakfast. Children welcome.
Open: All year. Restaurant (dinners only), piano bar, cocktail lounge.
Facilities and local attractions: Nature trails; eight tennis courts, tennis clinics offered. Safe swimming at Carmel River Beach; short walk to beach, Carmel Mission. Drive to Point Lobos, Big Sur. Party Barn available for parties, dancing.

A friend waxing nostalgic about his college days (more than thirty-five years ago) remembered when he and his friends would drive down to Carmel from San Francisco to dine and dance at the Mission Ranch. It's downright reassuring to see that places that gave us happy memories are still around and looking good.

The Mission Ranch is charming a new generation with its historic buildings, 🖝 hundred-year-old cypresses, and its outlook

76

on the rugged beauty of Point Lobos. The restaurant still serves hearty dinners, and the piano bar—how's *that* for nostalgia?—still gives repressed saloon singers an atmosphere for crooning.

One change at the Ranch is that the family homestead is now a bed and breakfast inn. The Farmhouse, built a century ago, was home to the Martins, a family of Scottish immigrants who came to California in 1856 and bought large acreage encircling an old Spanish mission.

The two-story, white frame house, sitting under several enormous cypress trees, is now sound-proofed and newly decorated in a homey, not high-fashion style. The large rooms are furnished very simply with odd pieces from the 1920s and 1930s. Bathrooms are large too, with showers added, and complimentary toiletries. A spacious parlor has Victorian sofas flanking a wood-burning fireplace, and a television and telephone are in the room.

The dining room is where a generous continental breakfast is set up buffet style in the morning: fruit, juices, breads, cold cereals, coffee, and teas.

This is an atmosphere different from the usual Carmel lodgings—an authentic ranch, not a manicured resort. And it's a mere few blocks from the chichi streets of art galleries and stylish shops. Twenty acres to roam and enjoy, with long vistas of fields and water. Bring the children.

How to get there: At Carmel, exit State Highway 1 on Rio Road west, toward the ocean. Immediately past the mission, turn left on Lasuen Drive; follow around to the Ranch on your left.

❧

J: The *mission just up the road is officially "San Carlos Borromeo de Carmelo," a romantic gem in the mission chain, with a Moorish tower and tranquil gardens. It's the resting place of Father Junipero Serra, who founded nine missions and died there in 1784.*

The Sandpiper Inn
Carmel-by-the-Sea, California
93923

Innkeepers: Irene and Graeme Mackenzie
Address/Telephone: 2408 Bay View Avenue; (408) 624–6433
Rooms: 15, all with private bath; 2 cottages.
Rates: $80 to $120, double occupancy; 2-day minimum on weekends.
    Includes continental breakfast, afternoon sherry.
Open: All year.
Facilities and local attractions: Ten-speed bicycles for rent, in-house library,
    color television in lounge. Golf, tennis club privileges by arrangement.
    Perfect location for walking Carmel Beach.

"We're different from those B&Bs," Graeme Mackenzie says
emphatically. "No miniature rooms here; no cold croissant and
call it breakfast; no rules and regulations saying you must do this
or you can't do that. *We're an inn!*"

The declaration is delivered in an unreconstructed Scottish
burr, and with a smile, but the message is clear: ☛ The Mackenzies are professional innkeepers, and not to be confused with those
other birds. Graeme has a wealth of experience in Europe, Hong
Kong, Bermuda, and Dallas, where he became president of a hotel
company.

Mackenzie's blue eyes are scornful as he relates the unbelievable behavior of some hosts who call themselves innkeepers. "Why, I know of one place that demands you take off your shoes in the house! Is that any way to treat a guest?"

Since returning to the Monterey Peninsula in 1975 and acquiring The Sandpiper Inn, Graeme and Irene have remodeled and redecorated the fifteen guest rooms and cottages. Now they all have private baths, queen- and king-size beds (Graeme recalls his unhappy encounters with small beds in other inns), and quilted bedspreads. They're furnished with country English and French antiques, and he's particularly proud of some recently acquired antique headboards. Freshly picked nosegays add to an impeccable, tranquil atmosphere, with no television or telephone to intrude.

Some rooms have wood-burning fireplaces, and others are situated to take full advantage of the inn's 🖙 sweeping views across Carmel Bay and out to the Pacific. The house is set only 70 yards from the beach in a quiet, private neighborhood. Just a quirk of luck—it was an inn before the strict zoning laws went into effect—accounts for its being there. The result is that 🖙 you feel like a house guest at someone's exclusive seaside home.

That's precisely the mood Irene and Graeme promote. They invite you to help yourself to glasses, ice, coffee or tea in the kitchen; ride one of their ten-speed bikes down the cypress-dotted streets along Carmel's beach; enjoy the warm English-feeling library, or relax by the fireside in the gracious living room ("lounge," to the Mackenzies) with sherry at 5:00 P.M.

How to get there: Take Ocean Avenue through Carmel to Scenic Avenue; turn left and proceed along the beach to the end. Just past the stop sign in the middle of the road, turn left at Martin. Inn is one block on the right at the corner of Bay View.

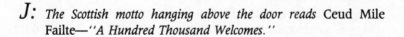

J: *The Scottish motto hanging above the door reads* Ceud Mile Failte—*"A Hundred Thousand Welcomes."*

Olive Metcalf

The Stonehouse Inn
Carmel-by-the-Sea, California
93921

Innkeeper: Virginia Carey
Address/Telephone: Eighth below Monte Verde (mailing address: Box
    2517); (408) 624–4569
Rooms: 6 share 3 baths.
Rates: $80 to $105. No smoking.
Open: All year.
Facilities and local attractions: Walk to Carmel Beach. Unique shops and art
    galleries two blocks away. Explore Point Lobos State Park two miles
    south. Seventeen Mile Drive at Pebble Beach.

Writers have always been attracted to the Monterey Peninsula. It's an atmosphere that seems conducive to creativity—
dramatic surfs, the misty cool weather, towering pines and
evergreen oaks, and the famous Monterey cypresses with their
twisted, gnarled shapes. It's inspiring even if you're only writing
post cards.

The original owner of The Stonehouse, Mrs. "Nana" Foster,
often invited notable artists and writers to stay in her Carmel
home. Sinclair Lewis, Jack London, Lotta Crabtree, and George
Sterling were among her guests. It seems to still reflect the old,
quieter Carmel, when it first became an artist colony.

This is just the kind of sprawling, old-fashioned vaca house many of us would choose—if a staff came with it. It's large and luxurious, with a completely stone exterior, hand-shaped by local Indians when it was built in 1906. It's surrounded by wonderful gardens and a big, broad, partially glassed-in front porch, with pots of flowers and comfortable chairs and sofas.

There's a warm, colorful living room with a large stone fireplace. Fine furniture and white wicker with bright cushions are all put together so tastefully with vivid rugs, plants, flowers, books, and *things*, you tend to think it just happened. On consideration, you realize it's been done artfully, that it's invitingly clean and fresh, and that innkeeper Virginia Carey is a pro.

Two bedrooms on the main floor and four upstairs have board and batten walls painted white that are typical of early Carmel houses. They're beautifully decorated in soft colors (peach, ivory, mossy green, pale blue), with quilts and antiques. Each room is reminiscent of the artist or writer for whom it was named. The Jack London has dramatic, gabled ceilings, a bed and a day bed set in brass, with a ceiling fan and a glorious ocean view. The Lola Montez has a four-poster bed, a gabled ceiling, and a view of the garden.

You eat well here, too. Breakfast is the only meal served, but it's a full and proper one. There are always several juices, at least two fresh fruits, at least two homemade breads or muffins, and homemade granola. Then Virginia serves a hot entree that changes daily, and plenty of fresh coffee and tea.

How to get there: Exit State Highway 1 on Ocean Avenue; continue into town to Monte Verde. Turn left two blocks to 8th Street; turn right. The inn is in the center of the block.

J: *When you gather around the fireplace for wine and hors d'oeuvres, you're likely to meet people who have been returning to The Stonehouse for years.*

olive Metcalf

Vagabond House Inn
Carmel-by-the-Sea, California
93921

Innkeeper: Honey Jones
Address/Telephone: Fourth and Dolores (mailing address: Box 2747); (408) 624–7738
Rooms: 11; all with private bath, most with fireplace, kitchen, or small refrigerator. Television; telephone.
Rates: $70 to $110; lower winter rates.
Open: All year.
Facilities and local attractions: Walk to Carmel shops, art galleries, restaurants, beach. Short drives to Pebble Beach golf courses, Big Sur, Point Lobos.

It's hard to believe that this romantic inn ever had a military connection, but it did. It was built during World War II to provide lodging when nearby Fort Ord was bursting at the seams.

A more poetic part of its history is that the poet Don Blanding lived here in the '40s, but no one seems to know if the house was named for his poem *Vagabond House,* or if he named his poem for the house.

The shake-roofed, oak-shaded Vagabond has heart-robbing qualities that have won it a loyal following through the years. Its half-timbered look is English Tudor, perfectly appropriate for the picture-book village of Carmel. The flagstone courtyard dominated by old and very large oak trees is the focal point for each of the rooms. Its lush scene of camellias, rhododendrons, hanging plants, ferns, and flowers is really quite magical.

The bright, airy, and especially spacious rooms are constructed of knotty pine, brick, and barn board. Decorating themes range from nautical to early American to Victorian. Each room is supplied with its own coffeepot, freshly ground coffee, and a decanter of cream sherry.

Continental breakfast is delivered to your room or served in the patio. It's most pleasant to fix a tray from the selection of juices, fruits, muffins and rolls, boiled eggs, and cheeses, and then take the newspaper and repair to the courtyard. The news goes down better this way. And, what better place to plan a day than under a hanging pot of brilliant fuchsias?

The management here at Vagabond House also owns Lincoln Green, a cluster of four spacious English country-style cottages. They're in a quiet, residential neighborhood near the ocean and the Carmel River. Each beautifully decorated unit has a living room with fireplace, separate bedroom, and kitchen. There is no food service here, but guests are invited to come up to Vagabond House for breakfast, if they wish.

How to get there: From State Highway 1, take Ocean Avenue turnoff to downtown Carmel. At Dolores Street, turn right to 4th Street. The inn is on the right.

※

J: *It is worth remembering that winter visits to Carmel have some distinct advantages: fewer people, lower rates, and, while reservations are still needed for weekends, you can often find appealing lodgings on the spur of the moment.*

olive Metcalf

Robles Del Rio Lodge
Carmel Valley, California
93924

Innkeeper: Glen Gurries
Address/Telephone: 200 Punta Del Monte; (408) 659–3706
Rooms: 31, including some cottages; all with private bath and cable
television, some with fireplace and kitchenette.
Rates: $59 to $139, includes generous continental breakfast.
Open: All year.
Facilities and local attractions: Cantina serves wine and beer. Exceptional
restaurant, The Ridge, serves lunch and dinner. Swimming pool; tile
hot tub with Jacuzzi; sauna; tennis. Surrounding woodlands to hike.
Ten minutes from Carmel attractions.

Driving the twisting road up to Robles Del Rio gives you a
feeling that you're deep in the heart of California countryside,
though it's only a ten-minute drive from Carmel. The lodge looks
just right for its rustic setting. Surrounded by live oak trees and
perched on the mountaintop (well, high hill) surveying the valley
below, this is true country-inn feeling. A tree-shaded flagstone
terrace extends from the lodge with flowers in profusion, a pool,
Jacuzzi, and outdoor fireplace to be enjoyed night and day.

It was built in the 1920s, the oldest resort still operating in the
Carmel Valley. The lodge is now owned by the Ron Gurries family

with son Glen and his wife Adreena as resident managers. Former long-time owner Bill Wood lives just across the road. He ran the place for over forty years and approvingly watches the renovations and improvements going on. He can reminisce about the early days of the lodge, when Arthur Murray would check in for a month or so, when Alistair Cooke visited after the war, and how the swimming pool was dug with horse and plow because they couldn't get a tractor up the crooked road.

Six rooms are in the main lodge; the others are in separate buildings scattered over nine acres. These rooms are unpretentious but entirely comfortable, and the views are wonderful. Some have a rustic board-and-batten decor, and others have a more contemporary country look using Laura Ashley fabric. Expandable options available in the cottages with outfitted kitchens and fireplaces are convenient for longer stays.

Beginning with a bountiful breakfast buffet set in the main lodge living room, good food is a big part of the Lodge's appeal. With a crackling fire going to chase away the morning chill, much of the original 1920s furniture still in place, and wide views of the valley, this room has a good feeling.

Lunch or dinner in The Ridge restaurant, also in the main lodge building, is a dining experience equal to the best available in Carmel or Monterey. Chef Daniel Barduzzi has extensive credentials from Europe and the East Coast, but he's now a California specialist. He relies on Monterey agriculture for daily deliveries of whatever is freshest and best. If he can be beguiled out of his kitchen, you will meet an example of what Gallic charm is all about.

His wine list, too, has a deliberate regional focus. (Did you know more grapes are grown in the Monterey region now than in Napa?) Notice the hand-painted china, the fresh flowers, the broad deck overlooking the valley. What a seat to watch a fog bank form over Carmel and quietly roll in. A fresh rockfish soup and a chicken breast stir-fry with ginger, bell pepper, and tomatoes were pretty impressive, too.

How to get there: From Highway 1 at Carmel, drive east on Carmel Valley Road about 13 miles to Esquiline Road. Turn right and follow the signs up the hill to the lodge, about 1 mile.

Olive Metcalf

Stonepine
Carmel Valley, California
93924

Innkeepers: Owners Gordon Hentschel and Noel Irwin-Hentschel; resident manager, Richard Buelow
Address/Telephone: 150 East Carmel Valley Road; (408) 659-2245
Rooms: 12 suites; all with private bath with Jacuzzi and cable television, most with woodburning fireplace.
Rates: $150 to $500 double occupancy, including continental breakfast. Exclusive use of the chateau (up to 16 people) $3,500 per night; Paddock House exclusive (up to 8 people) $1,000. Children welcome in Paddock suites.
Open: All year. Dinner by reservation.
Facilities and local attractions: 330 acres of meadows, gardens, and woodlands to explore over miles of riding and running trails or by horse-drawn Victorian carriages. Swimming pool; tennis court; croquet; archery range; soccer field. Health club, steam bath. Equestrian Center; instruction, moonlight hayrides. Minutes from Carmel, Monterey, Big Sur. Facilities for small or large parties, business gatherings.

If F. Scott Fitzgerald had wanted Gatsby to make his splash in California's Carmel Valley instead of East Egg, the once-private estate of Stonepine would have been the perfect background.

Fitzgerald missed it, but you need not. The splendid Mediterranean-style house is now a remarkable country inn.

When you press the button that opens an electric gate guarding a mile-long road to the main house, you enter a world of quiet luxury and ☞ 330 acres of natural beauty. After three years of restoration and redecoration, the Chateau Noel has eight magnificent suites, and four less formal suites in the Paddock House.

The common rooms include an elegant foyer, living room, dining room, and handsome library paneled with burnished nineteenth-century French oak. Every detail is first-class, even to the library shelves stocked with hardback copies of current titles and classics. Across the back of the estate is the ☞ loggia with stone arches supported by centuries-old columns from Rome. In daylight, you look out to gnarled olive trees and gardens that frame a rolling meadow. At night, it's a romantic place to watch the sunset or dine by a blazing fire.

In the early 1930s, the estate was the foremost thoroughbred horse–breeding farm in California. (The owner was the daughter of the Crocker banking family of San Francisco, and the social set motored over from Pebble Beach to play polo and ride.) Today, the ☞ Equestrian Center is the primary atttraction at Stonepine with the finest examples of classic breeds in residence. Debby and Tommy Harris run the center. They give English and western riding lessons and two-day equestrian clinics—beginners welcome. Tommy's drives around the estate and moonlight hayrides are popular with guests.

To dine here is to feast on superb food and drink served on Limoges, Waterford, and Baccarat with sterling silver at a prix fixe of $40 per person. If you want to entertain, a creative ☞ staff will produce a unique party with music, food, and entertainment. A recent Civil War extravaganza even had hairdressers and costumes for the guests—everything but live bullets in the battle re-enactment that took place off the loggia.

How to get there: From Highway 1 proceed east on Carmel Valley Road past a 13.0 mile marker; Stonepine will be on your right. Pick up telephone at the gate for entry. Complimentary ☞ airport pickups available in a Phanton V Rolls Royce. Monterey airport 30 minutes from Stonepine.

olive Metcalf

New Davenport Bed and Breakfast Inn
Davenport, California
95017

Innkeepers: Marcia and Bruce McDougal
Address/Telephone: 31 Davenport Avenue; (408) 425–1818 or 426–4122
Rooms: 12; all with private bath.
Rates: $55 to $105, single or double occupancy, with $10 charge for each
   additional guest. Expanded continental breakfast with champagne
   included. Children over 12 welcome, but pets not allowed. No
   smoking.
Open: All year. Lunch and dinner.
Facilities and local attractions: Folk art, textiles, pottery, other crafts in the
   Cash Store. Beach walking, whale watching; near state parks, Santa
   Cruz, University of California campus. Cabrillo Music Festival each
   summer.

You can talk to native Californians who have never heard of
Davenport—and that's just fine with most of the citizens of this
town. But there it is, halfway between San Francisco and Carmel,
smack dab on one of the most spectacular coastlines anywhere.

The McDougals saw it as the perfect site for their pottery
gallery (Bruce once taught pottery) and decided to build a new

Davenport Cash Store. The original Cash Store occupied the same corner for many years during the first half of the century when Davenport was a thriving town with a cement plant, hotels, and businesses. When Marcia and Bruce rebuilt, they added delightful accommodations and a restaurant.

The Cash Store is a gathering place for local artisans. It sells their 🖝 wares in pottery, textiles, wood, and glass. The original jewelry, especially, took my eye.

Some of these arts and crafts articles also decorate the eight bedrooms above the store. Each one has a cheerful mixture of antiques, ethnic treasures, and local arts. The pleasant rooms all open onto the balcony that wraps around the building.

Beside the Cash Store is the oldest remaining original building in Davenport. The McDougals have renovated it to provide a warm sitting room and four bedrooms. These rooms are smaller than the new ones over the store, but they're fresh and pretty, with quilts and an old-fashioned appeal. The 🖝 quiet garden patio here is another attraction. In the sitting room are books, a comfortable sofa and chairs, coffee makings, and an ocean view. Breakfast for all guests is served here, including 🖝 champagne, fresh juice, coffee, teas, and homemade pastry.

In the restaurant your eyes go from one interesting display to another: costumes from Yugoslavia, Mexican rugs, African masks, and handcrafts from around the world. The menu seems to offer as wide a variety of dishes as the decor is varied—and the bakery is outstanding. My luncheon choice of shredded, cooked chicken on a fresh tortilla topped with spicy salsa, cilantro, avocado, and lettuce was a winner.

After lunch, walk across the highway and down a short path to savor the discovery of 🖝 a secluded stretch of sandy beach. It could be awfully pleasant to take a blanket and a book, maybe some provisions from the restaurant, and spend a few hours here listening to the surf.

How to get there: On California Highway 1, 9 miles north of Santa Cruz.

The Jabberwock
Monterey, California
93940

Innkeepers: Jim and Barbara Allen
Address/Telephone: 598 Laine Street; (408) 372–4777
Rooms: 7; 3 with private bath, 4 share 2 baths.
Rates: $85 to $160, including full breakfast and evening aperitifs and hors
d'oeuvres. No credit cards. No children; no pets.
Open: All year.
Facilities and local attractions: Airport pickups by arrangement. Walk to
Cannery Row, Monterey Bay Aquarium, restaurants. Short drive to
Carmel, Pebble Beach.

Have you ever breakfasted on Snarkleberry Flumptious? How
about Burndt Flambjous? You'll recognize the inspiration of 🖙
Lewis Carroll nonsense as the theme of The Jabberwock, with
originally named breakfast dishes, decor, and room names. There's
also a Burbling Room (a telephone nook), and The Tum Tum Tree
(a refrigerator stocked with complimentary soft drinks).

Now I'm the first to admit that a little whimsy oozes like
chocolate on a hot day—and can be just as sticky, but the
innkeepers use this bit of fancy with a winning sense of fun. It
seems only to enhance the charm of a well-run, solidly comfortable
inn. As a kid, Jim Allen loved the poem "Jabberwocky" from

90

Through the Looking Glass (he says it was the only one he ever learned), and he and Barbara thought it was the perfect name for their inn.

The towered and turreted 1911 house sits on a hill in a neighborhood four blocks above Cannery Row. A glassed-in veranda wraps around two sides of the building and overlooks their colorful English garden and beyond to Monterey Bay. A chalkboard on the wall lists each room name, and beside it, the first names of the occupants. Barbara says she wants everyone to be on a first-name basis when a five o'clock bell summons guests to the veranda for aperitifs and hors d'oeuvres.

Every room is engagingly decorated with elegant antique beds, beautiful linens, and down pillows and comforters. Robes and every toiletry you might have forgotten are thoughtfully provided. The third floor has an arrangement two couples will enjoy—two bedrooms, The Mimsy and The Wabe, share a bath and a private sitting room that has views all the way to Santa Cruz.

When you breakfast by the fireside in the dining room, the name of the day's special dish is etched in reverse on a glass sign. You have to hold it up to a mirror to read it. Notice the clock on the mantle, too. It's backwards!

Steady yourself, and have a brillig day. Retire with one of the house volumes of Lewis Carroll, and the homemade cookies and milk Barbara sets out.

How to get there: Exit State Highway 1 at Munras Avenue. Take an immediate left at Soledad Drive; then turn right at Pacific Street. Continue as name changes to Lighthouse. Turn left at Hoffman; proceed two blocks to Laine Street. Inn is on the left corner, number 598.

J: ☞ *The Allens will prepurchase your Aquarium tickets so you can go when you please and not stand in line.*

Olive Metcalf

Old Monterey Inn
Monterey, California
93940

Innkeepers: Ann and Gene Swett
Address/Telephone: 500 Martin Avenue; (408) 375–8284
Rooms: 10; all with private bath, most with fireplace.
Rates: $130 to $195, full breakfast included. No credit cards. No children;
　　no pets; no cigars.
Open: All year.
Facilities and local attractions: Short walk to historic district of Monterey,
　　Fisherman's Wharf, shops, restaurants. Monterey Bay Aquarium.
　　Short drives to Carmel, Pebble Beach, Point Lobos State Reserve, Big
　　Sur coastline.

Let's discuss lodgings for particular people. Does the word
rustic give you a headache? When the phrase "Victorian charm" is
mentioned, do 'you have an acute attack of nausea? Do you feel
that anything built after World War II is faintly tacky? Have I got
an inn for you!

The Old Monterey Inn is an elegant architectural gem built in
1929 and until recently has always been a private residence. It's a
half-timbered, Tudor-style house sitting on an oak-studded hillside
in a quiet residential neighborhood. More than ☞ an acre of
astonishingly beautiful gardens surround it and give each room a

view of begonias, fuchsias, hydrangeas, and wooded banks of ferns and rhododendrons.

Ann and Gene Swett are the proprietors of this paradise, the family home where they raised their six children. Their hospitality and these beautifully appointed rooms are all the most discriminating guest could want. Choose any room and you can't go wrong, but the Library captured my heart with book-lined walls, a stone fireplace, and a private sun deck overlooking the garden. Everyone who stays in the Ashford Suite plots a return to this triumph of refined chic: a sitting room in Ralph Lauren sheets, separate dressing room, and large bedroom in antique pine.

Eight of the ten rooms have wood-burning fireplaces. All of them have luxuries like elegant linens, goosedown comforters, the gleaming wood of period furniture, family antiques, and bathroom items you might have forgotten. Other personal touches include a refrigerator stocked with complimentary juices and soft drinks, and the loan of an outfitted picnic basket for a day's outing. The Swetts include a list of the best delis, the most interesting picnic sites, and directions for getting there.

Another fireplace is in the elegant step-down dining room where breakfast is served. You can have breakfast sent to your room, but it's awfully grand to sit around the long oak table with your hosts and meet the other lucky people who are here. Fresh fruit compotes and things like coddled eggs, Belgian waffles, or Orange Blossom French toast are featured.

In the evening, a fire burns in the living room and the Swetts join their guests for wine and cheese. It's another lovely room, with oriental rugs and fine furniture. The ultimate standard of good taste runs throughout the house: comfort and quality, without pretention.

How to get there: Take Munras Avenue exit from Highway 1; make an immediate left on Soledad Drive, then right on Pacific. Continue ⁶⁄₁₀ of a mile to Martin Street on the left. Inn is on your right at number 500.

✳

J: *If checking into an inn is buying a bit of magic for your life, get ready to be enchanted.*

Olive Metcalf

The Centrella
Pacific Grove, California
93950

Innkeeper: Diana Vandergrift
Address/Telephone: 612 Central Avenue (mailing address: Box 884); (408) 372–3372
Rooms: 26, including suites and cottages for 2 and 4; all but 2 with private bath.
Rates: $65 to $175, including breakfast, wine and hors d'oeuvres. No pets; children under 12 in cottages only. Handicap accessible room. Two-night minimum on weekends.
Open: All year.
Facilities and local attractions: Bayside walking-bicycle path. Walk to Cannery Row, Monterey Bay Aquarium. Nearby 17-mile drive, Carmel, restaurants, shops.

Time your journey down Highway 1 to arrive at The Centrella in time for the social hour, 5:30 to 6:30 P.M. Its inviting living/dining area offers just what a weary traveler needs: decanters of wine and sherry and a ☛ substantial cocktail buffet: rye bread sliced thin, pâté, cheese spreads, hard cheese, crackers, guacamole and tortilla chips, marinated artichoke hearts, and dieter's delight—crudités.

It's difficult, but use some moderation at this repast, or you'll tend to tune out the good information that Diana and her staff have about the excellent choice of restaurants you can walk to in the area or that are just a short drive away. It's tempting to just relax by the fire in this pleasant room and read. There are books and magazines about, good reading lights, even an in-progress stitchery project set up with an invitation to contribute a few stitches.

Unlike so many inns of this vintage, The Centrella was never a private home. Built in 1889, it was described by the Monterey newspaper as "The largest, most commodious and pleasantly located private boarding house in 'The Grove.'" It's now listed in the *National Register of Historic Places* and has survived restoration beautifully, earning several design awards.

Guest rooms are decorated and appointed for comfort, but old touches remain. I liked the big claw-footed bathtub, the high ceilings, and the quilt in my room. But the good firm bed, a telephone, and an ice machine down the hall were appreciated, too.

Cottages in the back garden are a good arrangement for family vacations. One that sleeps four has an attractive sitting area, fireplace, television, small refrigerator, and wet bar.

Breakfast in the dining room is an easy introduction to a day of touring. A morning paper is at the door of your room, and the full breakfast buffet has all you require. A friendly staff going in and out of the adjoining kitchen might even pop your Danish into the oven for a few minutes, if you ask.

How to get there: From Highway 1, take Del Monte/Pacific Grove exit. Continue on as street name changes to Lighthouse, then to Central. Inn is on the right.

J: *I had an early-morning walk along the Bay Shore—just me, the scuba divers, and the seals.*

Olive Metcalf

The Gosby House
Pacific Grove, California
93950

Innkeeper: Kelly Short
Address/Telephone: 643 Lighthouse Avenue; (408) 375–1287
Rooms: 22, including 16 in main house; 20 with private bath, 7 with
  private entrance.
Rates: $85 to $125, full breakfast, afternoon wines and hors d'oeuvres
  included. Smoking and children in newer rooms only.
Open: All year.
Facilities and local attractions: Bicycling and walking paths along shoreline;
  Victorian architecture in Pacific Grove; watch seals, otters, and
  migrating whales. Close to golfing, tennis; deep-sea sport fishing,
  charter boats, tours available.

The Gosby House is a 🖙 showcase Victorian, vintage 1887,
the kind you turn around to look at again as you drive by. Though
it was built as a private residence, it's not a newcomer to the
proliferation of elegant inns in this area. It's been providing
accommodations to Monterey Peninsula visitors for nearly one
hundred years.

The inn's current brochure includes the Oscar Wilde quota-
tion, "I have the simplest of taste. I am satisfied with only the
best." Oscar would not be disappointed were he to magically

check into Gosby House. He'd be captivated right at the front door with the brimming pots of bright flowers clustered on the steps, and with the rich, colorful interior. And he'd appreciate the quiet, private places to relax throughout the house and along the brick garden paths.

You've seen dark, serious Victoriana? This is cheerful, playful Victoriana. (One does hope Herself would have been amused.) In the elegant parlor are polished woods, fine antiques, and comfortable English and French furniture around the fireplace. There's also a carousel horse, old teddy bears, a set of *Winnie the Pooh* volumes in the bookcase, and a grand glass-door cabinet filled with antique dolls. Guests gather here for afternoon tea or sherry, fresh fruits, and hors d'oeuvres.

In the handsome dining room, a large buffet is covered in the morning with an array of fresh fruits, cereals, hot breads, a hot dish like a frittata or quiche, and granola and yogurt—for yogurt parfaits.

The charm doesn't fall off when you go upstairs. Bedrooms are a special delight in a house of this style. With turrets and dormers you get window seats to be decorated with fat cushions in bright prints, and cozy slanted ceilings with delicately colored wallpapers. Fluffy comforters, good reading lights, and a hand-written card welcoming you by name are nice touches.

Oscar surely would have appreciated the teddy bear waiting on the bed.

How to get there: From San Francisco, take Highway 1 south past Monterey; exit at Highway 68 west to Pacific Grove. In town, follow Forest Avenue to Lighthouse Avenue; turn left, and go 3 blocks to the inn.

☀

J: *A wistful comment written by one guest in the register reads: ''I wish home was just like this!''*

Illustration: olive Metcalf

The Green Gables Inn
Pacific Grove, California
93950

Innkeepers: Roger and Sally Post
Address/Telephone: 104 Fifth Street; (408) 375–2095
Rooms: 11, including 1 suite and separate Carriage House accommodations; 7 with private bath, 4 share 2 full baths.
Rates: $95 to $150, breakfast included.
Open: All year.
Facilities and local attractions: Shoreline paths for bicycling and jogging; public beach, scuba diving, swimming, picnicking; short walk to Cannery Row, Monterey Bay Aquarium; close to golf and tennis.

Green Gables is a romantic gem of a Queen Anne–style mansion with a fairy-tale look about it, half-timbered and gabled, sitting above the shoreline of Monterey Bay.

Looking at the dormers and peaks of the roof line, you just know that the ☛ upstairs ceilings will be entertaining—and they are. One cozy accommodation tucked under the eaves is The Garret Room, an enchanting hideaway with dark beams against bright-flowered wallpaper. The Chapel Room is larger, also with a steep slanting ceiling, and tiny diamond-paned windows. The Gable Room, once a children's playroom, has a sitting area, a loft, and superb views. Adjoining the Balcony Room is a glassed-in porch fitted with tall camp chairs to enjoy the Bay view.

In the adjacent Carriage House accommodations, every room has a fireplace and bath, but the most romantic rooms are those in the main house. A suite off the living room is quite grand, with a fireplace, sitting room, and a large private bath. All the rooms are furnished with antique pieces, and beautiful fabrics cover the quilts and pillows. Fresh flowers and fruit, those gracious extras, are in every room.

The large living room and dining room are elegant, yet completely inviting. An ornate ceiling with delicate plaster designs painted in blue and apricot is impressive. Low tables and chairs are in bay-window alcoves facing the bay. A unique fireplace framed by stained-glass panels is flanked on either side with matching, dark blue sofas. Flowered draperies are at the tall windows, polished wood gleams, and tasteful accessories are everywhere. You'll feel terribly civilized having a nip of sherry and an hors d'oeuvre here in the afternoon.

The staff serves breakfast in a style appropriate to the surroundings—sitting down in the dining room. Juices and a wide offering of fresh fruits are followed by muffins, cereals, granola, and a substantial hot dish, perhaps a frittata or quiche.

How to get there: From San Francisco, take Highway 1 past Monterey and exit at Highway 68 west to Pacific Grove. Once in town, continue on Forest Avenue to the beach. Turn right on Ocean View to Fifth Street.

ప్ఞఁ

J: *Green Gables proves you* can *have Victorian charm, without a trace of cloying quaintness.*

Olive Metcalf

The House of Seven Gables Inn
Pacific Grove, California
93950

Innkeepers: The Flatley family (John, Nora, Susan, Ed, and Fred)
Address/Telephone: 555 Ocean View Boulevard; (408) 372–4341
Rooms: 14; all with private bath.
Rates: $85 to $155, with generous continental breakfast included. Two-
day minimum on weekends. No pets; no smoking.
Open: All year.
Facilities and local attractions: Four patios for sunning; shoreline paths for
bicycling, walking; short walk to Cannery Row, beaches. Close to all
attractions of Monterey Peninsula.

It was surprising to walk into this big, showy Victorian and
find, not the Victoriana I expected, but an  extraordinary
collection of fine European antiques. The Flatley family has
collected so much that visitors who have been coming to the inn
for years still find things they hadn't noticed before.

Guests here can enjoy the best of both times. While the house
and the antique collection are old, the quality of the linens,
bedding, and the plumbing is fresh and new. This is an especially
well-maintained inn.

The house was completed in 1886 and still has the same unobstructed view of Monterey Bay it had then. At the end of the century, Lucie Chase, a well-to-do widow and civic leader, added sun porches and gables, giving the house its amazing configuration.

Every room has excellent beds, good reading lights, a private bath, and elegant appointments. All have beautiful ocean views and a sitting area. Some of the newer bungalows behind the house are every bit as grand. No rustic country style here.

This is a fine house for relaxing, and the Flatleys think of every comfort. Tea is served in the afternoon on the sun porch or outdoors on the patio. There's always something homemade— shortbread, mini-muffins, and often Nora's homemade fudge. A television is on the sun porch, and an antique (working) telephone booth is in the hallway.

Breakfast is an elegant sit-down affair. Beautiful blue-and-white china is used on white linen at the dining room table. Silver platters of every available fresh fruit are always served along with fine teas and coffee, yogurt, and a variety of homemade breads and cakes, or Nora's apple cobbler.

How to get there: From Highway 1, take Pebble Beach/Pacific Grove exit. Follow signs to Pacific Grove, staying on Forest Avenue. Turn right on Ocean View Boulevard and continue 2 blocks to the inn at the corner of Fountain and Ocean View.

❀

J: *With a name like The House of Seven Gables, I felt there must surely be a Hawthorne Room—and there is—but the theme isn't labored. In all those nooks and crannies, alcoves and bays, I couldn't possibly have avoided naming at least a little closet "Hester," or perhaps putting a simple scarlet "A" on a door.*

The Martine Inn
Pacific Grove, California
93950

Innkeepers: Marion and Don Martine
Address/Telephone: 255 Ocean View Boulevard; (408) 373–3388
Rooms: 19; all with private bath and telephone.
Rates: $85 to $165, breakfast included. No children under 16; smoking
    only in rooms with fireplace.
Open: All year.
Facilities and local attractions: Conference facilities. Ocean-front views,
    paths for bicycling, walking; short walk to Cannery Row, Monterey
    Bay Aquarium, restaurants; close to tennis, golf.

Don't lose heart when you pull into the parking area of this
big pink palace and see how far above you the house is. As
befitting a palace, you merely step to the handy house telephone,
tell them you've arrived, and help will come.

The mansion looms 🖙 high on the cliffs of Oceanview
Boulevard overlooking the shore of Monterey Bay. It was built in
1899 and purchased by the Parke-Davis Pharmaceuticals family.
Looking at the distinctly Mediterranean style it is today, it's hard to
imagine that it was originally a true Victorian with cupola and
dormers, all changed over the years.

Mr. Parke was especially fond of exotic woods and employed

one craftsman to create ☞ Siamese teak gates, Honduras mahogany trim in the living and dining rooms, and a Spanish cedar staircase.

A huge parlor with one wall of windows looking to the ocean is the setting for afternoon wine and hors d'oeuvres while a baby grand player piano provides the background music. An extravagant breakfast is also served here. Lace-covered tables by the windows are set with juices and fruit. Then guests help themselves from a buffet in the formal dining room. The Martines' special collection of ☞ Old Sheffield and Victorian silver is used to display and serve the rest of the menu, perhaps omelets, pancakes, or eggs Benedict.

As you might suppose in a house this large, the bedrooms are spacious, almost regal. Many have a fireplace, and all are furnished in Victorian style with authentic antiques. Telephones in all the rooms are another convenience. A pleasant sitting room is also upstairs with a spectacular ocean view.

A courtyard, protected by the carriage house and a 14-foot wall, is at the back of the house. With a pond and an elaborate oriental fountain, the courtyard makes a lovely setting for a wedding. The Martines chose it for theirs.

One of the joys of staying in a grand house is all the special places in it to discover. Besides upstairs and downstairs sitting rooms, there's also a spa, a game room, and a marvelous library. It looks just the way a Victorian library ought to look—beautiful wood paneling, shelves of books and magazines, a fireplace, oriental rugs, and oversized dark furniture.

How to get there: From Highway 1, exit on Highway 68 west to Pacific Grove. Once in town, continue on Forest Avenue to the beach. Turn right and continue to inn on the right, between 5th and 3rd streets.

Olive Metcalf

The Old St. Angela Inn
Pacific Grove, California
93950

Innkeepers: Carmen and Donna Barbaro
Address/Telephone: 321 Central Avenue; (408) 372–3246
Rooms: 8, including 2 suites that accommodate 4; 5 with private bath.
Rates: $75 to $135, double occupancy, with champagne breakfast, after-
noon wine and cheese. $20 each additional person. No smoking.
Open: All year.
Facilities and local attractions: Jacuzzi hot tub. One block to ocean beaches,
parks; short walk to Monterey Bay Aquarium on Cannery Row.
Many excellent restaurants.

The Old St. Angela is a refreshing change in the midst of so
many Victorian inns. It was designed by a Boston architect, so it's
not surprising to find true Cape Cod details. It was built in 1910
and was the first Roman Catholic church in Pacific Grove, then a
rectory, later a, convent.

The house has an Americana theme, with mellow pine
antiques and country wallpaper. A large country-stone fireplace is
in the living room, an antique game table, beveled windows in
Dutch doors, and comfortable furniture in warm, earthy colors.
Among the handsome accents are duck prints, decoys, and a
collection of Currier and Ives prints.

Books all over the house are the best accent of all. The afternoon light in this attractive room, a glass of sherry, music, and a crackling fire add up to the perfect place to dispel the winter of your discontent.

·The bedrooms have a well-decorated country ambience— upscale country, that is, with tile bathrooms, fine linens, and down comforters. The Newport Room has a nautical feeling with a smart navy and brick color scheme. Ocean views from everywhere in the house are pleasing, but the best of all is from the Bay View Room. And you can't beat fresh flowers and fruit to give a room appeal.

Outside attractions are a white, latticed gazebo for dreaming under, and a hot tub that soaks eight friendly people. For a broader look at the area try the new walking trail beginning at Lovers Point at Asilomar and going to the Monterey Wharf. If you would rather bike it, the innkeepers will arrange for bike rentals and a picnic basket, too.

Breakfast in a solarium of glass, redwood, and tile is a memorable part of your visit. Champagne precedes fresh fruits, eggs, and pastries. Occasionally the host surprises guests with baked apples or cobbler.

The number and variety of restaurants nearby are almost overwhelming when it comes to choosing a dinner spot. Carmen suggests that a new French restaurant called Merloc's is proving to be especially popular.

How to get there: From San Francisco, take Highway 1 south; exit at Del Monte/Pacific Grove. Follow Del Monte Street. The name changes to Lighthouse, then to Central. Inn is on the left at 321 Central.

olive Metcalf

The Babbling Brook Inn
Santa Cruz, California
95060

Innkeepers: Tom and Helen King
Address/Telephone: 1025 Laurel Street; (408) 427–2437
Rooms: 12; all with private bath.
Rates: $85 to $135, full breakfast included. Seasonal discounts. Children over 12 welcome.
Open: All year.
Facilities and local attractions: Walk to Municipal Wharf, beach, boardwalk, specialty shops. Picnics, golf, tennis, whale watching, fishing, wine tasting at local wineries arranged.

Babbling Brook Inn couldn't be named better. It's built right over the sight and sounds of Laurel Creek, a bubbling natural brook which cascades at this point into a pond. ☛ Lush landscaping is around the pond and follows the creek through winding garden pathways and patios, complete with a covered footbridge and a gazebo.

The Ohlone Indians lived on the cliffs surrounding Laurel Creek and fished where the waterfall is now. A touring acting couple built a log cabin on the site in 1909, and some silent motion pictures were filmed here. Later owners included the flamboyant Countess (so she claimed) Florenza de Chandler, who added the upstairs and balcony.

Resident innkeepers, Tom and Helen King, bring plenty of travel know-how to running their inn. Twenty years in the airline industry took them to unusual lodgings the world over. What they aim to offer at this oldest and largest B&B in the area is comfort in a relaxed, friendly atmosphere. Most of us claim we love the simple country style, but we *do* like our conveniences. You'll lack nothing here, from private baths, telephones, fireplaces, and outdoor decks, to fresh flowers and a hidden-away television in every room.

The twelve guest rooms are divided among four buildings in the one-acre garden setting. Every room has been designed to provide maximum privacy and views of the lovely gardens. Each room is different, but the country French motif carries throughout. Most are named for impressionist painters, and the colors—delft blues, rich burgundies, and beiges—originate with the artist's works.

Breakfast here gives you options instead of enforced camaraderie. Help yourself from an attractive buffet presentation and join others in the dining area adjacent to the parlor, or take a tray to the deck for the morning sun or back to your room and your own private deck. Morning papers, even the *Wall Street Journal*, will be there along with selections from Helen's breakfast repertoire. At my last visit there were pitchers of ice water (innkeepers seldom think of this), fruit juice, croissants and jams, zucchini tart, hot "Pookie" muffins, fresh fruit Southern style (with flaked coconut), and red grapes in a fluffy fruit dressing.

The Kings also set out an early-evening wine and cheese selection to graze over while you check the local restaurant menus. Santa Cruz has so many outstanding places, it's good to have hosts who are up to date with what's new and good.

How to get there: From Highway 17 take Highway 1 toward Half Moon Bay and continue on Mission Street. Turn left on Laurel toward the ocean. The inn is on your right.

❀

J: *A word must be said about "Pookie" muffins—it's a Texas term of endearment. Helen doesn't serve them every day, but if you're lucky enough to be there when she does, I predict a day filled with life force!*

Olive Metcalf

Chateau Victorian
Santa Cruz, California
95060

Innkeepers: Franz and Alice-June Benjamin
Address/Telephone: 118 First Street; (408) 458–9458
Rooms: 7; all with private bath and fireplace.
Rates: $80 to $110, including expanded continental breakfast, afternoon
    wine and cheese. No pets; no smoking. Cannot accommodate
    children.
Open: All year.
Facilities and local attractions: Walk to beach, boardwalk, restaurants,
    shops. Local winter spectaculars include arrival of the monarch
    butterflies (October–March), elephant seals (October–February),
    whale migration (November–April).

It is amazing what people will do in the name of improving a
house. Chateau Victorian was constructed around the turn of the
century, a perfectly typical and lovable Victorian house. Then
came the 1950s with architectural philistines who decided that
graceful lines were old-fashioned and unfunctional. With righ-
teous fervor, bay windows and dormers were removed; thus, a
charming period house became a typical '50s tract house, with a
"picture" window.

Hooray for the arrival of **Fran**z Benjamin and friends! They set about turning the lamentable hybrid back into a cozy Victorian home with modern comforts to serve as an inn. Back came a graceful bay window, and fine tile baths for each bedroom were added. Franz landscaped a sheltered patio garden and renovated a cottage that opens onto it.

Then Franz individually decorated (with plenty of advice and help, he says) each room in beautiful colors to suit the era of the house—mauves, burgundies, and blues. He's chosen fine fabrics for bedcovers, draperies, pillows, and appealing window seats. The expected antique furniture pieces were added, including some particularly handsome armoires. Now we're talking about a pretty house!

The house sits high enough on a hill to offer a splendid ocean view from one of the rooms. Its location makes it an easy walk to restaurants, shops, and Santa Cruz's claim to fame, the last of the real boardwalks with its amusement park.

Breakfast, with the morning papers, is an expanded continental, meaning there's plenty of variety. Fine coffee and teas, juices and fruits, cream cheese, and croissants or other pastries are served from the dining-room buffet. You can eat there, or enjoy a sunny morning in the patio or on the decks.

How to get there: Driving south on Highway 1, exit on Bay. At West Cliff, turn left, then right on Beach to Main. Turn left at Main, and at First Street, turn right. Inn is on left. Off-street parking available.

❧

J: *This boardwalk has a major attraction: the* *oldest surviving roller coaster in California—tested by my daughter many times and rated a four-star screamer in all the books.*

Olive Metcalf

Cliff Crest
Santa Cruz, California
95060

Innkeepers: Sharon and Bruce Taylor
Address/Telephone: 407 Cliff Street; (408) 427–2609
Rooms: 5; all with private bath.
Rates: $70 to $115, full breakfast and afternoon snacks included. No
  smoking. No pets.
Open: All year.
Facilities and local attractions: Boardwalk attractions of Santa Cruz; Mon-
  terey Bay.

What a pleasure to stay in this well-maintained Queen Anne
Victorian. If you don't "ooh" and "ah-h" the minute you walk in,
you're just not a fan of Victorian style. Everything sparkles, from
the beveled glass front door, to the sitting room that opens onto a
☛ glassed-in bay solarium that looks out on the garden and patio.

This was the home of William Jeter. You do remember, don't
you, that he established Henry Cowell Redwoods State Park, was
interested in ecology, and was lieutenant governor of California in
1890? Of course you do. Jeter also had the good luck to have as a
personal friend John McLaren, the designer of Golden Gate Park in
San Francisco. McLaren planned the beautiful grounds around
this mansion.

Each of the bedrooms looks freshly decorated and offers special attractions. The smallest, the cozy Pineapple Room, is on the main floor and has pineapples carved on the four-poster queen-sized bed. The Rose Room is the largest and has an extra-long claw-footed tub in its bathroom across the hall and a sitting area with a view of Monterey Bay. All the bathrooms are a particular pleasure with their thick towels and terry cloth robes, shampoo, and lotions.

The sitting room is deliciously pretty: white wicker furniture against soft blue–gray woodwork and blue rugs. A white latticed archway opens to the solarium with two round tables and chairs. Across the top of the large bay window is a stained-glass border, and under the sills is an inside window box spilling over with Boston ferns. Can you imagine a cozier setting for breakfast?

Coffee is ready at 8:00 A.M., and the morning paper is there for a quiet beginning to the day. At nine you're served fresh juice and fruit. The entree might be French toast and sausages, or Egg Puffs with fresh muffins, or cinnamon–sour cream coffee cake. Sharon also makes some interesting phyllo creations that she arbitrarily names "Chef's Surprise Number 5" or "Number 8," or whatever she decides at the moment. In the afternoon, mineral water or iced tea and snacks magically arrive, accompanied by taped music.

How to get there: From Highway 17, exit on Ocean Street. Follow to San Lorenzo Boulevard; turn right. Go to stop light, and turn left on Riverside Drive. Go over bridge, turn right on Third Street; go up the hill to Cliff Street and turn left. Inn is on the left.

✳

J: *I concur with the feelings of a previous guest: "The ambience at Cliff Crest is warmth, charm, timeless. I feel the anxiety melting away."*

Olive Metcalf

The Darling House
Santa Cruz, California
95060

Innkeepers: Karen and Darrell Darling
Address/Telephone: 314 West Cliff Drive; (408) 458–1958
Rooms: 7 rooms in house, 1 self-contained cottage sleeping 4 to 5; with private and shared baths.
Rates: $50 to $115, continental breakfast included. No smoking.
Open: All year.
Facilities and local attractions: Walk to secluded beach, sailing; good place to see wintering monarch butterflies; Santa Cruz Boardwalk. Can accommodate weddings and small private parties.

If you guess from its name that this inn is a gabled Victorian, you would be way off-track. It's 🖝 a 1910 Mission Revival masterpiece sitting on the cliffs high above Monterey Bay. The owners and innkeepers, Karen and Darrell Darling, are simply calling it by their own name—although their children did have some doubts about the idea.

The house was designed by William Weeks, probably the most active architect on the Central Coast during the first decade of the century. He was known particularly for designing public buildings, but his talent and versatility can also be seen in the private homes he designed. Karen calls Darling House a "Colorado

Spanish" design, since Weeks and his clients the William Iliffs (cofounders of Denver University Graduate School) were both from Colorado, but Mission Revival is the true name of the popular style. The most striking features are the portico with its series of arches, the terra cotta tile roof, and beveled, leaded glass windows.

The imposing inn gives guests an opportunity to experience living in a period piece that is almost completely in its original state. Plumbing fixtures, for instance, are seventy-five years old and still working beautifully. Tiffany lamps and Art Deco (before its time) features are just as they were designed.

Bedrooms are large, and most have ocean views. One with an especially sweeping view has a big chair and a ☞ telescope ready for serious marine watching. Antique furnishings and beautiful details of ☞ inlaid woods on pillars, beams, and floors are fascinating to examine.

Breakfast is the only meal available, but Karen makes it special. She serves it family style in the oak dining room or on the ocean-side veranda: espresso, nut breads, croissants, granola, and fresh fruits. Whatever the menu, everything you eat is fresh or made from scratch.

Two just possibly connected extras offered by the Darlings are (1) they sometimes have home-grown walnuts for sale and (2) Darrell is a minister. So, should you decide to get married while you're at the inn, the clergy is on the premises and the rest of the guests could throw walnuts.

How to get there: From Highway 17, take Highway 1 north. Exit left on Bay Street, and turn right on West Cliff Drive. Inn is on the right.

❀

J: *A stroll down West Cliff Drive will bring you to a secluded beach. This stretch of the coast is a good place for tide-pooling, and for seeing the dizzying magic of wintering monarch butterflies.*

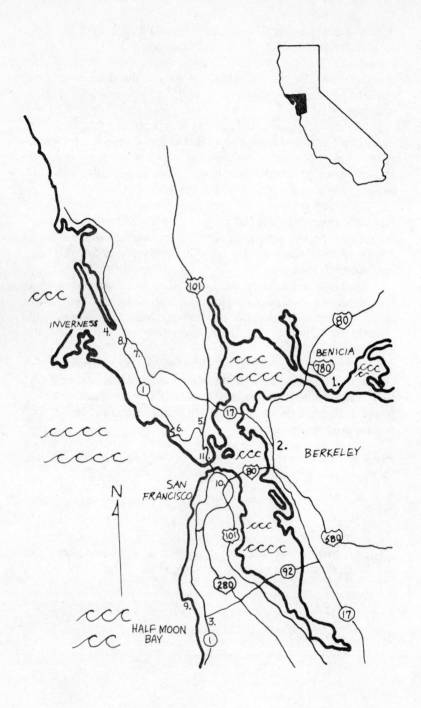

California: The San Francisco Bay Area

Numbers on map refer to towns numbered below.

olive Metcalf

The Union Hotel
Benicia, California
94510

Innkeeper: Andrea Barrett
Address/Telephone: 401 First Street; (707) 746–0100
Rooms: 12, including 2 suites; all with private bath, Jacuzzi, telephone, television, air conditioning.
Rates: $70 to $95 weekdays; $80 to $125 weekends, continental breakfast included. Special weekend package and corporate rate.
Open: All year. Lunch, dinner available Tuesday through Sunday. Brunch Saturday and Sunday.
Facilities and local attractions: Visit old capitol. Near Marine World Africa, USA. Open artisans' studios in glass blowing, pottery, sculpture; antique hunting. Marina, fishing, bird watching, picnicking. Guitar music in bar weekends.

Water, water, everywhere. Benicia is nestled on the north shore of the Carquinez Straits where the Sacramento and San Joaquin rivers flow into San Francisco Bay. When history and prosperity passed it by, this nineteenth-century town was largely forgotten. Once the capital of California, it boasts the 🖝 oldest standing capitol in the state.

The stately three-story Union Hotel was restored in 1980, but even before guest rooms were ready, its 🖝 authentically American food and regional dishes began attracting people to Benicia. The dining room is now presided over by Raymond Prevot, who is doing a varied continental menu. Chef Prevot was formerly with the Carnelian Room in San Francisco.

The second and third floors have been entirely rebuilt to make the twelve bedrooms. Each is large and airy, named for a different theme—Mrs. Miniver, Mei Ling, Summer Skies—has period furnishings, and uses large armoires for closets. The best views are from the Massachusetts Bay Room and from Louis Le Mad, where you look out at the Carquinez Straits and bridge. And the bathrooms are splendid. They're big and tiled, with some of the Jacuzzi tubs large enough for entertaining.

No, you're not roughing it at the Union Hotel. But I've always thought that was overrated, haven't you?

How to get there: From San Francisco, take Highway 80 north to Vallejo. Take Benicia turnoff; exit Second Street, turn left. Proceed to Military; turn right and go to first stoplight, which is First Street. Turn left and drive through town to the hotel on the right.

J: *Benicia is one of the last nontouristy, semi-undiscovered little towns left. I say, catch it while it's still free from the dreaded disease "Boutique-itis."*

Gramma's Bed & Breakfast Inn
Berkeley, California
94705

Innkeeper: Kathy Kuhner
Address/Telephone: 2740 Telegraph Avenue; (415) 549–2145
Rooms: 30; 28 with private bath.
Rates: $70 to $130, double occupancy. Breakfast included.
Open: All year.
Facilities and local attractions: Walk to University of California. Explore Berkeley shops, museums.

I love Gramma's because it takes many people's preconceptions about Berkeley and knocks them for a loop. The beautiful Tudor mansion with a sweet name (and no campy implications) has an atmosphere that surprises many visitors to this city of intellect and rebellion: Wholesome leaning to elegant is the feeling. It's the perfect antidote for outdated ideas of what goes on in Berkeley.

Go up a flower-lined walk and into a sunny living room where fat chintz-covered sofas and chairs invite you to "sit a spell." There's a pretty flower-tiled fireplace, and newspapers, magazines, and fresh flowers everywhere.

Beyond the light-filled dining room is a deck (Gramma would call it a back porch) and a cool grassy lawn. Tables and chairs are out here, along with pots of petunias, pansies, marigolds, white alyssum, and blue lobelia. It's a popular place for weddings and entertaining.

A portrait of Gramma—the real one, to whom the inn is dedicated—is on the landing on the way upstairs. Guest rooms are decorated in different colors but all in a country style. The antique furniture and handmade quilts are cozy. Some rooms have private decks, fireplaces, sitting areas, and access to the garden. The very nicest rooms are in the rear of the garden. They have fireplaces and windows on two sides.

The dining room has round tables with ruffled skirts to the floor and bright top cloths. One side of the room is all windows and offers a pleasant view of the garden. Dinner is not available here, but up and down Telegraph Avenue are some of Berkeley's best restaurants.

The breakfast served, as you might expect, is nourishing and substantial. (Would Gramma have served any other kind?) Juices and fresh fruit, muffins, and wonderful granola—the very thing to give you the energy to walk over to the university and raise Cain all day.

How to get there: From Highway 80 (the Eastshore) through Berkeley, take the Ashby Avenue exit; turn left at Telegraph Avenue. The inn is 3 blocks on your left at number 2740.

✳

J: *All that civility and charm . . . pretty radical stuff!*

Olive Metcalf

Old Thyme Inn
Half Moon Bay, California
94019

Innkeepers: Simon and Anne Lowings
Address/Telephone: 779 Main Street; (415) 726–1616
Rooms: 6; 4 with private bath including 1 with Jacuzzi, 2 with fireplace.
Rates: $55 to $105; reduced rates for weekdays and extended stays.
  Breakfast and early-evening beverage included.
Open: All year.
Facilities and local attractions: One mile to state beach. Explore sea life at
  Fitzgerald Marine Reserve. Whale-watching tours. Hiking, horseback
  riding. Fishing fleet at Princeton Harbor and pier. Walk Main Street
  with shops and restaurants. Spanishtown Art Center. Many local
  annual events including October Art and Pumpkin Festival.

Medical experts would surely agree that a two-day dropout
from routine can refresh spirits and do more for good marital
relationships than an entire season of watching Dr. Ruth. In
addition, it only gently dents a budget. All of which should have
Bay Area residents, especially, zipping down to the small coastal
community of Half Moon Bay. This short getaway destination is
just 45 minutes from the heart of San Francisco and a jog off the
highway—an unpretentious, pleasantly unchic, and, best of all,
☞ semi-undiscovered historic little town.

For lodging comfort, The Old Thyme Inn beautifully fits the bill for such a low-key holiday. The house is picturesque, dating back to 1899; it's freshly renovated, delightfully decorated, and sits right on the town's historic Main Street. You need not get in your car again until it's time to go home.

Actually, meeting Anne and Simon Lowings is reason enough to check into The Old Thyme. They're two of the most charming innkeepers you'll ever know. To my Anglophile ear, it helps, of course, that they speak English with a British accent—probably due to being born there. Simon, a former engineer, was once in the Silicon Valley whirl, but he and Anne elected to raise their two children in a slower-paced community. They restored this old house (and some of their stories about *that* enterprise sound like episodes from *Fawlty Towers*), Anne planted an herb garden, and Simon learned to cook. The whole family has become familiar with the joys of ☞ tide-pooling at the local Fitzgerald Marine Reserve, with the elephant seals that come ashore near here, and with walking and riding the hills and beaches all about them. You're quite likely to catch their enthusiasm for the area.

They've given a lot of care to the decorating, which has an herb theme. Each room has pretty wallpaper, comforters, English antiques, and an understated charm. The Thyme Room has a fireplace and a whirlpool tub (Simon denies it's the "Wild Thyme Room"). There are double and queen-sized beds.

A comfortable, homey sitting area ("lounge" to us Anglophiles) has a wood burning stove and English appointments and memorabilia. I especially liked sitting down to breakfast in the adjoining dining area under a portrait of the young Victoria. The menu would have pleased the old girl, I'm sure: fresh juice, homemade hot scones with marmalade, cold meats, and English cheeses, all topped off with a French cherry flan.

How to get there: From San Francisco, take Highway 280 south to Highway 92 and head west. At Main Street, turn left. The inn is on your right.

ক৯

J: *There are first-rate restaurants in the area. San Benito House is one you can walk to.*

San Benito House
Half Moon Bay, California
94019

Innkeeper: Carol Mickelsen
Address/Telephone: 356 Main Street; (415) 726–3425.
Rooms: 12; 9 with private bath, 3 share divided bath.
Rates: $49 to $108, including continental breakfast. Guests receive 10%
off in restaurant.
Open: All year. Dinner, Wednesday through Sunday; lunch, Friday and
Saturday, Sunday brunch; reservations advised.
Facilities and local attractions: Sun deck, sauna, croquet. Complete confer-
ence and wedding facilities. Thirty minutes from San Francisco
airport and Silicon Valley.

Here is a refreshing coastal wonder—an inn that takes dead
aim on European-style flavor and delivers it minus the pretensions
or obscene prices that often are part of the story. (Simple country
charm doesn't come cheap, you know.) Carol Mickelsen is the
owner and inspiration behind transforming the old Mosconi Hotel
into a hostelry in the European tradition. And she offers travelers
more than picturesque ambience.

Food—gloriously innovative, fresh, and colorful—is her forte.
She has seriously studied cooking and trained with famed French
chefs Jacques Pépin and Roger Verge at Cannes. Now she has

promoted herself out of the kitchen most of the time, but directs four female chefs through the no-short-cuts facets of California cuisine, classic country French, and Northern Italian. On the October day I stopped, they were preparing fresh ravioli with an unusual spicy pumpkin filling for lunch.

Meat and fish are impeccably fresh and often grilled on mesquite. And the vegetables are something to write home about. Most of them come from Carol's large garden: delicate lettuce, green beans, baby carrots, and fresh herbs. Two memorable cakes are among an array of dessert specialties: a lemon almond, and a dense chocolate called Queen of California.

Dinners are served in a dining room with brass chandeliers, blue cotton tablecloths, bright peach napkins, and a profusion of fresh bouquets. All around is an ☞ exceptional collection of original paintings by early 1900s coastal artists, particularly Galen Wolf and Greer Morton.

French doors lead onto a large ☞ redwood deck overlooking the English Garden. Here's the place to have lunch on a summer day, or to gather around the massive fire pit at night when the fire is lit to sip cognac and stargaze.

The stairway to the upstairs begins at an elaborate mirrored hallpiece and continues under an ornate cornice. Carol found many of the decorative accessories on trips to Europe. The stained-glass partitions she bought are a unique touch in the bathrooms. Bedrooms on the garden side are the most elaborately decorated with antique light fixtures, brass beds, and walls painted in vivid colors, some with stenciled details. It's pleasant having coffee makings up here, and a small deck off the end of the hallway.

How to get there: From San Francisco, take Highway 280 south to Half Moon Bay. Turn west at Highway 92 to Main Street; turn left. Inn is on the right at the corner of Mill Street. From the south, Highway 1 passes through Half Moon Bay.

✿

J: *As I write, a laudatory review of San Benito House has just appeared in* Gourmet. *Now the cat's out of the bag.*

Olive Metcalf.

Blackthorne Inn
Inverness, California
94937

Innkeepers: Susan Wigert and Bill Hemphill
Address/Telephone: 266 Vallejo Avenue (mailing address: Box 712); (415) 663–8621
Rooms: 5; 3 share 2 baths. Not convenient for children.
Rates: $105 to $165, with extended continental breakfast.
Open: All year.
Facilities and Local Attractions: Decks for sunning, hot tub. Point Reyes National Seashore, nature walks, wildflowers, bird watching.

"This is really an adult treehouse," says Susan Wigert. This
☞ fascinating redwood, cedar, and fir structure began with a small cabin built in the 1930s. Now it rises through the treetops to four levels, joined by a 40-foot spiral staircase. Flanked with decks and balconies, approached by walkways and bridges, the building is crowned with the ☞ octagonal Eagle's Nest Room. Your first adventure after arriving will be exploring the ways around it.

The inn was designed by Bill Wigert, Susan's husband, and she and her brother Bill run it. In addition to milling some of the wood from trees on the site, Wigert made the construction quite a salvage operation. He's used beams from San Francisco piers, boulders from seven counties for the walk-in fireplace, and huge doors rescued from the old San Francisco Southern Pacific building.

The main level has a large, airy living room with skylights, comfortable furniture, and a stone fireplace. The sounds of Handel (or was it Vivaldi?) came from a stereo the afternoon I arrived, cats snoozed, and the wine tray was ready. All good signs.

Adjoining the living room is a glass-enclosed solarium where a California-style continental breakfast is served: juice, fresh fruit, quiche, pastries, yogurt, and granola. This is the only meal served at the inn, but guests often walk or drive into the village to buy picnic munchies to lunch on back at the house while enjoying the decks.

Dinner choices in this coastal area used to be slim pickings, but these days in the villages there are cafes, a French restaurant, two Czechoslovakian ones, a bakery that makes a great pizza, and at Chez Madeline, a daily changing menu of fresh fish and local food prepared expertly. The innkeepers are happy to help you choose and make reservations.

Guest rooms are attractive and cozy, some with pitched ceilings and arched windows, some with small decks. A 2,500-square-foot sun deck surrounds the main level of the house—with a fireman's pole to slide down, if you're nimble. Another deck on the hillside has hot and cold tubs, and on the roof is a private sun deck for the Eagle's Nest.

This is a unique spot, for the young at heart.

How to get there: From San Francisco, take Highway 101 through Olema toward Inverness. Turn left at the Inverness Park Grocery onto Vallejo Avenue two miles south of Inverness. The inn is on your right.

✳

J: *Innkeeper Susan Wigert says she recently traveled in Mexico and on the East Coast and came home to Blackthorne convinced that she lives in paradise.*

olive Metcalf

Mountain Home Inn
Mill Valley, California
94941

Innkeeper: Charlie Leep, manager
Address/Telephone: 810 Panoramic Highway; (415) 381–9000
Rooms: 10, including suite with wheelchair access; all with private bath
   and deck.
Rates: $95 to $175, with extended continental breakfast.
Open: All year. Lunch, dinner, Sunday brunch. Wine bar.
Facilities and local attractions: Walk to Muir Woods, hike up Mt. Tamalpais,
   great eating.

This inn has it all: knock-your-socks-off views of the Bay and Marin hills, fascinating architectural design, luxury rooms, a lauded restaurant, and a professional staff just dying to pamper you. Even the twisting drive up to its mountain perch is beautiful.

Longtime Marin residents remember the inn on the slope of Mt. Tamalpais through many incarnations. It was built in 1912 by a Swiss couple supposedly homesick for an Alpine view. Most recently it was a German beer-and-sandwich place serving dusty hikers. What a difference a few mil' makes.

A blond hardwood interior softly announces "California chic," with cathedral ceilings and ☞ pillars of redwood still covered with bark. Muted colors—beiges, apricots—are punctuated with unusual hickory furniture pieces.

Guest rooms are sleek and serene, each with its own deck to enjoy the sweeping view. Appointments include grand tubs (some with Jacuzzis), complimentary toiletries, thick robes, and towels. Guests have a private dining room/lounge with fireplace and outside deck. If you've stayed the night, enjoy the daily papers and a buffet breakfast here, or in your room: hot and cold beverages, fresh fruits, pastries, and the ubiquitous California breakfast statement—yogurt and granola.

At the heart of the inn is the beautiful bar and intimate dining room with deck overlooking the dazzling view. The no-smoking rule in the dining rooms speaks to the ☞ serious way they regard food. Menus change twice a month to reflect the availability of seasonal fresh fish and produce. A mesquite grill and the trendy ingredients are here—status greens like radicchio, baby vegetables cooked *al dente,* and pastas—but with this kitchen's own artful stamp on them. The day I visited, two offerings were grilled swordfish with sun-dried tomato butter and stewed mushrooms, and a whole chicken breast stuffed with feta cheese and thyme. ☞ Homemade ice cream made with fresh berries is a specialty, and so is the bittersweet chocolate cake.

How to get there: From San Francisco, cross the Golden Gate Bridge, and take Mill Valley/Stinson Beach exit to Highway 1 junction. Turn left at light; follow signs to Mt. Tamalpais State Park. Road becomes Panoramic Highway; follow 8 miles to the top. Inn is on the right.

olive Metcalf

The Pelican Inn
Muir Beach, California
94965

Innkeeper: Barry Stock
Address/Telephone: Muir Beach; (415) 383–6000
Rooms: 7; all with private bath.
Rates: $105 to $125, with full English breakfast.
Open: All year. Lunch, dinner, bar serving wine and British ales. Closed Mondays, except to inn guests.
Facilities and local attractions: Point Reyes National Seashore, beachcombing, bird watching, hiking, Muir Redwood Groves.

That fourth-generation publican who built The Pelican Inn, Charles Felix, has retired. But fear not. "Rule Britannia" still applies. Barry Stock and his wife Pamela have arrived from Devon, England, to keep the British tradition of innkeeping alive and chipper.

Just twenty minutes from the Golden Gate Bridge, this ☞ replica of a sixteenth-century English country inn has white stucco and is crisscrossed with dark beams. It seems a proper spot, considering that it was here on the Marin Coast that Sir Francis Drake beached his *Pelican* (renamed the *Golden Hind*) some 400 years ago and claimed California for Queen Elizabeth I and her descendants forever.

You enter a cozy English pub with low beams, dart board, and a good stock of brews. Almost everything here came from the inn Felix previously owned in Surrey. The four-centuries-old paneled bar is packed on weekends with San Franciscans and guests who enjoy traditional lunch fare like fish n' chips, bangers, and mash.

An adjoining dining room has a huge fireplace and sturdy, dark tables and chairs. The dinner menu appropriately offers roast beef, Yorkshire pudding, and mixed English grill among its choices. Breakfast also is served here or in your room. It is big and English: juice, eggs, bacon, bangers, tomatoes, toast, and marmalade.

The bedrooms upstairs are wonderfully English. Beds have a brocade-draped half-canopy called a "half-tester." The device was once used not for decor, but to keep small rodents who might be frolicking in the thatched roof overhead from falling on your face while you slept. Other "mod cons" (modern conveniences) are a stone with a hole hanging over each bed to ensure no rickets in case of pregnancy. Former innkeeper Felix, who claimed a trust in every known superstition, successfully kept witches and evil spirits away with buried bones under the hearth and holly over the doors. Stock continues The Pelican as a safe haven with a garlic wreath at the entrance to ward off vampires and beasties of the night.

Mr. Stock takes the profession of publican seriously and laments mere B&Bs' calling themselves inns. The Pelican is in the traditional mold, where the innkeeper is a public servant and feels it his duty to see that you are lodged, fed, and looked after properly.

How to get there: From San Francisco, take Highway 101 to the Stinson Beach/Mill Valley exit. Follow Highway 1 to the Arco gas station; turn left and continue for 5 miles to Muir Beach.

✳

J: *I'm a pushover for an innkeeper who calls out as you're leaving for a walk on the beach, "Better take a woolie with you, do!"*

olive Metcalf

Roundstone Farm
Olema, California
94950

Innkeeper: Inger Fisher
Address/Telephone: 9940 Sir Francis Drake Boulevard (mailing address:
P.O. Box 217); (415) 663–1020
Rooms: 4; all with private bath, some with fireplace.
Rates: $95 to $105 with fireplace, two-night minimum on weekends.
Breakfast included. Smoking on the deck. Cannot accommodate
children or pets.
Open: All year.
Facilities and local attractions: Point Reyes National Seashore. Walk the
Earthquake Trail. Visit the lighthouse, Chimney Rock. Picnics. Bicy-
cles, horses available nearby. Bird watching. Whale watches January
through April. Walk Inverness for small shops, unique crafts. Excel-
lent restaurants.

Just an hour's drive north of San Francisco is Point Reyes
National Seashore, an ink blot-shaped peninsula of dramatic
impact. This 🐦 stunning convergence of land and sea, of ham-
mering surfs and treacherous riptides, of windswept beaches and
steep cliffs is a thrilling place for nature lovers. You don't go in the
water here; you watch it respectfully. There are carpets of California poppies in the spring, tidepools of sea life, tule elk, sea lions,

130

migratory birds, seals, and, in winter, whales migrating to Baja. The weather varies from hour to hour: warm and sunny to sudden chilling fogs.

Fresh from exploring this wild seashore, how lovely to return to the tranquil comforts of a country inn, beautifully designed and tastefully decorated. Roundstone Farm is a new inn in the area with just those qualities. Its understated, fresh look is a compliment to the Point Reyes terrain. Inger Fisher is both the designer and owner of Roundstone. She has owned the land a long time, but she waited and planned until she could build just the inn she wanted. "I've accomplished my dream—so far," she says.

The farmhouse of cedar batten and board has a long living room with a 16-foot ceiling and skylights. Books, a stereo, and comfortable upholstered furniture are inviting. One long side opens to a broad deck overlooking a pond and meadow where deer and horses graze. Mrs. Fisher also raises horses on the ten-acre ranch. ☞ Her Connemaras, Arabians, and quarter horses are beautiful sights, too. What a fresh-air spot to read in and gaze at the rolling hills with Tomales Bay beyond.

Each of the guest rooms is a quiet retreat. Ours had sea-spray soft colors, a handsome pine armoire, and fireplace with tiled hearth. With a cozy down comforter, excellent bed, and good reading lights, what more could you want? Breakfast, that's what.

Inger serves in a raised dining room that looks over the living room and out to the meadow and hills. Some of us had taken an early-morning walk along the earthquake trail of the San Andreas Fault, and her hearty breakfast was thoroughly enjoyed: fresh juices, egg and sausage torte, homemade chunky applesauce, hot homemade bread, jams, and coffee that kept coming while we sat around the table and talked.

How to get there: Ten miles north of the Golden Gate Bridge on Highway 101, take the San Anselmo/Richmond Bridge exit. Proceed west on Sir Francis Drake Boulevard approximately 20 miles. Roundstone Farm is 300 yards before (east) the intersection with Highway 1.

❋

J: *The legacy of good innkeeping has traveled a reverse direction in this instance: from son to mother. Jackie and Ron Fisher, Inger's son and his wife, became innkeepers first at the beautiful Mangels House in Aptos.*

Holly Tree Inn
Point Reyes Station, California
94956

Innkeepers: Tom and Diane Balogh
Address/Telephone: 3 Silverhills Road (mailing address: Box 642); (415) 663–1554
Rooms: 4, all with private bath. 1 cottage with private bath, fireplace.
Rates: $70 to $120, including tax and full breakfast. Children welcome.
Open: All year.
Facilities and local attractions: One mile from Point Reyes National Seashore. Area offers horseback riding, hiking, fishing, boating, bird watching, mushrooming, nature walks. Unique shops, fine restaurants. Horses boarded.

There is something especially pleasing about fine houses built before World War II: They're modern enough for comfort, yet old enough to have a spacious elegance few of us enjoy at home. Holly Tree Inn has those qualities, and sits on ☞ nineteen lush acres of lawns and gardens. It was built in 1939 by a Swede with a British wife, who probably accounts for the arbor of holly trees, the English laurels, lilacs, privet, and the herb garden.

The house is decorated in understated British taste that suits it perfectly: Laura Ashley prints, plump upholstered chairs and sofas, antiques, fresh flowers, and whimsy. A row of tiny wooden buildings ranges across both fireplace mantels in the dining and living rooms. A guest sipping a sherry in the big sofa might look at it for some time before realizing it is Point Reyes in miniature—made by innkeeper Tom Balogh.

Bedrooms are each different and delightfully English. The smallest, Mary's Garden Room, is done in a red-and-green-sprigged Ashley print and opens onto a patio and perennial flower garden. The larger rooms are equally tasteful and have beautiful views.

Diane's enthusiasm for decorating this great house extends even to a newly tiled bathroom sink. She pointed out the pretty gray-green color of the grouting. "Did you know grout comes in almost any color you want? It doesn't have to be white!"

Christmas at Holly Tree Inn is special. Polished wood gleams in the glow of both blazing fireplaces, and there are decorations galore. Santa made an unexpected appearance once by way of a working electric dumbwaiter beside the fireplace, usually used for bringing up logs.

Mid-January is ☞ whale-watch time on cool, misty Point Reyes Peninsula. The Baloghs arrange for a naturalist to speak about the phenomenon to guests, followed by a short drive out to the coast to watch the migration.

A fine breakfast is served in the dining room—juice, fresh fruit, bran muffins or croissants, homemade poppy-seed bread, several cheeses, and then something special, like individual asparagus soufflés. For other meals, there is a wide choice of good restaurants in the area.

How to get there: From San Francisco, exit Highway 101 north at Sir Francis Drake Boulevard. Stay on Drake 45 minutes to Olema and turn right onto Highway 1. Drive 1 block north, then turn left onto Bear Valley Road. At Holly Tree Inn sign, turn left onto Silverhills Road. Turn left at second driveway. Look for Holly Tree Inn sign.

Olive Metcalf

Pillar Point Inn
Princeton-by-the-Sea, California
94018

Innkeeper: Mary Lococo
Address/Telephone: 380 Capistrano Road (mailing address: P.O. Box 388,
El Granada); (415) 728–7377
Rooms: 11, including 1 room equipped for handicapped; all with private
bath, fireplace, media center, refrigerator, telephone.
Rates: $100 single to $122 double occupancy Sunday through Thursday;
$135 to $145 weekends; $20 additional person. No pets; no children
under 12. Full breakfast included.
Open: All year.
Facilities and local attractions: Active harbor and marina. Grey whale
migration watch December through March. Año Nuevo Reserve, 35
miles south. Conducted nature tours at Fitzgerald Marine Reserve.
Walking tour of Half Moon Bay. Fine coastal restaurants. Facilities for
weddings, business meetings; conference room.

Just 25 miles south of San Francisco on Highway 1, the new
construction is taking on a New England look. In the Princeton-
by-the-Sea/El Granada area they're even calling themselves Cape
Cod on the California coast. The Pillar Point Inn is one of the
newer additions to the scene, a handsome Cape Cod–style building
that opened in 1985.

There's a clean, windswept look to the frame structure with a white picket fence and flowers running along its length. A reception/parlor area looks smart with a cherry-red sofa and upholstered chairs arranged before a fireplace decorated with blue-and-white tiles. Beverages and afternoon tea are set out here or on the harbor-view deck. Touches of wood and brass against soft blue-gray colors and fresh flowers tell you at once that this is ☞ an impeccably maintained inn.

All but one of its eleven luxurious rooms overlook the colorful Pillar Point Harbor. The fussiest traveler should be happy with the soft, easy-to-take colors, cuddly European-style featherbeds, and beautifully tiled fireplace and hearth. Hidden behind cupboard doors is an entire media center: television, video player, and radio. Topping off this full slate of appointments is a mini-refrigerator, telephone, and first-rate bathroom, some of which have a private steam bath. One room has wheelchair access and a bathroom specially fitted for a handicapped guest.

A cheery breakfast room with pine-top tables and cottage curtains is another pleasant spot. Innkeeper Mary Lococo serves a full breakfast here including fresh fruits, juices, and a variety of homemade hot dishes.

This is ☞ a great stretch of the coast to explore: a busy fishing fleet and wharf, a variety of vessels, both commercial and pleasure craft, and an active boat-building industry, where you can watch even wooden boats in various stages of completion. Just four miles south, the old town of Half Moon Bay is wonderful to walk with its unique shops and an art center called Spanish Town. The town is the scene every fall of an enormously popular pumpkin festival, but most of the time you'll find far fewer people around here than in other coastal communities. Best of all is the nature and marine life to observe here, from the great elephant seal herds to the California grey whales' migration.

How to get there: From San Francisco, drive south 25 miles on Highway 1 to Princeton-by-the-Sea. Turn into the harbor on Capistrano at the traffic light.

Olive Metcalf

Alamo Square Inn
San Francisco, California
94117

Innkeepers: Wayne Corn and Klaus May
Address/Telephone: 719 Scott Street; (415) 922–2055
Rooms: 12, including 3 suites; all with private bath, telephone. Television available.
Rates: $65 double to $225 for 2-bedroom suite. Full breakfast included.
Open: All year.
Facilities and local attractions: Historic Alamo Square District for walking, viewing Victorian architecture; 10 blocks west of San Francisco Civic Center; close to Golden Gate Park. Facilities and catering for weddings, small private parties, and seminars.

These two San Francisco mansions on Alamo Square, lovingly restored and now maintained as an elegant inn, are just another grace note added to this historic district. The area escaped the great fire of 1906 and still has hundreds of picturesque houses that have survived since it was a popular suburb in the 1880s and 1890s. Some of the city's most beautiful examples of Victorian architecture face Alamo Square, a small park on a sloping hillside.

Innkeepers Corn and May have constructed a solarium and conservatory filled with flowering plants and greenery that joins an 1895 Queen Anne mansion to an 1896 English Tudor. Just looking at this verdant space makes you think of the possibilities, like hosting an elegant little party.

You see why prospective brides frequently choose the inn as the scene of both their wedding ceremony and reception; it's a romantic house. There are two parlors furnished in a blend of Victorian and Oriental styles, a grand staircase for a smashing entrance, and a large formal dining room.

The innkeepers have been restoring the two mansions for over ten years, but Corn says it is still an inn in transition. Guest rooms are comfortably decorated with antique touches. Some have gas fireplaces, and one unit overlooking the rose garden has a full kitchen. Some rooms overlook the park, others have garden views, and one of the suites has a balcony with a panoramic view of the city. This suite in Art Deco style also has a sunken Jacuzzi.

Klaus is a professional chef and takes pride in his breakfast productions. It's a hearty, sit-down meal in the dining room, but it can also be delivered to your room or served in the garden. Gorgeous fresh raspberries were the stars of the fruit selection when I visited. Then there was juice, cheese omelets, and the chef's specialty, ☞ homemade Danish and other breakfast pastries. (He makes special hors d'oeuvres too.)

Both Wayne and Klaus know San Francisco well. They're ready to help guests with information about what's happening in town, the best play, or the newest restaurant.

How to get there: From Highway 80 going north to the Golden Gate Bridge, take Fell Street west about 7 blocks. Turn right at Scott Street to number 719, on the left.

❄

J: *This is just the kind of neighborhood to walk when you want to get a feel for San Francisco: a park and greenery, picturesque houses, hills, and views.*

Olive Metcalf

The Archbishops Mansion
San Francisco, California
94117

Innkeepers: Jonathan Shannon and Jeffrey Ross
Address/Telephone: 1000 Fulton Street; (415) 563–7872
Rooms: 15; all with private bath and telephone; all but 2 have fireplace.
Rates: $100 to $250, continental breakfast included. Two-night minimum
   on weekends.
Open: All year.
Facilities and local attractions: Dinners, business meetings, private parties,
   weddings catered by arrangement. Near San Francisco Opera House,
   Davies Symphony Hall, Galleria Design Center, Moscone Convention
   Center.

Let us not pussyfoot about the kind of establishment this is:
opulent, romantic, dramatic, and *grand* will do for starters. Messrs.
Shannon and Ross call themselves innkeepers, but the lodgings
and service they offer give the term a new dimension.

This 🖝 impressive mansion in the Alamo Square District was
built in 1904 as the private residence of the archbishop of San
Francisco and his entourage. It survived the 1906 earthquake and
became headquarters for a citywide effort to rebuild San Francisco.
Pope Pius XII stayed here in the mid-1930s while he was still a
cardinal. It was purchased by Ross, a trained architect, and

Shannon, a fashion designer, and they've combined their considerable talents to restore it.

You enter a great hall with an elegant parlor on one side and ahead a 🖙 magnificent three-story open staircase covered by a 16-foot stained-glass dome. The architecture is French Empire. The intricate ceiling details, splendid rugs, antiques, and lush draperies could convince you that it was a European palace. But there are unexpected treasures, too, like Noel Coward's 1904 Bechstein grand piano in the reception hall and a large Victorian Pier mirror from Abraham Lincoln's Springfield home.

Each of the luxurious bedrooms is designed to reflect the atmosphere of a particular opera. The most opulent is the Gypsy Baron Suite with its large sitting area before a baronial fireplace and a stunning four-poster canopied king-sized bed. The Rosenkavalier Suite has gracefully curved construction, even in the thresholds and bookcases.

Cosi fan Tutte, La Tosca, and Madama Butterfly all have 🖙 exceptional antiques and exquisitely embroidered linens. Don Giovanni has an intricately carved bed that is just one of the prizes in a house full of treasures. Some of the bathrooms are like good-sized rooms (Carmen's has a fireplace) with oriental rugs, chandeliers, and tall stands for keeping the champagne cold while you soak in a hot tub. Surely, *you* don't tub without champagne at the ready?

Guests gather for wine in the afternoon in a downstairs parlor. Breakfast is served in the enormous dining room or delivered to your room in a French picnic basket. Several 🖙 salons are available for small conferences or where the hosts cater dinners or cocktail parties by prior arrangement. The surroundings are palatial but warm, with all the personal attention you could desire.

How to get there: From Van Ness, take Fulton Street west to Alamo Square. Inn is on the right, number 1000.

J: *Jonathan Shannon says: "Innkeeping is a theatrical event; it's nice to provide guests with an environment they don't have at home."*

Olive Metcalf

The Bed and Breakfast Inn
San Francisco, California
94123

Innkeepers: Marily and Robert Kavanaugh
Address/Telephone: 4 Charlton Court; (415) 921–9784
Rooms: 10, including penthouse; 6 with private bath.
Rates: $68 to $129; $189 for penthouse. Light breakfast included.
Open: All year.
Facilities and local attractions: Located on one of the most fashionable
    shopping streets in San Francisco; restaurants, shops, Victorian
    architecture. Bus line to downtown.

You say you want intimate ambience . . . Cotswolds-cozy
atmosphere . . . in San Francisco? It awaits you, with elegance,
down a narrow cul-de-sac off Union Street.

Occasional guests have been heard to utter the word *alley*—
probably some down-to-earth midwestern types—but the preferred location description here is "mews," or possibly
"courtyard." Whatever you call it, it *is* adorable. Red geraniums in
window boxes stand out against the blue and white exterior of the
inn, which is really three restored Victorian houses. ☞ You'll be
greeted like an old friend. Sit down on the white wicker settee and
have a glass of sherry.

The breakfast room just off the entrance can entertain a china lover for hours. Much of Marily's collection of Spode, Copeland, and Wedgwood, among others, is displayed along with a vast number of teapots. Even better, it's all used on pretty linen settings for morning and afternoon tea. You can breakfast on a different china setting every day in a garden patio, or be served in your room. You'll get the *Chronicle* and freshly ground coffee or English teas, fruit, and hot "good things" like croissants or sticky buns.

Rooms are decorated with extraordinary flair using family heirlooms from England. They all have the bright, fresh look of just having been redone. Dainty Laura Ashley print is in a delicate room called Celebration; grass cloth and rattan furniture in Mandalay. Other rooms are Covent Garden, Green Park, and Kensington Garden, which opens to a flower-filled deck behind the inn. The Mayfair is a private flat with living room, kitchen, latticed balcony, and spiral staircase to the bedroom loft.

A small library room downstairs is a cozy retreat with a television, games, and books. You're invited to brew yourself a cup of tea, if you like. Very personal service is the pride of everyone around here.

Within a two-block circle around the inn are dozens of interesting restaurants. Perry's is one that's always fun—one of San Francisco's most famous bars, specializing in interpersonal relations and great hamburgers.

How to get there: From Van Ness Street, take Union Street west. Between Laguna and Buchanan streets, turn left into Charlton Court.

✳

J: "Masterpiece Theatre" *buffs will love the "upstairs" treatment you get here. If the* Titanic *hadn't failed her, Lady Marjory would have been right at home.*

Olive Metcalf

Hermitage House
San Francisco, California
94115

Innkeeper: Jane Bertorelli; owner, Marian Binkley
Address/Telephone: 2224 Sacramento Street; (415) 921–5515
Rooms: 5; all with private bath, television, and telephone; some with fireplace.
Rates: $80 to $120, double occupancy, extended continental breakfast included. Long stays given special rates.
Open: All year.
Facilities and local attractions: Good public transportation to downtown; near Presbyterian Hospital. Beautiful neighborhood for walking. Restaurants close by.

This seventeen-room Greek Revival house, built between 1900 and 1903, displays some of the most 🖝 stunning use of redwood you'll ever see in a private home. The present owners did a lot of scrubbing, rubbing, and oiling to restore the original beauty, and the results are a masterpiece. From the entryway, with its beautiful carved redwood detail in pillars, beams, and stairway scrolls to the superbly carved mantels, it is a unique interior.

Seven working fireplaces are in the home, including one in the large living room. Wine is served here in the evenings, a tastefully decorated room with comfortable furniture and fresh flowers. Just off it is an alcove room that was once used as a chapel. It's a particularly pretty spot for weddings.

Despite the old-time formality of a grand house, the atmosphere is comfortable and unpretentious. The morning routine, for instance, accommodates the most finicky early-morning riser. A generous and beautifully arranged breakfast buffet is provided in the dining room. You can help yourself and eat here, or take it to a less formal room with your morning paper.

The rooms are beautifully decorated and have added thoughtful touches like fresh flowers, radios, private outside telephone lines, televisions, and alarm clocks. The Judge's Study on the third floor under the eaves is especially inviting and cozy with paneling, shelves of books, and a marvelous view of the city. At the top of the stairs on the third floor is a porch with another city view, which is, in Jane's words, "an absolute sun trap."

An out-of-towner will love walking this most San Francisco of neighborhoods. It is only minutes from Nob Hill, Japan Town, and some of the city's most glamourous restaurants. Just a couple of blocks away is the upper Fillmore, a district that's becoming quite chic with boutiques and quaint restaurants. A garden, a sheltered patio, and off-street parking are other conveniences for a city inn.

How to get there: From Van Ness Avenue, turn west on Sacramento Street to the inn on your right.

$$*$$

J: *If you know a morning grouch who's coming to San Francisco, steer him to this understanding inn.*

olive Metcalf

The Mansion Hotel
San Francisco, California
94115

Innkeeper: Robert Pritikin
Address/Telephone: 2220 Sacramento Street; (415) 929–9444
Rooms: 19; all with queen-sized bed and private bath.
Rates: $89 to $200 double occupancy; $74 to $150 single. Full breakfast included.
Open: All year. Restaurant serves dinner weekends and most weeknights.
Facilities and local attractions: Concerts, billiards, Bufano Sculpture gardens.
A neighborhood of splendid San Francisco homes; cable car four blocks away; tennis courts nearby. Weddings, parties, and conferences catered.

In the words of Monty Python, ☞ and now for something completely different: a twin-turreted Queen Anne Victorian that has nightly magical séances; real British masters like Turner and Reynolds on the walls; pigs, rendered in all media, throughout the house; rooms of fine antiques, funky junk, and cages of doves; a neighborhood polling place whose costumed staff offers voters beverages and venison pâtés from silver platters . . . it's all The Mansion!

Ad man Robert Pritikin has been called eccentric and whimsical, but he also may be the most original innkeeper in the city.

144

His inn is a little quirky, but it's lavishly decorated and great fun. Parlor, billiard room, and kitchen are splendid. Even more elegant is the crystal-chandeliered restaurant opening onto a garden of flowers and ☞ Bufano sculptures. This magnificent marble and bronze collection constitutes the definitive display of the artist's works.

It's the ☞ pigs, in porcelain, painting, and sculpture, that tell you a sense of humor is loose here. The perfectly reasonable explanation for the swine element in the midst of Victoriana is that they're to pacify Claudia, the Mansion ghost. She kept pigs in this house where she lived and died, and according to demonologists, her "extremely heavy" (but not negative) presence is still in the mansion.

Claudia appears nightly in the music room in her empty Victorian wheelchair and invisibly plays selections requested by the guests. Sometimes the concert closes with ragtime or a Sousa march, assisted by the audience members, who have been supplied with cowbells, maracas, and tambourines. ☞ Weekend concerts feature innkeeper Pritikin on the Concert Saw and other class acts.

Up the grand staircase are guest rooms in turn-of-the-century-style decor with modern plumbing, telephones, and other contemporary comforts. Some have balconies and marble fireplaces; each has a private speaker which plays classical music when you wish.

Dinners served in the lovely dining room are produced by David Coyle, formerly personal chef to the Duke and Duchess of Bedford. They win raves from restaurant critics and, at the current prix fixe of $30, are a bargain in this city. He also does a first-rate British breakfast including Earl Grey tea (and coffee), fruits, juice, toasted crumpets, eggs, bangers, and Chef Coyle's au gratin potatoes. Coffee is always ready in the kitchen for guests to help themselves.

How to get there: Entering the city from the east or south, follow signs to the Golden Gate Bridge until you come to the Van Ness exit. If you are entering over the Golden Gate Bridge, follow signs to downtown and Lombard Street. Go east on Lombard to Van Ness and turn right. From Van Ness Avenue, turn west on Sacramento to the Inn on your right.

J: *This is a classy place to fulfill the need of people who visit San Francisco searching for something offbeat.*

Olive Metcalf

Petite Auberge
San Francisco, California
94108

Innkeeper: Carolyn Vaughan
Address/Telephone: 863 Bush Street; (415) 928–6000
Rooms: 26, including 1 suite; all with private bath, 18 with fireplace.
Rates: $105 to $195, with generous continental breakfast and afternoon
   tea. Parking $15 per day.
Open: All year.
Facilities and local attractions: Walking distance to San Francisco's theater
   district, shopping, Nob Hill, Union Square, fine restaurants, cable-car
   connections.

Hard to believe, but in the very heart of downtown San
Francisco is an inn with all the 🐦 ambience of a French country
inn. Not rustic-country, mind you, but classy-country. Step into
the blue canopied entrance from busy Bush Street and you enter a
warmly inviting lobby of large, brick-colored tiles that look old
(but probably aren't), oriental rugs, fresh flowers, and a carousel
horse that for some reason looks French.

But everything looks French with bright Pierre Deux fabric
designs on lampshades, picture mats, and French Provincial
furniture. (Robin, at the desk, told me that the Pierre Deux
company, by the way, was begun by two men both named Pierre;

146

thus the "deux.") White porcelain ducks sporting ribbons around the neck, and grapevine wreaths entwined with ribbons give the impression of perennial springtime, French style.

Upstairs, even the smallest rooms are impeccably decorated with every possible convenience. Handsome armoires hide TVs. ☞ Good reading lights are on either side of the beds, which have beautiful linens and lacy pillow shams. On an antique writing desk is a hand-addressed welcome letter for the expected guests.

One of the medium-size rooms has space for a creamy tiled fireplace, rose loveseat, blue wingback chair, and a window seat. Bathroom fixtures have elegant porcelain handles, and special toiletries and thick towels await.

What makes this an inn instead of an elegant, small hotel? ☞ Hands-on taking care of you, that's what. Do you want to be picked up at the airport, have your car parked, or have your shoes shined? Do you need someone to handle those tiresome details of dinner reservations and theater tickets? Would you like to lay on a smart dinner party but abhor the crassness of a public restaurant?

Relax, mon ami. All can be arranged. Downstairs from the lobby is a comfortable lounge, dining room, and courtyard garden. Breakfast is served here mornings; tea, wine, and nibbles in the afternoons. The inn offers an attractively presented and satisfying breakfast, with fresh fruit, juices, cereals, homemade breads and pastries, and an ever-changing main dish.

How to get there: From Union Square, go left (west) on Sutter Street to Taylor; turn right, go to Bush; turn right. Inn is on the right at number 863.

J: *I've always loved the pastoral life. It's good to see it thriving here on Bush Street.*

The Spreckels Mansion
San Francisco, California
94117

Innkeeper: Kathleen Austin
Address/Telephone: 737 Buena Vista West; (415) 861–3008
Rooms: 10; all but 2 with private bath.
Rates: $88 to $190, breakfast included. Two-night minimum on weekends.
  Cigars discouraged.
Open: All year.
Facilities and local attractions: Small conferences can be accommodated.
  Beside Buena Vista Park; neighborhood of beautiful homes; walk to
  Haight Street, shops and restaurants; fifteen minutes from Union
  Square.

The Spreckels Mansion is one of the city's fine "country inns." When it was built in 1887 for a nephew of Adolph Spreckels, the famous sugar baron, it really was a country estate, probably an hour's carriage drive from downtown San Francisco. Sitting high on Buena Vista Hill, the inn has the advantage of beautiful views and the privacy of an ☞ interesting neighborhood. Jack London and Ambrose Bierce once lived here. More recently, the top-floor ballroom was a recording studio for a rock band, and the guest house next door was owned by a rock musician, Graham Nash.

148

A two-bedroom suite now covers the entire third floor of the mansion. It has a marble fireplace and kitchen and is understandably expensive. But the pleasures of this grand house are in the smaller rooms, too. Five guest rooms in the mansion and five in the guest house are each an achievement in comfortable elegance. There's no getting away from the fact that they *are* grand, but nothing about the decor is stiff or off-putting. Most have fireplaces and views of either Buena Vista Park or Golden Gate Park and the ocean.

A broad central hallway, oriental rugs on parquet floors, chandeliers, stained glass, and fresh flowers reward every guest. To sit in the handsomely decorated library/parlor, with its dramatic wallpaper and myriad bookshelves, is to enjoy a kind of old-world experience most of us find only at special inns like this. Sipping wine by the fireplace in these surroundings is bound to make you feel rather elegant. So will the continental breakfast and morning paper delivered to your room on a silver tray.

High standards of taste and talent and lots of money have brought the mansion back to architectural prominence, but it's the 🖝 tender loving care lavished on guests that ultimately makes it an exceptional inn. Help is on the spot if you want touring suggestions or reservations made. Kathleen has a knack for coming up with exactly the kind of restaurant to suit your mood, from the newest undiscovered treasure to a little place with great French food and a quiet jazz piano.

How to get there: From Van Ness, take Fell Street west to Masonic, and turn left. At Fredrick, jog left to Buena Vista. Follow to inn on your left.

✳

J: The world does not exist to satisfy your every whim, but they don't know that at The Spreckels Mansion. Lucky you.

olive Metcalf

Victorian Inn on the Park
San Francisco, California
94117

Innkeepers: Lisa and William Benau
Address/Telephone: 301 Lyon Street; (415) 931–1830
Rooms: 12; all with private bath.
Rates: $75 double occupancy to $225 for suite for 4. Continental breakfast
   included; not convenient for children. Two-night minimum on
   weekends.
Open: All year.
Facilities and local attractions: The Panhandle and Golden Gate Park for
   walking and bicycling; De Young Museum, California Academy of
   Sciences, Japanese Tea Garden.

When Queen Victoria celebrated her Diamond Jubilee in
1897, the Victorian Inn on the Park was built by a local lumberman
for his son Thomas Clunie. The Clunie House reflected the family
business with its intricately paneled entry and parquet floors
lavishly inlaid with oak, mahogany, and redwood. The history of
the ornate house progresses from first owner Clunie, who became
a state senator and United States congressman, to a recent cult
group who held rebirthing rites in a hot tub in the basement!
   Since the Benaus rescued it, they have restored and decorated
the house as an inn with faithful attention to turn-of-the-century

details. Lisa and her mother chose the antique pieces. There are fascinating old photographs on the walls and a red velvet upholstered Queen Anne sofa and chair in the parlor. They've found, or had designed, some of the most flamboyant fringed lampshades I've ever seen . . . and they look wonderful in rooms this size.

Six guest rooms are upstairs, another four in what was once the ballroom on the top floor, and two more bedrooms in the basement. The largest room has a fireplace and a good view of the Panhandle, but the most unusual is the Persian Suite, with exotic fabric covering a multitude of pillows and draping a sitting area tucked under a dormer window. All the rooms have pretty comforters and down pillows.

My favorite room is the library downstairs. It's rather dark, with lots of wood and books, and very cozy. The Benaus will pour the sherry.

Breakfast, served in your room or in the dining room, consists of fresh fruit, juice, croissants, homemade breads, and cheese. The morning *Chronicle, New York Times,* and *Wall Street Journal* are on hand. The Benaus will give you good ideas for dinner choices nearby, or they'll arrange small catered dinners at the inn.

How to get there: From Highway 101 north, take Fell Street toward Golden Gate Park. Inn is on the right at Lyon Street.

✺

J: *One of the world's zaniest races, the annual San Francisco Bay to Breakers, goes right by the inn's front door. Each May for seventy-five years, world-class runners race from San Francisco Bay, up the murderous Hayes Street hill, and out Fell to Ocean Beach. The event has grown to be the city's best party, with 100,000 runners, many in outrageous costumes. You could have a front-row seat here to see all the sights—and they're astounding.*

olive Metcalf

The Washington Square Inn
San Francisco, California
94133

Innkeepers: Nan and Norman Rosenblatt
Address/Telephone: 1660 Stockton Street; (415) 981–4220
Rooms: 15; 10 with private bath, 4 shared, 1 half-bath.
Rates: $75 to $160, including continental breakfast. Children welcome.
   Telephones; television available on request at no charge.
Open: All year.
Facilities and local attractions: Great walking area of San Francisco: restaurants, shops, markets. Close to cable car line; one block from Telegraph Hill; easy walk to Ghirardelli Square, the Cannery, financial district.

The inn faces Washington Square, in the heart of North Beach, to my eye the 🖝 most colorful neighborhood in the city. Saints Peter and Paul Church dominates one side of the square; on the other sides are wonderful restaurants (the Washington Square Bar and Grill is the mecca for politicians and literary types), shops, and markets displaying fresh pasta, salamis, and produce. In the park a covey of shining black bangs clutching brown bags (a Chinese kindergarten class) settles down on the grass for a picnic lunch. Several old men practice *tai chi* exercises, oblivious to the bustle on all sides. Over all is the aroma of freshly ground coffee.

You can see much of this scene from the comfort of the inn's lobby/sitting room. There is a handsomely carved fireplace, comfortable provincial furniture on a blue rug, magazines, and books. A big basket of fresh fruit looks as if you're actually supposed to take a piece. Continental breakfast with freshly squeezed juice is served here or in your room. Since this is North Beach, with some of the best restaurants and bakeries anywhere, the croissants and pastries will be the best. Afternoon tea is served here, too, with tiny sandwiches and shortbread.

The inn is as ☞ convenient for business travelers who want a personal atmosphere as it is for families who want bedroom-sitting room combinations with sofa beds that sleep four. From hiring you a stenographer, to packing a picnic lunch, to arranging baby-sitting or tours, the staff is ready to help. High-anxiety types may find that the most considerate personal service is an innkeeper who will find at 10:00 P.M. that aspirin or Alka Seltzer you forgot to pack.

The rooms are pure pleasure. Nan Rosenblatt is a San Francisco designer and has decorated them with English and French antiques and a good eye for comfort. She has chosen bright French floral fabrics for quilted comforters and matching canopies. Some rooms look out on a small courtyard, and those in front overlook the square and a bit of city skyline.

The colors, aromas, and sights of North Beach are the very essence of San Francisco. And you can ☞ walk to most of the city's attractions from this location.

How to get there: From Van Ness, take Union Street east; turn left on Stockton. The inn is on your right.

Olive Metcalf

Casa Madrona Hotel
Sausalito, California
94965

Innkeeper: John Mays
Address/Telephone: 801 Bridgeway; (415) 332–0502
Rooms: 34; all with private bath.
Rates: $75 to $185 for rooms; cottages, $140 to $160; 3-room suite, $300.
   Continental breakfast included.
Open: All year. Lunch, dinner, beer and wine bar.
Facilities and local attractions: Sausalito's shops and galleries, ferryboat rides
   across the bay, fine dining. Hiking, bicycling.

John Mays knows how to create an atmosphere. He's turned
this luxurious, old mansion perched on a hill above Sausalito into
☞ one of the most romantic inns you'll find. Of course, he has a
lot going for him with a town almost too winning for words and
spectacular views of the yacht harbor.

Casa Madrona is more than one hundred years old. Time had
taken its toll on the former residence, hotel, bordello, and boarding
house when John Mays rescued it in 1978. It nearly slid off the hill
during the rains of '82, but renovations already begun saved it
from gliding away.

Since then he's added an elegant tumble of cottages that
cascade down the hill to Sausalito's main street. Each one is

different, with dormers, gables, peaked roofs, and hidden decks. Amazingly, the whole gray-blue jumble lives perfectly with the old mansion.

You've seen "individually decorated" rooms before, but these beat all. Mays gave each one of his new hillside cottages over to a different Bay Area decorator. The range of their individual styles resulted in rooms with themes from nautical to equestrian (The Ascot Suite), to a Parisian Artist's Loft. Most have private decks and superb views. And since it *is* fabled, sybaritic Marin, there are luxurious tubs for two (sometimes elevated and open to the room), refrigerators stocked with fruit juice and mineral water, and fresh flowers. (But no peacock feathers.)

If you're indifferent to unique rooms surrounded by lush gardens, exotic bougainvillea and trumpet vine spilling over decks and walkways, perhaps elegant food will ring your bell. A beautiful wine bar and uncluttered dining room in the old house on top of the hill are lighted and decorated to enchant. Only white linen on round tables and fresh flowers compete with the view from the deck of the bay and Sausalito Yacht Harbor . . . that is, until the food is served.

We began with a California cuisine standard, radicchio and Belgian endive salad with baked chevre (goat cheese). Perfection. Our waiter was agreeable when I ordered another first course (angel hair pasta with roasted peppers and mussels) instead of an entree. (I love places that encourage you to order by *your* appetite instead of *their* rules.) Others at our table raved about grilled swordfish with a red pepper butter and rack of lamb with a watercress pine-nut pesto. The meal could not have been lovelier.

How to get there: Cross the Golden Gate Bridge; take Alexander Street exit to center of town. San Francisco Airport pickup available. Ferry service from San Francisco.

✳

J: *If this inn can't rekindle a dying ember, no place can.*

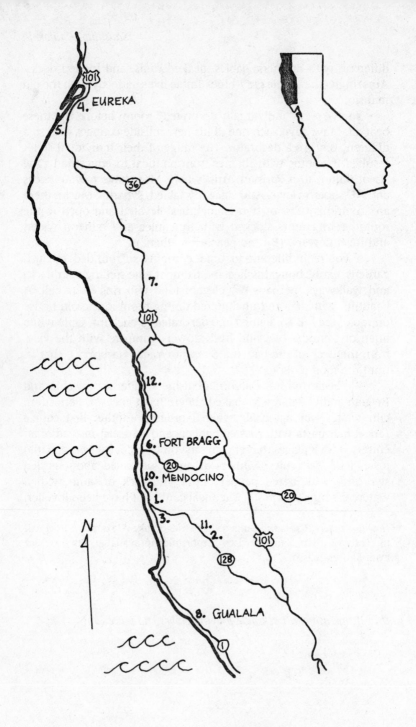

101

4. EUREKA

5.

36

7.

101

cccc
cccc

12.

1

cccc

6. FORT BRAGG

20

10. MENDOCINO

9.

1.

20

3.

11. 2.

101

128

8. GUALALA

1

cccc
cccc

N

California: The North Coast

Numbers on map refer to towns numbered below.

olive Metcalf

Fensalden
Albion, California
95410

Innkeepers: Frances and Scott Brazil
Address/Telephone: Highway 1 (mailing address: Box 99); (707) 937–4042
Rooms: 7; all with private bath.
Rates: $70 to $125 for suite, including breakfast. No smoking.
Open: All year.
Facilities and local attractions: Seven miles from Mendocino for fine restaurants, shopping, art center, galleries, theater. 1½ miles to Albion and Navarro rivers for swimming, fishing, canoeing. Hiking, biking terrain.

Humming down California Highway 1, roof back, sea breezes blowing, and Willie Nelson on tape singing his heart out, I nearly ignored a sign that read "Fensalden." Fortunately, I followed the narrow road a quarter mile back into the hills and discovered a stunning inn.

It belongs to Frances and Scott Brazil, who fell in love with the place when they were guests, bought it, and moved north from Los Altos to make it their "early retirement" home. No wonder! The twenty acres of rolling, wooded land overlooks the spectacular Mendocino Coast, and the two ramshackle buildings that were once an 1860s stagecoach stop and tavern were transformed by the former owners into a handsome country inn.

The two-storied, cedar-shingled structure, with dormers and balconies, looking out to the ocean seems to blend naturally into the land. Every step of renovation and decorating has been done with reverence for this beautiful site. It was named Fensalden (accent the middle syllable), which in Norwegian means "home of the mist and the sea."

You enter a small parlor with a fireplace. The interior walls are the original rough-hewn redwood with each window and door framed in oiled redwood trim. A hall leads to a large common room with an ocean view through rows of cypress trees lining the headlands meadow. You often see deer grazing here. A grand piano (Frances plays) dominates the room that also holds comfortable sofas and chairs, a wood-burning stove, and a couple of Charles Russell prints.

At the east end of the room, windows look out at the flower garden entrance. Here is the large Victorian oval table where Frances serves a full breakfast. Her apple puff pancake is a favorite, but she has a variety of egg dishes, hot muffins, and plenty of fresh juice and coffee. For other meals, there are excellent restaurants within a short drive.

The seven bedrooms are beautifully simple. Down comforters are inside colorful cotton covers—such a fresh, clean idea, I wonder why more innkeepers don't use them, instead of quilts that can't be laundered after each guest. The baths are particularly attractive. Ceramic tile showers and sinks made by local potters are works of art.

How to get there: Driving north on Highway 1, the inn is 1½ miles past the intersection of Highways 128 and 1. Driving south on Highway 1, the inn is 1½ miles past Albion.

✳

J: *Away from highway noise here, you can stand among the wild-flowers or tramp over the meadows and hear only ocean and wind.*

Olive Metcalf

The Toll House
Boonville, California
95415

Innkeeper: Beverly Nesbitt
Address/Telephone; 15301 Highway 253; (707) 895–3630
Rooms: 5; 2 with private bath.
Rates: $60 to $100, including country breakfast and complimentary wine.
  Each additional person, $15. No pets; no young children. Smoking
  discouraged.
Open: All year. Evening meals by special arrangement.
Facilities and local attractions: Large yard with gazebo, hot tub, barbecue.
  Television in sun parlor. Short drive to wineries and fine restaurants.

The Toll House, a picture of apple-pie rural America, sits in
the beautiful, secluded Bell Valley in the heart of Mendocino
County. The 1912 house is six miles up the road from Boonville
and was once the headquarters for the vast sheep grazing Miller
Ranch. It became known as Toll House because the family that
maintained the road charged loggers to haul their redwood over it
to the inland mills.

In Beverly Nesbitt's hands it has become a well-maintained
inn that draws you into its homey atmosphere. The big shaded
yard with a hammock, gazebo, and a hot tub are welcome sights
to city-weary eyes. Guests have the run of the kitchen during the

day to help themselves to coffee and snacks. In your room, more relaxing spirits await: a carafe of local Parducci wine.

The sunny bedrooms have a refreshing absence of frills. Two rooms upstairs with a shared bath are done in pastels, with windows situated to let the sun spill in. The large Blue Room is even more inviting—to masculine tastes, perhaps—with a private bath and a fireplace. All the rooms have queen-sized beds with an additional daybed. Everybody loves the main floor's library, which features a private bath, a fireplace, and book-lined walls. Behind the house is the Bicycle Shed, a captivating room with twin beds and wood paneling—though you do have to cross the patio and enter the house to use the bathroom.

A big country breakfast starts the day in the dining room, on the patio, or in the delightful sun parlor. Fresh juice and fruit are followed by one of Beverly's specials: omelets, waffles, or pancakes, and warm gano sauce (see J's comment). The atmosphere here is so cozy that you may want to request dinner when you make your reservation. With advance notice you can have an intimate dinner for two or a five-course feast, often featuring local lamb. If you go out for dinner, try the sophisticated cooking at the Floodgate in Navarro, just a fifteen-minute drive to the coast.

How to get there: Traveling north from San Francisco, take Highway 101 to Cloverdale. Turn west on Highway 128 and follow to Boonville and Highway 253. Turn northeast. The inn is about six miles up the road. Or take Highway 101 to Ukiah and then Highway 253 (Boonville Road) as it twists over the mountains to Boonville.

J: *This valley is the home of "Boontling," a peculiar, contrived jargon spoken here and even taught in the schools between 1880 and 1920. A sprinkling of it survives today. A cup of coffee at a Boonville cafe is a* horn of Zeese. *The* Buckey Walter *is a pay telephone. At The Toll House you might have* florries (*light biscuits*) *or* gano sauce (*applesauce made from the apple orchards of Anderson Valley*).

Ol.ve Metcalf

Elk Cove Inn
Elk, California
95432

Innkeeper: Hildrun-Uta Triebess
Address/Telephone: 6300 South Highway 1 (mailing address: Box 367);
(707) 877–3321
Rooms: 8; 6 with private bath, some with fireplace.
Rates: $138 to $168 weekends and holidays, AP; $88 to $118 midweek,
breakfast included. No pets. No smoking.
Open: All year. Dinner on Saturdays and holidays.
Facilities and local attractions: Beach walks, secret caves, seals, exotic birds.
White-water tours. Restaurants, wineries nearby. Fifteen miles south
of Mendocino galleries, shops, theater.

Elk is a small village on a bluff overlooking the ocean, as fresh
as the winds that blow over it. There are a few surviving Victorian
houses, as is this 1883 inn, but it is ocean lovers who come to Elk.
From the bluffs behind the inn there is a ☞ spectacular ever-
changing view of the Pacific. A short staircase leads down the bluff
to an expansive, driftwood-strewn beach with a fresh-flowing
creek that meets the ocean.

The main house is where all meals are served. Adjacent to it
are four individual units, recently remodeled. Two of these have
free-standing fireplaces, high, beamed ceilings, and skylights. All
of them have bay windows looking out to the ocean view.

Hildrun-Uta's decor is nicely done, with appealing individual touches in each cottage. One has handmade doors more than a hundred years old; another has bits of stained glass worked into the framework; still another has a sunken bedroom from which the bay window looks to the ocean. Given the dramatic beauty of this stretch of coastline, I applaud her determination to not squander any opportunity for viewing it. There is a window seat in one cottage that is seemingly on the very edge of the bluff, and even a shower (with a mural of handpainted tiles) has an ocean view. Decanters of sherry or wine and fresh flowers welcome you.

Breakfast and Saturday night dinner at Elk Cove are part of the experience. Hildrun cooks everything herself. With the help of two daughters, she serves on fresh linens and pretty china in her newly remodeled dining room that runs across the ocean side of the inn. Her German background is reflected in the French and German specialties she prepares. The breakfast star is Eierkuchen, an impressive German eggcake served with fresh berries, applesauce, or raspberry sauce. Dinner entrees might include Sauerbraten, Rouladen, Coq au Vin, Ling Cod Veracruz, or Veal Ragout. A good selection of wines is available, many of them local and unique to the inn.

How to get there: From San Francisco, take Highway 101 to Cloverdale, then Route 128 to the coast. Turn left on Highway 1; go 5 miles to Elk. The inn is on the ocean side of the highway south of Elk.

✳

J: *Take your sneakers and a sweater for brooding (and usually blustery) beach walks.*

Olive Metcalf

Harbor House
Elk, California
95432

Innkeepers: Helen and Dean Turner
Address/Telephone: 5600 South Highway One (mailing address: Box 369);
   (707) 877–3203
Rooms: 10, including 4 cottages; all with private bath; each has fireplace
   or parlor stove except 1 room with private deck.
Rates: $135 to $195 for two, includes breakfast and dinner, MAP. Each
   additional person $45 per day. Ask about midweek winter rates. No
   credit cards; not suitable for children or pets.
Open: All year. Dinner by reservation.
Facilities and local attractions: Private beach, fishing, ocean kayaking with
   guide. Close to Mendocino shops, galleries, restaurants. Forest walks.
   Local wineries.

   The windswept solitude of this stretch of Northern California's
shore is one of nature's tens. And for an inn on the bluffs above the
rocky coast, Harbor House has it all: a 🖙 dramatic location,
unique architecture, fresh decor, and fine food.
   The house was 🖙 built in 1916 entirely of virgin redwood by
the Goodyear Redwood Lumber Company as a place to lodge and
entertain their executives and guests. In the 1930s it was converted
to an inn and has variously faded and flourished over the years.

164

The inn's newest owners are warm hosts, who understand exactly what a spell this inn casts.

The large living room, completely paneled in redwood with a high-beamed open ceiling, sets the tone: quiet and unpretentious. Comfortable sofas and a piano are grouped on a rich Persian rug before a huge fireplace, with books and a stereo nearby. (Christmas here sounds wonderful—the redwood room glowing in firelight, a giant tree, roasting chestnuts, festive dinners, and music from local musicians.) Bedrooms and cottages are freshly decorated, many with pastel watercolor prints by a local artist of flowers and birds indigenous to the area.

☛ Ocean views from the dining room are breathtaking. On blustery North Coast days, some guests choose to spend the day here watching the churning surf. It's comforting to know you don't have to leave this warm atmosphere to find a restaurant. Wonderful food is in store for you here.

The Turners subscribe to that old verity of California cooking: Use only the freshest, best ingredients possible, and keep it simple. ☛ Many ingredients are plucked right from the inn's own garden. What they don't grow, they purchase from the finest local sources, like baby potatoes and the locally raised lamb. Fresh fish is often featured, prepared with Harbor House nuances. All the breads and breakfast pastries are homemade. Desserts also tend to reflect whatever is fresh. Typical are poached pears with raspberry sauce, or a sweet flaky pastry stuffed with apricots and cream. A fine California wine list and a good selection of beers are available. Dinner is a fixed menu, changing every night, but with advance notice, they'll try to accommodate any special dietary needs.

Mendocino's attractions are only twenty minutes farther north, but I'm all for staying right here. Walking the beach, discovering the secluded patios and paths—one leads to a waterfall and grotto—these are the quiet seductions of the inn. If you're in during the day, a bottle of local wine and a cheese platter from the kitchen are available to hold body and soul together until dinner.

How to get there: From the Bay area, take Highway 101 to Cloverdale, then Highway 128 west to Highway 1. The inn is 6 miles south on the ocean side of Highway 1.

J: Plan on long romantic dinners.

Olive Metcalf

Carter House
Eureka, California
95501

Innkeepers: Mark and Christi Carter
Address/Telephone: 1033 Third Street; (707) 445–1390
Rooms: 7; 5 with private bath, 2 share a bath.
Rates: $65 to $165 double occupancy; breakfast included.
Open: All year.
Facilities and local attractions: Dinners and special events catered at the
house. Walk renovated Old Town waterfront, shops, restaurants.
Victorian architecture tours; salmon fishing; Fort Humbolt. Drive
south to Avenue of the Giants; north to Redwood National Park.

Sitting in the splendid parlor of Carter House sipping wine, a
guest from Ohio declared that he had "built a good many houses
in my time" and this house couldn't possibly be new. "No one *does*
work like this anymore."

But you do if you're Mark Carter and grew up in Eureka near
the 🖝 famous Carson Mansion, probably the single finest example
of Victorian architecture in the country. Carter renovated other
houses by the same architects, and, with an old book of their
designs, he decided to construct one from scratch.

With a crew of three, Carter built the four-story redwood
mansion, handcrafting the intricate wood moldings and detailings.

166

His only deviation from the Newsom plan (aside from modern baths) was a bay window that splashes light into the entryway. Instead of heavy Victorian decor, Mark and Christi kept the walls white (allowing the beautiful wood to stand out even more), put down white marble in the hallway, and decorated with a few outstanding antiques and oriental rugs on polished oak floors. A changing gallery of paintings and ceramics by local artists, plants, and fresh flowers complete the remarkable, light-filled *new* Victorian.

One of the seven guest rooms is a suite, complete with sitting room, fireplace, private bath, and Jacuzzi. Three rooms with high-vaulted ceilings, designer linens, and antiques are on the top floor; three more rooms and a sitting room with a television are below the parlor.

Mornings begin with a newspaper at your door, then a lavish breakfast served in the dining room. On my visit, we started with fresh raspberries and juice, proceeded to hot breads and eggs Benedict, and finished with Christi's wonderful apple tart.

The Carters have added the newly restored Hotel Carter—all peach and white with bleached pine antiques—to their domain. Guests get the full Carter House breakfast treatment, but they also serve elegant dinners here. It would be a shame to drive all the way up here and miss this outstanding food.

The Carter lodgings are hospitable places to get acquainted with Eureka—and you should. Mark smiles at people who think that because the town is remote, it must be a cultural wasteland. The truth is, it's a stimulating community of writers, artists, and craftspeople, with five theater companies and higher theater attendance per capita than in San Francisco!

How to get there: Highway 101 into Eureka becomes Broadway. At L Street, turn left. Inn is on the corner.

✳

J: *A friend of Mark's tells that a few years ago he'd often lock up the restaurant he managed and see Mark drive by—at 2 A.M. He wondered what his married friend was doing out at that hour and learned later that new father Mark, rather than have his guests disturbed, lulled his crying son back to sleep out driving. Is that an innkeeper?*

olive Metcalf

Old Town Bed &
Breakfast
Eureka, California
95501

Innkeepers: Leigh and Diane Benson
Address/Telephone: 1521 Third Street; (707) 445–3951
Rooms: 5; 3 with private bath, 2 share a bath.
Rates: $50 to $75; singles deduct $5. Includes full breakfast, evening
    beverage, and cheese. No smoking.
Open: All year.
Facilities and local attractions: Walk to waterfront, Old Town, Victorian
    architecture, Carson Mansion, shops, restaurants, Theaters, muse-
    ums. Fishing.

I can almost feel sorry for the thousands of visitors to
California every year who think everything worth seeeing is
contained between Los Angeles and San Francisco. Tell them
about the Redwood Empire that stretches more than 400 miles
from San Francisco into Oregon and their eyes glaze. But that's
okay with the rest of us. That reluctance to go beyond the
well-traveled areas of the state is what keeps vast regions of
California still an unspoiled scenic wonder.

After living in many countries and states, Leigh and Diane

Benson decided to put down roots in the heart of the redwood country. Their decision brought them to Eureka, the commercial center of Northern California, and to this 1871 Victorian. The house is the one-time residence of William Carson, a local lumber baron. Its location at the entrance to Old Town is ideal for walking that ambitious waterfront revival of Eureka's Victorian past.

The Bensons have obviously found a new life they love. Their inn is neat as a pin, with fresh flowers in every room from their almost year-round gardens. Diane likes touches of whimsy, such as teddy bears on all the beds and rubber ducks by the claw-footed tubs. There is also a cat in residence.

Bedrooms are spacious, airy, and attractively decorated. The largest room is The William Carson with a queen-sized bed and private, old-fashioned bathtub in the room. But it's hard to resist one called Sarah's Rose Parfait, with a raspberry carpet, lace curtains, and pretty floral wallpaper. The Maxfield Parish Room features his artwork, oak antiques, and a shared bath with tub. This is the room for watching sunsets. Sumner's Room, the smallest, has a double bed and a private bath with shower.

This is one of the few inns that give a break to the solo traveler. A deduction of $5 from the rate schedule offers an attractive package to a single or business traveler who wants an inn atmosphere rather than a hotel.

A full breakfast is served in the country kitchen, sometimes warmed by its wood-burning stove. A variety of egg dishes, homebaked muffins, coffee cake or biscuits, and a variety of fresh fruit are typical fare.

Since breakfast is the only meal provided, the Bensons like to keep up to date on all the restaurants in town so they can help their guests choose one.

How to get there: Going north on Highway 101, proceed through Eureka and turn left on R Street. Go 2 blocks to Third Street; turn left. The inn is 1½ blocks on the right.

J: *Diane has had so many requests from guests for her breakfast recipes that she's put together her own cookbook. Selling nicely, she reports.*

Olive Metcalf

The Gingerbread Mansion
Ferndale, California
95536

Innkeepers: Wendy Hatfield and Ken Torbert
Address/Telephone: 400 Berding Street; (707) 786–4000
Rooms: 9; all with private bath, 3 with fireplace.
Rates: $75 to $135, double occupancy; singles deduct $10. Includes
   generous continental breakfast. No pets, no children under 10. No
   smoking.
Open: All year.
Facilities and local attractions: Bicycles loaned. Walk Victorian Ferndale,
   theater, art galleries, shops, restaurants. June Scandinavian Festival,
   August Ferndale Fair, May three-day World Champion Kinetic
   Sculpture Race (in which "cheating is not a right—it's a privilege").
   Bird-watching reserve at Russ Park; walking tours of Pacific Lumber
   Co.; Humbolt Redwoods State Park.

   The Victorian village of Ferndale is far enough off Highway
101 to have remained a secret for a long time. Now, however,
increasing numbers of travelers are discovering it and experiencing
that special pleasure of finding a still-little-known treasure.
   Except that every owner of a Victorian has obviously hired a

color consultant and a painstaking crew with brushes to decorate his or her fairy-tale house, ☞ the town has virtually not changed since the 1800s. There are no traffic lights, no parking meters, no mail delivery (citizens pick up at the post office). A village blacksmith is more than local color for the tourists; he uses his hammer and anvil to fabricate practical tools and decorative items. And one of the few remaining Carnegie-endowed public libraries is still in business, circulating books.

Visitors can sample this slice of old-time Americana from a ☞ spectacular turreted, gabled, and elaborately trimmed Queen Anne inn. The Gingerbread Mansion is renowned for being one of the most photographed Victorians in northern California, but fame hasn't turned its head. Wendy and Ken run a first-class inn, paying ☞ attention to little things that you'll remember: robes and luggage racks, a turned-down bed at night, a hand-dipped chocolate at bedside and an early morning tray of coffee in your room. They'll provide boots and umbrellas if you forget yours and lend you a bicycle, too, from their yellow-and-orange fleet painted to match the inn.

Even if you stay in a smaller room, be sure you get a look at some of the suites. These attractive young innkeepers have decorated all the bedrooms elegantly, romantically, and amusingly. They're always happy to tour you around the mansion for a view of all the rooms that aren't occupied. The Gingerbread Suite has a prim and proper sitting area, *and* ☞ twin claw-footed bathtubs sitting toe to toe on a raised platform surrounded by a Victorian railing. The Fountain Suite bath has twin tubs side by side facing a mirrored wall reflecting the flames in a Franklin stove and a full view of the room. What a marvelous place for a leisurely, meaningful conversation.

When breakfast is served you'll have homemade muffins and cakes along with juice, fruits, cheeses, and hard-boiled eggs. Wendy also serves an afternoon tea and cake spread in one of the downstairs parlors.

How to get there: Exit Highway 101 just north of Fortuna. Cross over Eel River Bridge, and proceed west 5 miles to Ferndale's Main Street. At the green Bank of America, turn left. Go 1 block to inn on corner.

Olive Metcalf

The Grey Whale Inn
Fort Bragg, California
95437

Innkeepers: John and Colette Bailey
Address/Telephone: 615 North Main Street; (707) 964–0640; in California,
(800) 382–7244
Rooms: 14; all with private bath. One room adapted for handicapped.
Rates: $60 to $125, double occupancy; $45 to $90, single; $100 to $125,
three people; $110 to $140, four people. Full breakfast buffet. Cribs
not available. Inn is appropriate for children over 12. No-smoking
rooms. No pets.
Open: All year.
Facilities and local attractions: Conference room for small meetings. Television room with VCR. Walk to depot for Skunk Train, shops,
restaurants. Drive to redwood forests, hiking trails, state parks,
beaches, Noyo Harbor fishing. Local events: March Whale Festival;
July Salmon Barbecue; September Paul Bunyan Days.

The Grey Whale was the first bed and breakfast in Fort Bragg,
and many people still think it's the best. The weathered redwood
building has the spare, straight lines of New England architecture,
and looks suitably sea-bleached and salty. The perception is
enhanced by the 🐋 hand-carved whale on the front lawn created
by Byrd Baker, artist and leader in the "Save the Whales"
movement.

The inn was originally built in 1915 as the Redwood Coast Hospital. Owners John and Colette Bailey converted it to an inn in 1976, adding their own warm, colorful touches. They have a deeply felt interest in the community and its artists, reflected in the local work decorating the walls.

Wide, carpeted hallways and spacious rooms afford unusual privacy and quiet. Both the prices and the variety of facilities make it a ☞ convenient inn for families. Some rooms sleep up to four and have kitchenettes, some have a fireplace, and others have ocean views. A fireplace lounge on the first floor is stocked with magazines, scrapbooks of information about the area, and games.

The Baileys continually refresh and improve the inn. Their way of gradually achieving a no-smoking environment is pretty clever: as a room is redecorated, it becomes a no-smoking room.

On the second floor, the breakfast room has a refrigerator that guests can use. A morning buffet is spread here of fruits, breads, custard or yogurt, and a hot entree. Scrambled eggs and crispy fried potatoes would be typical. You can eat here and meet other guests, or after sizing up the conversational possibilities, you can take a tray back to your room.

Straight directions don't begin to tell the story of driving to the North Coast. One suggestion is to take Highway 128 west out of Cloverdale over to the coast. You'll maneuver steep climbs and tight curves before dropping down into beautiful Anderson Valley with many wineries to explore. Once through the redwood groves along the Navarro River, you'll meet Highway 1 and climb to the headlands looking out at the Pacific. Don't take your eyes off the road until you pull over, but the views are breathtaking. The point is . . . *great scenery takes time.* If you drive Highway 1 all the way from San Francisco, allow about six hours to Fort Bragg.

How to get there: In Fort Bragg, Highway 1 becomes Main Street. Driving north, the inn is on your left.

❋

J: 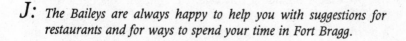 *The Baileys are always happy to help you with suggestions for restaurants and for ways to spend your time in Fort Bragg.*

Olive Metcalf

Pudding Creek Inn
Fort Bragg, California
95437

Innkeepers: Marilyn and Gene Gunderson
Address/Telephone: 700 North Main Street; (707) 964–9529
Rooms: 10; all with private bath.
Rates: $49 to $78, double occupancy; includes breakfast.
Open: All year, except 3 weeks in January.
Facilities and local attractions: Western depot for Skunk Train; walk to Glass
   Beach, shops, restaurants. Party boats at Noyo Harbor; July Salmon
   Barbeque. Mendocino Coast Botanical Garden three miles south.
   Pudding Creek State Beach open for picnicking, swimming, fishing.

What's an inn without a story? Pudding Creek's tale is that a
Russian count with a mysterious past came to the area in the
mid-1800s, bringing money that everybody assumed to be ill-
gotten. He started a bottling plant, prospered, and built four houses
in Fort Bragg, including this one. He changed his name to Mr.
Brown, and took a bride who wore the first wedding dress
advertised in the Montgomery Ward Catalog. Pictures of the
couple, and the wedding dress, are displayed in the parlor.

If this adds an information overload to your historical trivia
quotient, simply enjoy the cheerful, easy atmosphere you'll find
here. The inn is really two houses connected by ☛ an enclosed

174

garden. Even on the blustery day I visited, it was warm in the garden, and the fuchsias, begonias, and ferns were thriving. This is the choice spot, weather permitting, for afternoon wine and cheese.

On other days, guests gather in the parlor or poke around the country store on the first floor of one of the houses. The store stocks a jumble of souvenirs, local art, gifts, handcrafts, and a collection of Depression glass.

Breakfast is served in the parlor or in the old-fashioned kitchen. Marilyn serves homemade coffee cakes, a hot egg dish, and juice, along with fresh fruit and coffee. This is the only meal served, but she has plenty of suggestions for dinner at good local restaurants.

The bedrooms are decorated in a combination of early American and Victorian furniture, colorful quilts, and pretty flowered wallpaper. A room named for the count is, naturally, a touch more royal, with cranberry velvet accents, redwood paneling, a king-sized brass bed, and stone fireplace.

How to get there: Highway 1 becomes Fort Bragg's Main Street. Traveling north, the inn is on the right.

J: *If you don't know about the Skunk Train—it is a forty-mile trip on a standard gauge passenger railroad through mountainous terrain between Fort Bragg and Willits. A big tourist attraction.*

clive Metcalf

Benbow Inn
Garberville, California
95440

Innkeepers: Patsy and Chuck Watts
Address/Telephone: 445 Lake Benbow Drive; (707) 923–2124
Rooms: 56, including terrace- and garden-level rooms with television; all
  with private bath.
Rates: $78 to $220, EP. Off-season rates: April 1 through June 15; October
  and November.
Open: April 1 to December 1; December 18 through January 2. Bar, dining
  room open to public for breakfast, lunch, dinner, Sunday brunch.
Facilities and local attractions: Hiking, swimming, picnics at Benbow Lake;
  bicycles, boat rentals, tennis, horseback riding; nine-hole golf course.
  Scenic drives through redwoods. Shakespeare-on-the-Lake, mid-
  August. Special inn events: Halloween Ball. November wine tasting,
  Christmas and New Year's Eve celebrations.

Californians call this territory the Redwood Empire, and the
Benbow Inn is surely one of its castles. Driving north on Highway
101, you see it rising four stories high in ☞ Tudor elegance,
situated among tall trees and formal gardens on the shores of
Benbow Lake and the Eel River. It was designed in 1926 as an inn
and enjoyed some grand years. In 1978, the Wattses rescued it
from fading elegance and have been steadily restoring and improving it.

For all the fresh refurbishing and additions, Patsy and Chuck have managed to keep a kind of old Hollywood baronial feeling in the main lobby that's fun: a large stone fireplace, oriental rugs, antiques, and grand-scale furniture. Tea and scones in the afternoon and an Afghan hound that lounges about looking elegant add to the Hollywood atmosphere. Looking at an old guest register, I saw that fifty years ago Mr. and Mrs. Basil Rathbone checked in—with valet/chauffeur. Charles Laughton stayed here, too, memorizing his lines for *Mutiny on the Bounty* and reading in the evenings to the Benbow family and staff.

Nostalgia stops when it comes to accommodations. New bathrooms, thick towels, great beds, and attractive decor are the rule in the main building. A nice touch in every room is a basket stocked with paperback mysteries. Garden- and terrace-level rooms are even more deluxe, all with decks overlooking the garden and river.

Dinner in the handsome dining room is a dressy (in California, that means shoes, no jeans), candle-lit affair. If you're a guest at the inn, you'll be greeted by name at the door. The menu is not trendy, but includes a variety of fresh fish, good beef, and veal in particular. Several low-fat entrees are offered with calorie count listed for guests who notice those things. For those who don't, there's a gorgeous white chocolate mousse with fresh berries.

How to get there: Two hundred miles north of San Francisco, 2 miles south of Garberville, on Highway 101.

*

J: *The Benbow is not inexpensive, but it's not for snobs either. When I visited, it had a full house of mostly affluent-looking middle-aged couples and honeymooners. But when a party of latter-day hippies arrived for dinner, infant in arms, they were greeted as warmly as any other guests.*

The Old Milano Hotel
Gualala, California
95445

Innkeeper: Leslie Lincheid
Address/Telephone: 38300 Highway 1; (707) 884–3256
Rooms: 9, including 2 cottages; 3 rooms with private bath, 5 share 2 baths.
Rates: $75 to $160, with full breakfast. Two-night minimum on weekends.
   No children under 16; no pets. No smoking.
Open: All year. Dinner served Wednesday through Sunday, $18.
Facilities and local attractions: Hot tub; massage therapy available. Beach
   walks, fishing; explore coastal towns. Wedding facilities.

The Old Milano Hotel has the right patina of age to look engagingly romantic. At the same time, it's a pleasure to stay where all appointments are fresh, clean, and where everything *works*. This well-maintained country inn has a special setting—three sprawling acres on the Mendocino Coast. You can stroll through the English gardens or relax on the broad lawn and watch the churning surf.

Two indoor sitting rooms have plants, fresh flowers, and cozy chintz-covered sofas to snuggle in by the huge stone fireplace. Afternoon wine tastings here give you a chance to sample some of Mendocino's vintages.

Guest rooms upstairs blend antiques, armoires, floral wallpapers, and handmade quilts. Five of them have ocean views, and one overlooks the garden. The rooms are refined, but not exclusively feminine. Men will enjoy the spacious master suite, which has a private bath and a separate sitting room with a superb view of the ocean and "Castle Rock."

Two cottages on the grounds give you the ultimate in privacy. The Passion Vine Cottage has a sitting area and Franklin stove. ☞ The Caboose, which really is an old caboose, is tucked among the cedars.

Breakfast is served in your room, outside on the patio, or in the dining room. Along with the standard fare of homemade breads, fresh fruits, and yogurt are the Old Milano's private blend coffee and unique teas.

Dinner, even though it is open to the public, has an intimate atmosphere. At least six entrees are offered each night, usually three meat and three fish. The inn's cook, Jutta Juengung, makes up a different menu every day, so that the freshest foods can be used. She is famous for her hors d'oeuvres, things like fresh mussels and ☞ miniature thick-crusted pizzas made with goat cheese and tarragon. Her desserts are worth the calories, maybe an apple custard cake or a deep-dish fruit pie. Many brides who choose The Old Milano for their reception ask Jutta to make the cake.

Don't miss trying the ☞ terrific outdoor hot tub on a point overlooking the surf. Guests reserve it to assure privacy. Nearby are several skilled massage therapists the innkeeper will schedule for you also.

Does this sound like a place to drop in for a few days and recharge your batteries? You're right.

How to get there: On the ocean side of Highway 1, 1 mile north of Gualala; 100 miles north of San Francisco.

Olive Metcalf

St. Orres
Gualala, California
95445

Innkeeper: Rosemary Campiformio
Address/Telephone: 36601 Highway 1 (mailing address: Box 523); (707) 884–3335 or 884–3303
Rooms: 8 in the inn share 3 baths; 10 cottages, all with private bath.
Rates: $50 to $65 double occupancy in the inn; $75 to $140 in the cottages. Breakfast buffet included. No pets.
Open: All year. Dinner. Beer and wine bar.
Facilities and local attractions: Hot tub, sauna. Beach access, walking, picnics. Visit Fort Ross.

Non-Californians see the ☞ spectacular Russian architecture of St. Orres tucked away above Highway 1 and tend to think it is another example of the native penchant for theater. Actually, a historical basis for the style is found only a few miles south at the trading fort the Russians built in the nineteenth century when they traded in furs and employed the Aleut Indians to hunt the sea otter.

Fort Ross is restored to look as it did while the Russians were in residence, but St. Orres stands as an architectural fantasy of the heritage. It's an intimate hideaway built of hundred-year-old timbers and hand-carved redwood, with stained-glass windows and onion-top turrets capped by copper, octagonal roofs.

180

You enter through a trellis-covered patio to a cedar lobby, an attractive bar, and plant-filled solarium. The dining room is in one of the stunning domed towers that rise more than fifty feet, with row after row of windows and stained glass.

Each bedroom in the inn is a cozy redwood snuggery with a built-in double bed covered with a unique handmade quilt. The baths are "his," "hers," and "ours," the third one being a large, tiled tub with dual shower heads. Two front rooms have French doors that open onto ocean-front balconies.

The more spacious accommodations are the ten cottages surrounding the inn. The most rustic is The Wildflower cabin, one of the original buildings on the property. It has a double bed on a sleeping loft, with a skylight above and a hideabed downstairs. There's a kitchen, bath, wood-burning stove, and an outdoor hot-water shower.

For more luxury, try The Rose Cottage, with architectural details similar to those of the inn. It has a carpeted living room with fireplace, kitchenette, and French doors opening onto a sun deck with an ocean view. Pine Haven is the newest cabin. All the cottages have breakfast delivered to their door in a basket.

You should not be surprised that the food is as outstanding as the architecture. Begin with Russian caviar and close with Chocolate Decadence; in between, the menu is continental. It changes according to what is fresh and special, but the specialty is 🖝 rack of lamb with a Dijon mustard crust.

How to get there: On Highway 1, between Gualala and Anchor Bay, the inn is on the inland side.

☀

J: *Gualala, by the way, is pronounced "Wallala." It's not Spanish, but rather a Spanish version of the Pomo Indian word meaning "where the waters meet."*

Olive Metcalf

Whale Watch Inn
Gualala, California
95445

Innkeepers: Irene and Enoch Stewart, and Beth Bergen
Address/Telephone: 35100 Highway 1; (707) 884–3667
Rooms: 18, in 5 buildings; all with private bath.
Rates: $125 to $200 for two; $20 each additional person. Extended
continental breakfast included. Smoking on decks only; no pets.
Two-night minimum on weekends.
Open: All year.
Facilities and local attractions: Selected wines and champagnes available.
Whirlpool baths. Private stairway offers beach access. Hiking; nearby
golf and tennis facilities.

If the quaint appeal of the North Coast's old accommodations
escapes you, Whale Watch may be just the contemporary luxury
answer to your desires. On two cliff-side acres, it consists of five
architecturally striking buildings with spectacular ocean views. It
is the ultimate adult getaway designed for privacy, personal
service, and with incomparable scenic beauty.

Every bedroom is stunningly decorated with elegant furniture,
some custom-designed Queen Anne, some hand-carved pieces, a
fine Bombay chest here, a yew-wood library table and chest there.
Amenities? Merely fine linens and down comforters, ice makers,

skylights, fireplaces in most rooms, and your private deck looking out at the rugged surf.

If sybaritic bathrooms are your thing, these take you to the outer limits of the bathing experience. In one, a spiral stairway flows from the bedroom up to the second level capped by a skylight roof to a two-person whirlpool, separate shower, and lounging area with a fabulous view of the Pacific below.

Many rooms are on two levels, and all of them are large. Some units are self-contained and designed for longer stays with fully equipped kitchens.

The original Whale Watch building was the former home of Irene and Enoch Stewart. The redwood-and-glass house has a huge, hexagonal living area with a circular fireplace and a sweeping Pacific view. The area is used as a gathering place for inn guests and has comfortable sofas and chairs, game tables, taped music, books, and wonderful spots to enjoy the view. The two bedrooms in this building open off of this impressive room.

Continental breakfast is served to guests in their rooms. A short drive up or down the coast brings you to some excellent restaurants—St. Orres, for one.

How to get there: Take Highway 101 to Petaluma and proceed west to Highway 1. Or, take Highway 101 to 4 miles north of Santa Rosa and proceed west to Highway 1. Follow Highway 1 north to Whale Watch at Anchor Bay, 5 miles north of Gualala on the ocean side. Fly-in: Ocean Ridge Airport.

Olive Metcalf

Glendeven
Little River, California
95456

Innkeepers: Jan and Janet deVries
Address/Telephone: 8221 North Highway 1; (707) 937–0083
Rooms: 12, including 2-bedroom Barn Suite; all but 2 with private bath.
Rates: $80 to $200 weekends, holidays and August; off-season rates
Monday through Thursday. $15 less for single occupancy; two-night
minimum on weekends. Continental breakfast included. Smoking
only on decks, terraces, and evenings in sitting room. Children by
arrangement.
Open: All year.
Facilities and local attractions: Beautiful gardens. Beach walks. Picnics on
headlands. Close to Mendocino galleries, restaurants, and shops.

The delights of California's North Coast have little to do with
sunshine and blue skies. It's the bluffs, the rugged coastline, and
the misty cool climate that seduce those of us who love it. But
unpredictable weather makes the comfort of your lodging all the
more important. Glendeven is an inn that pleases, rain or shine.

It is an 1867 farmhouse of Maine-style architecture, set back
on a headland meadow from the Mendocino Coast, surrounded by
fields and trees. The atmosphere in the pleasant living room pulls
you in to nestle before the fire and enjoy the view through a wall

of windows to a brick patio and the meadow beyond. A piano for impromptu musical urges, a good stereo for those of us less inclined, books, a tray of sherry, and a quiet rural setting—this is the stuff of a country inn.

The deVrieses have an eye for contemporary art—ceramics, paintings, and sculpture—that they display engagingly in their vintage house. I wanted to buy half a dozen pieces in the house—and they *are* for sale, even though price tags aren't on them. There are also some fine antiques and just plain comfortable furniture.

These are beautifully done guest rooms. Every one is a pleasure with fireplaces, commanding views—some with French doors leading to private balconies—and attention to detail. In the farmhouse, one of my favorites is ☞ The Garret, a large attic room with dormer windows and splendid vistas. Stevenscroft, a separate building in back, has four elegant rooms with tiled baths. The Barnhouse Suite, an 1800s hay barn, is now a spacious two-bedroom suite and the newest addition. Like the others, it exudes the Glendeven style: warm, comfortable, subtle elegance.

Breakfast included excellent coffee (ready for the early risers), a fresh fruit bowl, boiled eggs, and just-baked raisin-bran muffins. It seems to be a good time to hear the latest reports on local restaurants. There are some outstanding choices in the vicinity that the innkeepers will tell you about.

Two acres of grounds and gardens invite you to stay right where you are, even though Mendocino is just up the highway. A ☞ path to the beach is an easy walk and a wonderful place to spend the day. With notice, the innkeepers will prepare a tidbit basket for you to take along.

How to get there: On California Highway 1 traveling north, just past Van Damme State Park, the inn is on your right.

✱

J: *If you don't enjoy Glendeven, you're just not inn material.*

185

Olive Metcalf

Heritage House
Little River, California
95456

Innkeeper: Gay Dennen Moore
Address/Telephone: 5200 Highway 1; (707) 937–5885
Rooms: 70; all with private bath.
Rates: $95, one person, to $270 for two-person suite, MAP. Each
   additional person $50. No credit cards; no pets.
Open: Closed December and January. Restaurant serves breakfast, dinner;
   full bar.
Facilities and local attractions: Walking paths through woods, along beaches.
   Reading, relaxing. Mendocino nearby for art galleries, unique shops,
   restaurants, theater.

Above the dramatic Mendocino Coast in 1949, the late
innkeepers L. D. and Hazel Dennen set about restoring the original
1877 farmhouse of Mr. Dennen's grandfather. Since then, Heritage
House has become a classic. Without ever advertising, defying time
and fashion, it goes on pleasing and setting a 🖝 high standard for
a country inn. It is now run by their daughter, Gay.

The 🖝 site is magnificent: forests of eucalyptus and redwood
meet green pasture lands with sheep grazing, and then stretch to a
rocky, churning sea coast. The present sedate atmosphere belies a
fairly wild past. In the early 1930s, Baby Face Nelson used the

cove below the house for his bootleg operations, concluding one of his last deals in the house. As late as the 1940s, Chinese immigrants were smuggled into the country here. Today it is one of the more formal inns along the coast, with gentlemen "encouraged" to wear jackets and ties at dinner.

A few guest rooms are in the main building, but most are in cottages tucked into the landscape. As the rooms were built and remodeled through the years, the spirit of 1877 has been kept with furnishings and names inspired by early-day buildings of the area, like Scott's Opera House and Schoolhouse. A two-story unit, The Watertower, has a circular stairway leading from a living room to a bedroom. Most rooms have fireplaces or Franklin stoves.

A glass-domed dining room (one area is nonsmoking) has superb ocean views and a fresh, airy feeling that make it as inviting at breakfast as it is for candle-lit dinners. Breakfasts are hearty: a cereal, fruit and juice buffet, followed by eggs Benedict, a choice of breakfast meats, and dollar-sized pancakes. By the time you return to your room, the sharp staff has made the bed and refreshed your bathroom. Dinner menus change nightly. Perhaps a creamy potato soup, greens mixed with pine nuts and Smithfield ham, rare beef tenderloin or Pacific snapper with sauce mousseline, fresh vegetables, and fettuccine, ending with an almond cream cake. The wine list is extensive.

The comfortable lounge has an enormous fireplace and sweeping views of the rocky coastline. Don't expect television or video games; you come here to read, look, and relax. And the walks are major pleasures.

How to get there: On Highway 1, the ocean side, between Albion to the South and Little River to the North.

❁

J: *Anyone who gets bored on the Mendocino Coast should apply for a new soul.*

olive Metcalf

Little River Inn
Little River, California
95456

Innkeepers: Charles D. Hervilla and Susan Kimberly
Address/Telephone: Highway 1; (707) 937–5942 reservations; 937–5051 restaurant.
Rooms: 54, including inn rooms, cottages, motel-type units; all with private bath.
Rates: $56 to $70 in the inn; cottages $70 to $200, some with fireplaces; EP. $10 per extra adult; ☛ no charge for children under 12. No credit cards; no pets.
Open: All year. Breakfast, dinner daily. Bar.
Facilities and local attractions: Lighted tennis courts. Golf course (nine holes), pro shop, putting greens; hiking, bicycling Van Damme State Park; beachcombing, good tide-pool exploring. Minutes from Mendocino art galleries, antique shops, restaurants.

Anyone who has driven north on Highway 1 along the dramatic Mendocino coastline has seen this rambling white inn off on the right. It looks "New England" because it was built in 1853 by a pioneer from Maine, Silas Coombs.

Three generations later, the parlors are lobbies and dining rooms, and the conservatory is the bar. The long front porch used to be the place to watch for arriving schooners. Now it's where you follow the movements of the salmon fleet and, during the winter months, a favorite place for watching the migration of gray whales.

The range of accommodations here means you can have exactly what tickles your fancy. Rooms in the inn are decorated in early California style with antiques. If you prefer more modern appointments, try the motel wing. The pleasant, single-story rooms have big decks looking out at the ocean. Quiet spots to read are interrupted occasionally by deer wandering in the meadow below.

The cottages are especially cozy when you want to snuggle in for a few days. They have one or two bedrooms, some with sitting areas and fireplaces. One of my favorites for many years and through several refurbishings is the ☞ Van Damme Property. It sits across the road from the inn with three other units directly above the rugged coastline.

A continuous refurbishing of the inn goes on, but long-time fans will notice a new flair in recently done rooms. Ms. Kimberly has an eye for comfortable furnishings and tasteful appointments.

Little River's dining room is known up and down the coast for fine cooking. ☞ Whatever is freshest from the sea will be on the menu, along with good steaks and other choices. Salmon, abalone, snapper, and ling cod are specialties, and they are prepared with the delicate touch fresh fish deserves. (It ought to be a crime for kitchens to *claim* that they specialize in seafood when their only technique is to beat, batter, and deep fry!)

There's a down-to-earth quality about food here that you get only when things are homemade. This kitchen makes soups from scratch and its own breads. For dessert, try a fresh berry cobbler with tender crust and softly whipped cream.

How to get there: Three hours north of San Francisco on Coast Highway 1. The inn is on the right just south of Mendocino. Fly-in: Mendocino County Airport, 2 miles from the inn.

Olive Metcalf

Rachel's Inn
Little River, California
95460

Innkeeper: Rachel Binah
Address/Telephone: 8200 North Highway 1; (707) 937–0088
Rooms: 5; all with private bath, 1 with fireplace. Access for the handicapped.
Rates: $85 to $95, double occupancy; $15 for third person. Full breakfast included. Two-night minimum on weekends.
Open: All year. Dinners by special arrangement.
Facilities and local attractions: Weddings and small receptions catered. Walk fields, headlands and beach; whale watching; skin diving cove; Van Damme State Park; Fern Canyon. Close to Mendocino restaurants, galleries, shops, theater.

If you like the wild, natural Mendocino atmosphere, but still want comfort, even elegance, in light-filled space, try Rachel's Inn. What a pleasure to see someone with Rachel Binah's talent and flair go into the inn business. She had been catering for ten years when she found a dishearteningly ramshackle 1870s house on the Mendocino Coast and decided to make it an inn. It took the confidence of a riverboat gambler to believe that an inn was hiding in that ruin, but Rachel has accomplished an impressive renaissance of the house.

190

The ☛ site is very special—ocean views, tall trees, and wind-swept meadows. And adjoining her property are eighty-two acres of state-owned land that runs right down to cliffs overlooking the ocean and that will remain in the natural state it is now.

The interior of the inn is as fresh and airy as the outdoor Mendocino breeze. Each room's construction and decor reflect a feeling for the coast setting and make the most of the superb ocean views. ☛ High, vaulted ceilings, white walls, and redwood trim detailings are in the large living/dining room. A crackling fire felt good, even on an August morning.

The bedrooms have the same uncluttered good looks as the rest of the house. Linens on the queen-sized beds are in soft muted colors—mauves, grays, and paisley. The Parlor Suite has a cushioned window seat, a separate sitting room with a piano, and an ocean view. The Blue Room has a private balcony, and the Garden Room has a fireplace and an outside entrance, convenient for a wheelchair. Several rooms have an extra single bed.

For someone with ☛ Rachel's catering experience, breakfast is a piece of cake. She offers juices, fresh fruits, homemade sausage or bacon, muffins, and an egg dish. But give her an event and she'll really start cooking—buffet receptions, weddings, or a seven-course dinner, like the one she was preparing the day I visited. She has a wine cellar at the inn.

How to get there: On Highway 1 immediately north of Van Damme State Park and 2 miles south of Mendocino, the inn is on the ocean side.

J: *Your first sight of this inn, painted a daring soft mauve, will tell you that there's a stylish innkeeper at work.*

Olive Metcalf

The Victorian Farmhouse
Little River, California
95456

Innkeepers: Carole and George Molnar
Address/Telephone: Highway 1 (mailing address: Box 357); (707) 937–0697
Rooms: 10; all with private bath, 6 with fireplace.
Rates: $75 to $85, with generous continental breakfast. No children; no credit cards.
Open: All year.
Facilities and local attractions: Walk to ocean; whale watching; picnics. Two miles to Mendocino restaurants, galleries, shops, theater.

When the Molnars were looking for an inn to buy, Carole favored gold rush country, but George had his heart set on the Northern Coast of California all along. When he talks about "the historic North Coast," you hear real feeling for the beauty and history of this rugged area. The Molnars had long collected antiques, so when they found this picture-perfect Victorian farmhouse near Mendocino, it was kismet.

The house was built in 1877 by John Dennen as a home for him and his wife, Emma. The Molnars' pride in it is apparent, and they've lavished their time and attention on making it a completely captivating inn. With just four guest rooms in the farmhouse, it has as 🖝 intimate and cozy an atmosphere as you'll find. Each room is a picture of Victorian charm with 🖝 period antiques, white eyelet dust ruffles, quilts on the beds, and wicker furniture. One room has an appealing cushioned window seat and a small sitting room that opens onto a deck. The Garden Room looks onto an 🖝 old-fashioned flower garden that is lighted at night. The views from upstairs are of apple orchards and ocean.

In the apple orchard behind the farmhouse, the Molnars have added six new rooms, all with private baths and fireplaces. They're decorated with antiques and dainty flower prints on the walls. Pretty views from here are of redwood and fir trees and the creeks around the farmhouse.

Each room has a small, round table set with crochet lace over a soft-color cloth and pretty china where you'll be served breakfast. The tray brought to your room will have whatever beverage you want—tea, coffee, hot chocolate—juice, fresh fruits, perhaps baked apples, yogurt, and homemade muffins and breads. Carole never wants guests to have the same breakfast twice during a visit, and when people settle in for a week or more, she laughs that she has to get creative.

In the small downstairs parlor, sherry is offered in the evening, and you'll see some of the clocks George has restored. Carole and George will show you menus of nearby restaurants, and there are some fine ones on this part of the coast. When I was there, an antique desk in the room held wine, stuffed animals, and family photographs—all recent gifts from guests who left feeling they had found a home away from home with the Molnars.

How to get there: Driving north on Highway 1, the inn is on your right between Heritage House and Little River.

❧

J: *The Molnars say you should see it in the spring when the daffodils flower and the orchard is in bloom.*

olive Metcalf

The Headlands Inn
Mendocino, California
95460

Innkeepers: Pat and Rod Stofle
Address/Telephone: Corner of Howard and Albion streets (mailing address: Box 132); (707) 937–4431
Rooms: 5; all with private bath and wood-burning fireplace; 1 with parlor stove.
Rates: $85 to $110, double occupancy. $20 for third person. Two-night minimum on weekends; three nights on holiday weekends. No credit cards; no pets; no children under 16. No smoking.
Open: All year.
Facilities and local attractions: Hiking the Mendocino Headlands; walk to galleries, shops, restaurants, Art Center, theater. Mendocino Botanical Gardens.

The lumber industry flourished along this coast a century ago, leaving this all-wooden New England–style town as a legacy. Among the remaining buildings is The Headlands Inn, named for the spectacular bluffs above the rocky shore. The shingled, rather stern exterior belies an 🖙 exceedingly warm and well-furnished interior.

The building began in 1868 as a small barbershop on Main Street. The barber, John Barry, added the second story as living quarters for his family. It also had a history as a "high class" restaurant, The Oyster and Coffee Saloon. In 1893, the house was moved to its present location on the corner of Howard and Albion streets by horses pulling it over logs used as rollers. From here, it has ☞ white-water ocean views looking over the inn's English-style garden, toward the tree-covered mountains beyond.

I could happily move into any one of these guest rooms. The décor is restful—fresh flowers, good furniture, tasteful appointments—with ☞ impeccable housekeeping. Everything from bed coverings to upholstery looks fresh and inviting. Most of the rooms have wonderful views, and each has a fireplace or country stove. Some furniture is antique, and other pieces, like several of the beds, are handsome products of contemporary craftsmen. A delightful sitting room is on the second floor, with games, books, and good reading lights.

Breakfasts are served on trays directly to each room. In comfortable surroundings like these it's an indulgence that pleases. The W. J. Wilson Room has a private balcony for breakfasting outside, but most chilly Mendocino mornings you'll prefer inside, perhaps in the Bessie Strauss Room with a view from its bay window of the English garden and the ocean.

Full breakfasts include a hot entree that changes daily: maybe tarragon-flavored scrambled eggs in whole wheat bread baskets or crepes filled with blackberries and topped with a walnut streusel. There also are home-baked muffins, the freshest fruits available, and specially blended coffee.

Beyond breakfast, the area offers some outstanding dining opportunities. You can walk to the renowned Cafe Beaujolais and several other possibilities, or just a few minutes' drive takes you to the homey Ledford House.

How to get there: Entering Mendocino from Highway 1, proceed two blocks on Main Street to Howard Street. Turn right, go 1 block to inn on the left.

❀

J: *The flower gardens, like so many in Mendocino, are very English and quite special. They appear to be completely natural, as if the flowers had popped up spontaneously.*

Olive Metcalf

Joshua Grindle Inn
Mendocino, California
95460

Innkeepers: Gwen and Bill Jacobson
Address/Telephone: 44800 Little Lake (mailing address: Box 647); (707) 937–4143
Rooms: 10; all with private bath. Access for the handicapped. No smoking.
Rates: $65 to $90, single or double occupancy; includes breakfast.
Open: All year.
Facilities and local attractions: Walk to coast headlands or beach; all Mendocino activities, shops, restaurants, Art Center, theater.

The beautiful Joshua Grindle Inn looks every bit as New England as it sounds. It is named for the man who built it in 1879, situated on two acres several streets above the bustle of Main Street, Mendocino. The white house is a picturesque sight itself, but from the slight hill it sits on, ☛ the views of ocean and rocky coast are glorious.

New England flavor at its best is throughout the house— comfortable, tasteful, and immaculate. Antiques that decorate each room are early American rather than Victorian. Fine woods and pieces from the Jacobsons' own collection lend a classic, unfussy feeling to the decor.

Guests are invited to use the light, airy living room with a

196

fireplace. There sits a fine piano that Gwen identifies as her mother's engagement ring. (Her independent-thinking mother scorned a traditional ring and opted for a grand piano instead.)

Gwen serves a full breakfast at an antique 12-foot-long, pine refectory table. A fine old hutch and a grandmother's clock make exactly the kind of cheerful, cozy ambience that draws people to country inns. Conversation hums over fresh fruit, eggs, and homemade coffeecakes and breads.

It is a short walk to explore the town's galleries and excellent restaurants, but you might choose this inn merely to experience the misty air of Mendocino in a comfortable, country atmosphere. All the guest rooms are appealing. The Library is a warm room with a four-poster double bed and a fireplace trimmed with tiles depicting Aesop's *Fables*. The Grindle, with a view of town and ocean, has a queen-sized bed and, for a third person, a twin bed. In the grounds behind the main house are two additional buildings with accommodations: two rooms in the cottage, and three in the newest addition, The Watertower. The decor is early American with pine antiques and beautiful quilts. Some rooms have fireplaces.

Fleet Admiral Chester W. Nimitz is a friendly presence around here, too—that's Chester, the inn dog, who was found abandoned on the Oakland, California, Nimitz Freeway.

How to get there: Going north on Highway 1, turn off to Mendocino at Little Lake Road (the exit past the main road into town). Inn is on your right in the first block.

J: *Even with the crowds that flock to Mendocino during summer tourist time, the atmosphere here is tranquil and rural.*

Olive Metcalf

MacCallum House
Mendocino, California
95460

Innkeeper: Patti Raines; owners, Joe and Melanie Redding
Address/Telephone: 45020 Albion Street (mailing address: Box 206); (707)
   937–0289
Rooms: 21; 7 with private bath; some rooms with sink.
Rates: $45 to $165 for 4-person suite. Special family and mid-week rates.
   Continental breakfast. Prefer cash or checks. Children welcome; no
   pets.
Open: All year. Restaurant serves dinner; full bar.
Facilities and local attractions: Walk to everything in Mendocino: restau-
   rants, shops, galleries, theater. Whale watching, fishing, hikes.

   Daisy MacCallum was the lucky bride who in 1882 moved
into this beguiling New England–style Victorian house, a gift from
her father. Gingerbread trim, gables, and a white picket fence
decorate the yellow house that sits on three acres.

   This is an inn for lovers of flowers and flounces, quilts and old
trunks. In the old house, the rooms have been cheerfully preserved, many still containing the ☞ original furnishings, Tiffany
lamps, and Persian rugs. Facilities are down the hall, but most
rooms have a sink. The third floor is a cozy haven with walls
papered with rotogravures of the period, and has a small parlor
with splendid views of the town.

Other accommodations are in cottages around the garden. Among these, The Watertower and The Green House have private baths and wood-burning stoves. The Carriage House is convenient for families or two couples, with two separate units, each with a Franklin fireplace and privacy. The most luxurious rooms are those in The Barn. The ☛ upstairs unit has a private deck with sweeping views and a sitting room with a massive stone fireplace.

The Gray Whale Bar and sun porch are additions so skillfully done you would think they were part of Daisy's house. Remember, a bar means music and laughter (naturally), so if you plan to rise early for bird watching, you might want one of the garden or barn suites, a little more removed from the action.

Rob Fertero oversees the restaurant. Dinners are served in the book-lined dining room at tables set with fresh flowers and oil lamps, before a huge cobblestone fireplace. Like all good chefs, he cooks what is freshest, and in season. No cans in this kitchen. Poached salmon with béarnaise sauce, bouillabaisse, beef Bordelaise, and veal and champignons are typical fare. On the porch off the bar, you can order light items rather than a full dinner. I had tasty homemade linguine with red peppers and snow peas. A continental breakfast is served strictly for house guests.

How to get there: From Highway 1, enter Mendocino on Main Street. On Lansing, turn right and go one block to Albion; then turn left. The inn is on the right in the center of the village.

olive Metcalf

Philo Pottery Inn
Philo, California
95466

Innkeepers: Judy and Bill Hardardt
Address/Telephone: 8550 Route 128 (mailing address: Box 166); (707)
    895–3069
Rooms: 4; 2 with private bath.
Rates: $60 to $75, including full breakfast. Smoking only on decks. No
    young children or pets. No credit cards.
Open: All year.
Facilities and local attractions: Explore Anderson Valley wineries. Pottery
    Gallery. Nearby Boonville restaurants, shops. Ocean forty-five min-
    utes away.

If you like an atmosphere more laid back than elegant, favor
conversation and good music rather than fine antiques and solitary
splendor, you'll find a haven at the Philo Pottery Inn.

The 1888 redwood house was once a stage-coach stop. The
setting is still rural with tall trees, a flower and vegetable garden,
and one of the largest blackberry patches in Mendocino County.
The main house is really a log cabin, an intimate lodging with
high-ceilinged common rooms, antique furnishings, a piano, and
an extensive library that guests can use. Former owners Jan Wax
and Chris Bing were ceramic artists who added decks, stained-

glass windows, and floor tiles they made in their backyard pottery studio.

There are only two bedrooms downstairs, each with private bath, and two bedrooms upstairs sharing a bath. All the better to enjoy chatting in the parlor with the innkeepers. Bill brings out wine, a few hors d'oeuvres, and turns on some classical music. As other guests arrive, they drift in to join the relaxed gathering.

Evening plans are tested, rejected, and enhanced with suggestions from Bill and Judy. A few minutes away in Boonville the local chiropractor runs a popular pub called the Buckhorn, where he serves his own homemade brew. By publication time, the Boonville Hotel will be reopened under new management. Or perhaps you're ready for a drive to the coast for dinner and some live music. The innkeepers know what's going on all over the area and make the reservations you need.

At the round dining-room breakfast table, you compare notes over fresh fruit cups, bread or muffins, eggs or pancakes, bacon or locally made sausage. Then a tour of the pottery gallery behind the main house is in order. Yes, the pottery *is* for sale, and you may not be able to leave without, at least, an original sugar bowl and cream pitcher.

How to get there: From San Francisco, take Highway 101 north to Cloverdale; follow Highway 128 west through the Anderson Valley to Boonville, then Philo. Driving south on Highway 101, exit at Highway 253, and drive through the Bell Valley to Boonville and Philo. Both are beautiful drives.

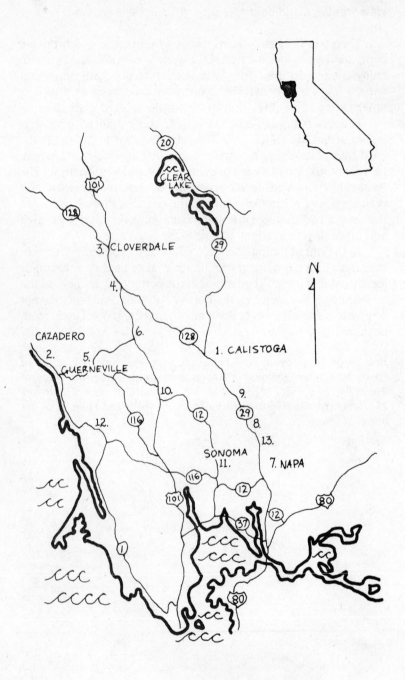

California: The Wine Country

Numbers on map refer to towns numbered below.

Olive Metcalf

Calistoga Country Lodge
Calistoga, California
94515

Innkeeper: Rae Ellen
Address/Telephone: 2883 Foothill Boulevard; (707) 942–5555
Rooms: 6; 3 with private bath, 1 common bathroom.
Rates: $75 to $85, with continental breakfast.
Open: All year.
Facilities and local attractions: Swimming pool. Visit neighboring wineries;
      hike; bicycle; picnic.

The silhouette of a weary Indian warrior on his tired horse is
on the sign at the lodge's entrance. It is an unusual but fitting
theme for an inn situated in the heart of Napa Valley wine
country; the ☞ beautiful wooded property promises a peaceful
retreat at trail's end.

When you open the door to the rambling, white 1930s stucco
house nestling in trees, you enter a thoroughly ☞ *uncommon*
common room. Tom Scheibal, the inn's first owner and a furniture
designer, removed all distractions to create one long open-beamed
space, as clean and bleached as a desert scene. The floors are wide
planks of whitewashed pine with textured rugs scattered about. At
one end is an old stone fireplace with a moose head over it
surveying the room.

The ☛ rustic pine furniture arranged in several groupings down the room was designed and built by Scheibal. Chairs and settees are softened with pads and pillows covered in natural canvas. On some he has splashed the fabric with ragged black splotches to resemble cowhide. The only color in the room comes from ☛ vivid Indian rugs on the walls and leafy green potted trees. Some aptly chosen black-and-white photos are a wonderful touch: Gary Cooper in a cowboy hat; Georgia O'Keeffe and Alfred Stieglitz.

A marble-top table is used for a continental breakfast buffet served on bright pottery. Very pleasant to help yourself and mosey out to the swimming pool terrace.

Bedrooms down the hall keep the southwest feeling with Indian artifacts and rugs and four-poster pine beds. The Mt. Helena room has a fireplace with deer antlers, Indian baskets, and a beige-and-carmel-spotted calfskin rug. The ☛ common bathroom in the hall will make you smile. It looks as if it is lined with cowhide. Every surface, walls and porcelain alike, is spotted with black and outlined with rope. In chic decorator circles, this is known as the "bovine motif." Downstairs, a low-ceilinged room with a stone fireplace is quiet and cozy, but you do have to go upstairs for the bath.

A basket of local restaurant menus is in the common room. The valley has such an embarrassment of famous places that you may arrive with several names you want to try. Rae Ellen is particularly enthusiastic about nearby Knickerbockers. Not only is the California-style fresh food excellent, but prices are surprisingly fair. She's happy to make any reservations you want.

How to get there: Follow Highway 29 through the Napa Valley to Calistoga; at the intersection of Highway 128, continue straight ahead a mile. The Inn is on the left side of Highway 128.

Olive Metcalf

Culver's, A Country Inn
Calistoga, California
94515

Innkeepers: Meg and Tony Wheatly
Address/Telephone: 1805 Foothill Boulevard; (707) 942–4535
Rooms: 6; each 2 rooms share a bath. Air conditioning.
Rates: $85 to $95, full breakfast included and evening wine. No children
    under 12; no pets; no smoking in bedrooms.
Open: All year.
Facilities and local attractions: Swimming pool, Jacuzzi, sauna. Tour win-
    eries. Mineral waters and mud baths nearby. Biking; hot-air balloon-
    ing; Calistoga restaurants, shops.

    Calistoga has been famous since the nineteenth century as a
health-spa town with mineral waters and mud baths. One of the
mansions built in the resort community then was that of editor
and publisher John Oscar Culver. His large, three-level Victorian is
now an ☛ immaculate, well-decorated inn.
    The inn sits on a hillside with a view of the Napa Valley and
Mount St. Helena from the big covered front porch. The grounds
are dotted with old shade trees, and a path leads around to a ☛
swimming pool (it's not heated, but you won't miss that during a
Calistoga summer), sun deck, and Jacuzzi elegantly nestled into
the back hillside.

Inside, there is a comfortable, colorful sitting room with mellow, pine floors, vivid oriental rugs, a red-velvet sofa, antiques, and a fireplace. The Wheatlys' British background is evident in curios and family photos, the china and silver collections, and the Delft displayed in the dining area.

At breakfast, guests gather at round tables in a light-splashed room adjoining the spiffy kitchen that recklessly sports an oriental rug. French doors open onto a patio for summer breakfasts. It is a fresh, appealing atmosphere with a dividend to the arrangement: While you sip juice, you can savor the aroma of homemade goodies baking and get suggestions about restaurants and local attractions. Scones or pastries are usually on the menu along with an egg entree. Fresh fruit, coffee, and a variety of teas are accompaniments.

Bedrooms are as light and airy as is the main floor. The upstairs four are furnished in Victorian and early-twentieth-century style. The three on the lower floor are in authentic Edwardian, Art Deco, and Art Nouveau. They are uncluttered and simply done, each benefiting from a few carefully selected furniture pieces and accessories.

At the end of the hall on the lower level is a first-class sauna with a shower beside it. Guests who are really "into" body shock can hop from one to the other. For really major body rejuvenation, the innkeepers will arrange for massage or mud baths—"the works"—at a nearby spa.

How to get there: Follow Highway 29 through the Napa Valley to Calistoga and intersection of Highway 128. The inn is ¾ mile north of Calistoga on the west side of Highway 128.

☀

J: *Meg hopes you'll notice her antique hutch in the breakfast area. It is dated 1875, the same year that the inn was built.*

Olive Metcalf

Larkmead Country Inn
Calistoga, California
94515

Innkeepers: Gene and Joan Garbarino
Address/Telephone: 1103 Larkmead Lane; (707) 942–5360
Rooms: 4; all with private bath; air conditioning.
Rates: $88 to $95, including continental breakfast and early evening refreshment.
Open: Year-round.
Facilities and local attractions: View vineyards from porch. Visit wineries, Calistoga restaurants, shops, mineral waters, mud-bath spas.

Between the Silverado Trail and the Sonoma Mountains runs the fertile Napa Valley. Acres of vineyards are criss-crossed with lanes. On one of them is a splendid white clapboard house with broad porches. You will not find a fluttering flag or a cute sign announcing the inn, merely a burnished brass plate with "Larkmead" on it. Drive through the old fieldstone gates and around the house to a 🖙 wisteria-covered loggia.

The main-floor living room and bedrooms are really on the second floor. Early in the century, the house was purposely built high by the Swiss owner, says Joan Garbarino, in order to catch the evening breezes and look out over his vineyards.

Guests are encouraged to enjoy the ambience of the sprawling house and grounds. The large living room is beautifully furnished with the Garbarinos' collection of antiques, handsome upholstered furniture, books, and paintings. Their Persian rugs are brilliant contrasts to dark wood floors. A crackling fire and a decanter of sherry invite arriving guests to a ☞ private, tasteful world.

The house is large, but Joan offers only four bedrooms. It is a matter of high standards ("I'm death on cleanliness!") and wanting to give personal attention to every guest. Bedrooms, named for Napa Valley wines, all overlook the vineyards and hills beyond. Beaujolais uses the open porch over the loggia. Chenin Blanc has a fresh green-and-white floral print on the walls, draperies, and a chaise. Chardonnay is decorated in Art Deco, and Chablis has an enclosed sun porch.

You breakfast in the formal dining room on ☞ Imari china with Grand Baroque sterling. Joan serves a beautiful arrangement of fresh fruit followed by individual baskets of hot breakfast breads with freshly ground coffee.

This is the only meal served, but the recent appearance of some exceptional restaurants in the valley attracts many people. The Calistoga Inn is a great favorite, with fresh menu changes daily and an adjoining pub.

How to get there: From San Francisco, take Highway 101; or from the East Bay, take Highway 80 to Highway 37. At Highway 29 continue north, and turn right on Larkmead Lane between St. Helena and Calistoga. For a more picturesque route, take any cross-valley road from Highway 29 to the Silverado Trail; follow north, turn left on Larkmead Lane.

J: *You can step right next door to the Hans Kornell Winery and see the process of making bottle-fermented champagnes.*

olive Metcalf

Wine Way Inn
Calistoga, California
94515

Innkeepers: Dede and Allen Good
Address/Telephone: 1019 Foothill Boulevard (Highway 29); (707) 942–0680
Rooms: 6; all with private bath, double and queen-sized beds; air conditioning.
Rates: $65 to $85, including full breakfast and afternoon beverage. Ask about off-season rates. Smoking discouraged; no pets. Children over 10.
Open: All year.
Facilities and local attractions: Expansive deck with views. Walk to Calistoga shops and restaurants, Sharpsteen Museum. Hot springs and mud baths. Hot-air ballooning arranged. Many noted wineries nearby. Bicycling, hiking. Picnic throughout the valley. Golf, tennis, swimming arrangements made at nearby resort.

People familiar with Highway 29 may wonder at an inn on that busy trail through the Napa Valley. But once you enter this warm 1915 Craftsman-style house, even the horde of summer and weekend tourists can be forgotten. This is a quiet, homey inn with the advantage of having everything in Calistoga within walking distance.

210

I have a nostalgic bias for houses this age. That sturdy, solid look, the beamed ceilings and built-in ☛ lead-glass cabinets in the dining room all give it a very livable charm. It's probably my midwestern roots that make it look familiar.

The Goods have run the house as an inn since 1980, and in all that time they have resisted the siren call of Victoriana—theme decor, or collections. Even more shocking—Dede admits to the absence of even one teddy bear, all the while insisting that this *is* an inn. They have had the nerve to keep it tastefully old-fashioned, comfortable, and, to my eyes, heartwarming. Yes, there are antiques, like Allen's grandmother's long, drop-leaf pine table, where breakfast buffet is spread. But the squashy sofas and chairs in the generous living room are covered with fresh, colorful fabrics and arranged for comfort before a fireplace that always has a fire in cool weather.

The bedrooms upstairs are light and airy with white tongue-and-groove walls. Fresh bouquets, attractive comforters, books, and Napa Valley watercolors are welcome touches. Dede's shower curtains will give you a smile.

On the landing in the upstairs hall a bulletin board holds a collection of the area's current attractions and events. Charming pictures of Allen's grandparents from their vaudeville days hang on the wall up here. Grandmother was a musician, and Grandfather was humorist Chic Sales. His book, *The Specialist*, about a man who specializes in building outhouses, is a unique bit of reading material in the bathroom.

A doorway here leads out to a surprisingly large, ☛ multi-level deck with a gazebo on the top level. There are splendid views over Calistoga toward the mountains from the upper level. It's a grand place to breakfast or have a late-afternoon glass of wine. A cottage tucked into the hillside (Calistoga) is the most private and spacious room of all. It even has its own little redwood deck.

Both the Goods contribute to an ever-changing breakfast menu that includes their baked specialties, fresh fruits, and different hot dishes like frittata or quiche. It's served in the dining room on blue-and-white local pottery with fresh flowers on tables set for two or four. This inviting room is morning sunny and evening cozy.

How to get there: The inn is on the left side of Highway 29 in Calistoga just at the corner where it turns right to go through the town, while straight ahead it becomes Highway 128.

olive Metcalf

Timberhill Ranch
Cazadero, California
95421

Innkeepers: Barbara Farrell, Frank Watson, Terran McDaid, Michael Riordan
Address/Telephone: 35755 Hauser Bridge Road; (707) 847–3258
Rooms: 10 seclulded cottages. Handicapped access.
Rates: $125 per person weekdays; $135 per person weekends, including all meals. Ask about seasonal rates. Cannot accommodate children. No pets. Smoking restricted to designated areas.
Open: All year.
Facilities and local attractions:  World-class tennis courts. Swimming pool, outdoor Jacuzzi. Hiking. Four miles to ocean beach. Close to Salt Point State Park, Fort Ross, The Sea Ranch public golf course.

When your stress level hits C above high C and you can't bear making one more earth-shaking decision . . . when you want to seclude yourself with nature (and a close, close friend) for some spiritual renewal . . . when you demand the best in fine food, service, and amenities . . . then head for Timberhill Ranch.

This classy resort on a very intimate scale is off the beaten track, perched high in the hills above the Sonoma coast. Once you've checked in at the reception and dining area, you're shuttled to your cottage in a golf cart, and not a telephone or a discouraging word will ruffle your brow until you grudgingly conclude it's time to go home.

Sonoma's fabulous climate, rugged beauty, unspoiled high meadows, and redwoods are undisputed. What's surprising is to find an inn with such luxury blending into these surroundings. All credit must be given to the two innkeeping couples who planned and built eighty percent of the resort themselves. Their vision accounts for keeping the ranch ☞ an underdeveloped oasis of tranquility; for only ten cottages, despite acres of land; for building their world-class tennis courts far from the swimming pool, because "when you're lounging quietly by the water you don't want to hear tennis chatter."

The spacious, cedar-scented cottages are situated for maximum privacy. Each has a stocked mini-bar, a fire laid, a well-appointed tile bath, handmade quilt on the queen-sized bed, comfortable chairs, good lights, and a radio. In the morning, breakfast is delivered to your door to enjoy on your private deck as you look out at a stunning view.

What more? ☞ Superb food served beautifully in an intimate dining room with windows overlooking hills and forest—but without reservations, hurry, hassle, or check to interrupt. (All meals are included in the rate.) The six-course dinners, for inn guests only, are what you might expect in one of San Francisco's finest restaurants. Here's a sample of one recent night: chilled artichoke with lemon mayonnaise, beef barley soup, salad with hearts of palm, raspberry sorbet, loin of lamb with red-pepper butter (among five other entree choices), and a dessert selection including puff pastry blackberry torte.

The four owners are hands-on innkeepers, always giving a level of ☞ personal attention far removed from a slick resort atmosphere. As one told me, "We really like taking care of people and giving them the kind of service and privacy *we* looked for when *we* used to get away." As I watched the reluctant farewell of one couple, the hugs and promises to be back soon, I decided that Timberhill has all the right stuff, including a warm heart.

How to get there: From Highway 1 north of Fort Ross, turn east on Timber Cove Road. Follow to Sea View Ridge Road. Turn left, follow to Hauser Bridge Road and inn sign on the right.

olive Metcalf

Vintage Towers
Cloverdale, California
95425

Innkeepers: David and Shawnee Bach
Address/Telephone: 302 North Main Street; (707) 894–4535
Rooms: 8; 6 with private bath. Air conditioning.
Rates: $55 to $85, including full breakfast. No chidren; no smoking.
Open: All year.
Facilities and local attractions: Russian River six blocks away for canoeing,
    swimming, tubing. Lake Sonoma boating, fishing, skiing. Equestrian
    trails, hiking. Bicycles available.

Vintage Towers is another of those grand Victorians built by a
lumber baron for himself. Simon Pinschower built this Queen
Anne in 1901, and it's had loving care through the years, most
recently with innkeepers David and Shawnee Bach.

They've remembered Pinschower by naming one of the tower
suites for him. A settee and chair upholstered in royal blue sit in
the bay window formed by the tower. The bedroom furniture has
belonged in Cloverdale families for more than one hundred years.
The tower suites are choice, but each one of the antique-appointed
rooms is pleasant.

One owner of the house had a penchant for adding 🖝 huge
floor-to-ceiling, many-drawered cabinets to the bedrooms. An

214

overnight guest is hardly going to use them, but I enjoyed just thinking about how I could fill them if they were in my house.

Pinschower did not scrimp on space. At the top of the stairs, what could have been an ordinary landing is, instead, an entire sitting room furnished with a wood-burning stove, a Victorian sofa, and a barber's chair. Wedding parties who have booked the whole house often set up the ironing board here and scurry back and forth between rooms in a flurry of activity.

The ☞ library is fascinating. More than 1,000 volumes are in the house, including handsome old sets of Dickens and Carlyle. Across the hall is the Music Room with a piano and a collection of offbeat instruments. The most unusual is a ☞ piano player—no, that is *not* a player piano. The old Chase-and-Baker oddity is fitted up with a roll of music, say a Scott Joplin rag, rolled up next to the piano, and its wooden fingers dash over the keyboard banging out the tune.

Breakfast is a substantial meal here: fresh fruit, eggs, and hot breads. For dinner, they will suggest several restaurants in town, or you might want to drive to Healdsburg for a big splash at Madrona Manor.

How to get there: From San Francisco, follow Highway 101 to center of Cloverdale. At first stoplight in town, turn right on First Street. Go 1 block to North Main; turn left. Inn is 3 blocks on the right.

Olive Metcalf

Campbell Ranch Inn
Geyserville, California
95441

Innkeepers: Mary Jane and Jerry Campbell
Address/Telephone: 1475 Canyon Road; (707) 857–3476
Rooms: 5; all with private and semiprivate bath and king-sized bed; most
  rooms with balcony. Air conditioning.
Rates: $70 to $100 per couple; $20 for additional person. Two-night
  minimum weekends, three on holidays. No smoking. Teenagers
  welcome.
Open: All year.
Facilities and local attractions: Swimming pool, hot tub, professional tennis
  court. Horseshoes, Ping-Pong. Bicycles available. Hiking. Russian
  River 3 miles, Lake Sonoma 4 miles for water recreation and fishing.
  Many nearby wineries, restaurants. Facilities for small business
  seminars.

Bring your camera to this thirty-five acre hilltop ranch. The
spectacular view over rolling Sonoma vineyards and a
profusion of flowers and plantings will have you snapping memories of your stay. It's a quintessential Northern California scene,
with the fresh air and vast open skies thrown in with the room
rate.

Suppose you want to stay a few days in the wine country, but you don't want to spend all your time touring and sipping. This is just the kind of inn you'll want: a modern ranch house with comfortable, impeccably maintained surroundings, an atmosphere of utter relaxation, and plenty to keep you entertained.

The Campbells are transplanted Pennsylvanians, who raised a family in this home and haven't lost their knack for making it a place to have fun. There's an elegant terrace and swimming pool and a 🖝 professional tennis court. They even keep an unlimited supply of lemonade and iced tea available. A big family room has a television, Ping-Pong, games, and a collection of model trains that will amuse a lot of males in particular. There's an attractive living room with a large fireplace, where you can relax or read.

The bedrooms are spacious, most with a deck overlooking the pool and the hills and vineyards beyond. Every room had a fresh bouquet from the garden. The bunkhouse, which accommodates four, is separate from the house. It's a more casual room than those in the house, but the beds are new, and it has a television. Jerry Campbell's aviary is nearby—a hobby and a business for him.

Save Room For Dessert is the name of Mary Jane Campbell's cookbook and a kind of second name for her. Those are usually her words as guests leave for dinner. When they return, she's ready with a 🖝 warm fresh-fruit pie and coffee every evening. Jerry says it's one of the most sociable times at the inn, sitting around the kitchen table or on the terrace under the stars. These are the special moments that get people hooked on country inns.

When you check in at the ranch you'll get a menu with a bounteous choice of fruits, breads, and breakfast entrees. All you do is make your selections and say what time you'll want it. Could you get used to this life?

How to get there: From Highway 101 at Geyserville, take the Canyon Road exit and follow west 1.6 miles to the inn.

J: *Nearly sixty wineries are scattered through the Russian River area, many with famous names like Korbel and Simi. Different from Napa Valley wineries, most here are small, family operated, with tasting rooms less crowded and time to visit, sometimes with the winemaker.*

olive Metcalf

Hope-Merrill House and Hope-Bosworth House
Geyserville, California
95441

Innkeepers: Bob and Rosalie Hope
Address/Telephone: 21238 Geyserville Avenue (mailing address: Box 42);
(707) 857–3356
Rooms: 5 in Hope-Bosworth; 2 with private bath, 1 with half-bath, 2 share
common bath. 5 in Hope-Merrill; 2 with private bath, 3 with sink in
room share common bath.
Rates: $60 to $80 at Bosworth House; $85 to $95 at Merrill House; full
breakfast included. Not suitable for children; smoking discouraged.
Open: All year.
Facilities and local attractions: Picnics, vineyard tours arranged. Explore
backroads, many small wineries. Russian River, redwoods, Lake
Sonoma, Warm Springs Dam close by.

Geyserville is a small town in the Alexander Valley, one of the
most beautiful—and least traveled—areas of California wine country. On the first day of September, the vines were hanging heavy
with ripe grapes, and the aroma of the crush just begun pervaded
the valley.

This pair of houses, facing each other across Geyserville's

main street, was restored as inns by the Hopes in 1980. The Hope-Merrill is the more splendid of the two, a redwood Victorian of the Eastlake Stick style popular in the 1880s. It was once an early stage stop. It has exceptionally beautiful dining and living rooms, with 🖝 handsome silk-screened wallpapers, antique furniture, and a collection of Victorian curiosities. The five bedrooms are strikingly decorated.

Both houses retain an atmosphere of the time they were built—old-fashioned yards, grape arbors, and at Hope-Merrill, a white gazebo. Ceiling fans are a modern touch that *look* old but do a good job of cooling on hot days.

The Hopes have devised a tour they call 🖝 "Stage a Picnic" to show guests the wine country. Two strawberry-roan draft horses pull a ten-person antique open-air stage right through the vineyards. You visit three wineries while your driver tells you about the grapes and relates tales of this old community. If your tour includes Trentadue Winery, the stage approaches it down a long grape arbor thick with green leaves and hanging bunches of grapes. People who have never before visited the wine country can't take pictures fast enough; and for those who are familiar with it, it's still a spectacular excursion.

Then comes Rosalie's gourmet picnic of local cheeses ˜nd smoked meats, seasonal fresh fruits and vegetables grown in Sonoma County, and her own prize-winning breads. She's well known as 🖝 an outstanding caterer, and the lunch is as beautiful to look at as it is to taste.

How to get there: From Highway 101, take Geyserville exit to 128; follow it into town past the Bank of America. Check in at Hope-Merrill on the left.

J: Get a map and drive or bike as many of these back roads as you can. They're special.

Olive Metcalf

The Estate
Guerneville, California
95446

Innkeepers: Darryl Notter and Jim Caron
Address/Telephone: 13555 Highway 116; (707) 869–9093
Rooms: 9; all with private bath, television, telephone.
Rates: $75 to $150, single or double occupancy. Two-night minimum on
weekends. Smoking only in public rooms. Cannot accommodate
children. No pets.
Open: All year.
Facilities and local attractions: Swimming pool, spa. Facilities for private
parties, small business seminars. Golf, tennis, horseback riding
nearby. Canoeing and other river activities. Explore Guerneville
shops. Many local wineries. Short drive to Sonoma Coast beaches.
Armstrong Redwood State Reserve two miles north.

The Estate is an unexpected taste of glamour in the forested
hills hugging the Russian River. As it twists through the Guerneville area, the river's beautiful natural setting has long been a
popular choice for "resorts," cabins, cottages, and campgrounds.
But . . . this is something quite different.

It's not always easy to relax in handsome surroundings, but
that's not the case in this Mission Revival-style house. It was built
as a private residence in 1920 by a financier, Ralph Belden, and

you know what grandiose ideas the wealthy in those days had when it came to building even their vacation homes. This one is imposing, but it remains an ☞ inviting country home. On the main floor, a large rock fireplace divides the living room from a many-windowed solarium. On the lower level, bedrooms open to still another comfortable sitting room.

The decor is *Architectural Digest*—with warmth. Darryl studied design in San Francisco, and the house shows it. There's no one "look," but rather an individual, personal style. He's designed stylish slipcovers for some of the chairs and smart divot covers for the beds. There are fine antiques among some just comfortable furniture. Both he and Jim are always looking for interesting pieces, but they admit that as much as they've bought, it seems to disappear in the large house.

Bedrooms are wonderfully romantic, and there's not a Laura Ashley in the lot. Billowing cotton draperies at an expansive bow of casement windows graced Number 4, my room. ("Cute" room names are out, says Darryl). A sitting area had two cushy lounge chairs, a settee, and a fresh bouquet of roses. The room had everything for comfort: television and telephone, down pillows and comforters, even the rarest of all inn appointments—good reading lights. When I returned from dinner, the drapes were drawn, bed turned down, and my robe laid out. (Next time I'll pack a prettier robe.)

Breakfast was prepared and served as elegantly as everything is done around here. On a terrace by the pool a table set with heavy silverware, linen napkin, silver coffee pot, and newspaper at hand was the right place to be on the sunny morning of my visit. The beautiful fresh fruit, hot muffins, and a bacon-avocado-tomato-sour-cream omelet were perfection.

This is a ☞ terrific place to entertain—one other person or a party. If you have four or more, the innkeepers will sometimes cater special lunches or dinners. They're working hard to make this classic house a class-act inn by applying a simple philosophy: only the best of everything.

How to get there: From 101 north, take River Road/Guerneville exit just past Santa Rosa; go west 14 miles to Guerneville. At the stop sign at Highway 116 and River Road, turn left, cross the bridge over River Road. The inn is ½ mile beyond the bridge on the left. Local airport pickup.

221

olive Metcalf

Ridenhour Ranch House Inn
Guerneville, California
95446

Innkeeper: Richard Jewell
Address/Telephone: 12850 River Road; (707) 887–1033
Rooms: 8; 5 with private bath. Wheelchair access.
Rates: $50 to $90, including full breakfast. Two-night minimum on
  weekends. Children over 10 welcome; no pets. Smoking only in
  living room.
Open: Closed December.
Facilities and local attractions: Quiet retreat; hot tub; croquet court. Hiking,
  bicycling, winery visits. Close to Russian River beaches; good restaurants. Dinners served Saturday night to house guests. Other meals by
  special arrangement. Private parties, meetings, and weddings catered
  when entire inn is booked.

The Russian River winds over two hundred miles of northern
Sonoma County. Near Guerneville (pronounced Gurn-ville,
please), it flows west through wooded mountains, redwood
forests, and vineyards to the Pacific. In this beautiful countryside,
Louis Ridenhour built a ranch house in 1906 on part of the
940-acre spread that his family had on both sides of the river.

222

Rick Jewell has owned the house since 1987. He has achieved an inn that blends a laid-back atmosphere with all the comforts of a private country home. There is a large country kitchen with Rick's professional-sized stove, freezer, and cooking equipment, a dining area, and a redwood-paneled living room. This is the kind of space that invites you to relax by the fireplace with lots of comfortable furniture, attractive rugs, greenery, and big-window views of the forested area along the river.

A smaller sun parlor–type room that Rick calls a "cold kitchen" is off the living room. It's a convenient place for guests to keep wine cold that they might have bought on a tour, or even to make themselves a sandwich.

Each bedroom has individual touches that please, along with decanters of sherry, fresh flowers, and tranquil views of the wooded setting. Some rooms have an early American look with brass beds and quilts; others have English antiques.

You can enjoy breakfast in the big kitchen or out on the patio: freshly ground coffee, fresh juices and fruits, Dutch Babies, crepes, or eggs Florentine.

Food is the aspect of innkeeping that particularly interests Rick. (I haven't met an innkeeper yet who claims making beds is the best part.) He looks forward to doing even more cooking in the future. At this writing, besides the big breakfasts, he is doing elegant Saturday night dinners for house guests. The menus, which change monthly, are elaborate and wonderful—appetizers like barbecued oysters, grilled marinated lamb, or Moscovy Duck for entrees, and desserts such as chocolate mousse swirl. Other dinners are available to guests by special arrangement.

Paths meander around the inn's informally landscaped grounds, under oak and redwood trees, and past a hot tub. One can walk to the neighboring Korbel Winery and visit their champagne cellars, or to secluded river beaches nearby.

How to get there: From Highway 101 north of Santa Rosa, take River Road exit. Drive west 12½ miles to entrance to the inn on the right, just 500 yards east of Korbel Winery.

J: *Your fresh breakfast fruit is often from the inn's own orchards: figs, pears, plums, apples, and, oh joy . . . fresh raspberries!*

Olive Metcalf

Camellia Inn
Healdsburg, California
95448

Innkeepers: Ray and Del Lewand
Address/Telephone: 211 North Street; (707) 433–8182
Rooms: 9; 7 with private bath, including 2 with Jacuzzi for two.
Rates: $55 to $95 double occupancy; rate includes full breakfast buffet, afternoon wine. No pets; children not encouraged. No smoking.
Open: Year-round.
Facilities and local attractions: Beautiful gardens. Swimming pool. Two blocks from town plaza's shops, restaurants. Visit Russian River wineries. Canoeing, fishing, swimming on the river.

This graceful Italianate Victorian is a wonderful setting for indulging fantasies of the leisurely "good old days," with you starring as master or mistress of the mansion.

Because you're decently rich, you have not one, but *two* connecting parlors with ☞ twin marble fireplaces. The rooms have long elegant windows, 12-foot ceilings featuring medallions and other architectural details. Oriental rugs and inviting sofas and antiques fill the rooms, which are decorated in warm salmon tones. A crystal decanter of sherry and fresh flowers are appointments you insist upon.

As the proper owner of one of the finest houses in town, you must perambulate the grounds to see that the roses and camellias are thriving and to pause by the tiled fishpond to count the stock. After a vigorous property inspection, you rest by the villa-styled swimming pool—just the shady spot for a sip of something bracing.

If your fancy today is a winery tour or dinner at a restaurant, your household staff is knowledgable about both. For dinner, a suggestion might be that you leave the carriage at home and stroll to the Plaza Grill on the town square. Most agreeable.

Later that night you step from an upholstered footstool to your four-poster, canopied, queen-sized bed and slip between crisp sheets. You prop yourself up on fluffy pillows and survey your big bedroom with lace at the windows and antiques. Soothing music lulls you to a well-deserved sleep. In the morning, confident that someone *else* is grinding Viennese coffee and squeezing fresh juice, you linger in your private bath with its marble shower, antique sink, and thick towels.

What a pleasure to enter a dining room that looks the way God meant it to look—spacious and substantial, with a 🖙 massive hand-carved mahogany mantel surrounding a tiled fireplace. Help yourself from the buffet offering fresh fruit, just-baked breads, soft-boiled eggs, and homemade jams. Have another cup of coffee and, if you *must* spoil the dream, face the morning newspaper.

How to get there: Driving north on Highway 101, take the second Healdsburg exit. Follow Healdsburg Avenue to North Street, and turn right. Inn is on the left.

☀

J: *I can't see why some people are always complaining about life's hardships. The world seems altogether orderly and pleasant to me at Camellia Inn.*

Olive Metcalf

Grape Leaf Inn
Healdsburg, California
95448

Innkeeper: Kathy Cookson
Address/Telephone: 539 Johnson Street; (707) 433–8140
Rooms: 7; all with private bath and air conditioning. Wheelchair access.
Rates: $55 to $95, including full breakfast and complimentary local wines
    and cheeses. No smoking.
Open: All year.
Facilities and local attractions: Walk to Healdsburg Square; restaurants,
    shops. Wine touring. Bicycling. Russian River boating, rafting,
    fishing. Lake Sonoma water sports. Fish Hatchery.

This sedate, lavender Queen Anne with the grape color trim is
a gingerbread deceiver. Who would think that behind its Victorian
façade are seventeen skylight roof windows, air-conditioned bedrooms, and seven private bathrooms, four with a ☞ two-person
whirlpool tub/shower?

The 1900-vintage home has undergone major renovations,
including the addition of an entire second floor under the existing
roofline. The four bedrooms and baths up here have an abundance
of appeal, due in large part to all the ☞ natural light from the roof
windows. They can be opened for fresh air, but even when closed,
you have magnificent views of the trees, mountains, and blue sky
of Sonoma.

Each of the upstairs guest rooms has a sloping roof, and you know how cozy that is. They are named and decorated after the varietal grapes grown in the surrounding countryside: Chardonnay, Cabernet Sauvignon, Merlot, Zinfandel, Pinot Noir, and Gamay Rosé. Colorful linens and puffy comforters decorate the iron and brass beds, all king- or queen-sized. The Chardonnay has a separate sitting area with a daybed covered in white eyelet and two stained-glass windows in shades of blue and purple.

Downstairs guests can enjoy a colorful parlor with a gray-floral-patterned sofa before the fireplace, as well as a living room, dining room, and kitchen. They are fresh, pleasant rooms to relax in, read, or sip a glass of wine. Outdoors under the trees, the umbrella tables are inviting, too.

A full breakfast is served in the dining room at a lace-covered table with fresh flowers. Fresh juice and fruit, home-baked breads and muffins, and an entree, such as a frittata, are typical.

For dinner, stroll to the square and try the Plaza Grill's mesquite-broiled fresh fish and meat. Also on the square is the Salame Tree Deli. It's a good supply station for picnickers. Choose from an assortment of cold cuts, cheeses, and wines; then head for the back roads—on bikes if you've brought them. And who would go to Sonoma without a bicycle!

How to get there: Driving north on Highway 101, take the second Healdsburg exit and follow into town. At Grant Street, turn right 2 blocks. The inn is on the right at the corner of Johnson Street.

☙

J: *Can anyone doubt that we Westerners are ready for hardship and sacrifice when necessary? The popular duo-bathing phenomenon proves we'd do* anything *to conserve water!*

Olive Metcalf

Healdsburg Inn on the Plaza
Healdsburg, California
95448

Innkeeper: Genny Jenkins
Address/Telephone: 116 Matheson Street (mailing address: Box 1196);
(707) 433–6991
Rooms: 9; all with private bath and air conditioning.
Rates: $55 to $115; substantial discounts mid-week and off-season. All
rates include full breakfast, afternoon refreshments. No children
under 7; smoking only on roof garden.
Open: Year-round.
Facilities and local attractions: Walk to Healdsburg restaurants, shops. Wine
tours; Russian River nearby for canoeing, fishing; picnics; good
bicycling area. Lake Sonoma.

Genny Jenkins looks around the small Victorian hotel she has
restored, shakes her head, and grins. "I didn't *need* this!" She
already owns a small B&B in St. Helena, but given her enormous
energy, the beautiful old Krause building on the Plaza had too
much potential to pass by.

Healdsburg is a 🖙 heart-tugger of a town, built around a
Spanish-style plaza with quaint storefronts and historic houses on

228

its backstreets. Genny has decoratively painted and trimmed her building with bright colors, divided the lower floor into attractive shops, and created a comfortable inn upstairs. The street-level entry and lobby are part of a gift shop and gallery showing original local art. Daughter Dyanne runs this operation. A paneled stairway leads up to a wide, tall-ceilinged hallway with ornamental architectural details, period lighting fixtures, and a lounge where guests can enjoy a collection of classic novels or watch television or video.

Rooms facing the plaza have graceful bay windows that make delightful sitting areas and some have fireplaces. Genny is constantly decorating with an eye for turn-of-the-century furniture and whimsy. Several bathrooms have new spectacular skylights over big, claw-footed tubs. "We really go in for an abundance of plush towels, bubbles, and rubber ducks," she says.

The room that captivated me is in back. Long ago, it was a photography studio. An entire wall—and these are 12-foot ceilings—is a slanted skylight. Besides the large bath and queen-sized bed, at no extra cost, you get a ceiling of clouds and sky. Imagine it for full moons!

A large flower-filled roof garden is one of Genny's best innovations. Breakfast is usually served out here at fancy, white iron tables and chairs: fresh fruit and juice, homemade goodies, and an entree of cheese, eggs, or meat combination. Sunday morning breakfast expands into a champagne brunch served until noon that is open to the public as well as houseguests.

Most guests walk across the square to the Plaza Grill for dinner. The innovative mesquite grill cooking, with the freshest ingredients, is winning many fans.

How to get there: Driving north on Highway 101, take second Healdsburg exit; turn right on Matheson Street, follow to town plaza. Inn faces the plaza. Coming from the north, take Mill Street exit to the plaza.

❀

J: *In 1901, the local paper said that this building was "a substantial ornament to the town." Healdsburg is lucky that the description holds true once again.*

olive Metcalf

Madrona Manor
Healdsburg, California
95448

Innkeepers: John and Carol Muir
Address/Telephone: 1001 Westside Road (mailing address: Box 818); (707)
    433–4231
Rooms: 18 and 2 suites; all with private bath.
Rates: $85 to $135, full breakfast included.
Open: All year. Dinner nightly, Sunday brunch.
Facilities and local attractions: Swimming pool. Convenient to golf, tennis,
    hiking, canoeing, fishing. Winery tours and picnics.

    Country inns are springing up in northern California faster
than yuppies are going out of style, but Madrona Manor stands
alone. First, it is a truly ☞ dramatic Victorian mansion sitting in
the midst of landscaped grounds and eight wooded acres. But even
more notable is its ☞ outstanding California restaurant, the only
one in Sonoma County rated 3-stars by *Chronicle* food critic
Patricia Unterman.
    Approaching the Italianate mansion up the long driveway
brings feelings of pleasant anticipation. Elegant accommodations
await inside: antique furnishings, period wallpapers and rugs, and
rooms with original plumbing and lighting fixtures. The third floor
has recently renovated rooms with fireplaces, queen-sized beds,

and antique reproduction furniture from Portugal. Less opulent but more modern rooms are in two other outbuildings and the Carriage House, where a fireplace has been added to the lounge.

The fine cooking is served in two high-ceilinged, attractive dining rooms. Former Chez Panisse cook, Todd Muir, runs the kitchen. He and his staff work in a modern kitchen (contrasting with the rest of the 1881 setting) complete with a wood-burning oven for bread and pizzas, a mesquite grill, and a smokehouse in back that produces smoked trout, chickens, and meats.

An a la carte menu of salads, pastas, and grilled main courses, or an elegant prix-fixe dinner ($42.50, at this writing) are available seven nights a week. My first course of individual goat-cheese soufflé was perfectly crusty on top with a softly oozing middle. Every element of the meal, down to dessert of amaretto-soaked cake with chocolate-ricotta filling, was meticulously prepared.

The wine list is both interesting and reasonably priced, which, even though this is the heart of the wine country, is not always true up here. Some selections from small local wineries are at near-retail prices.

Breakfast for guests is as carefully done as dinner. It includes their wonderful house bread, toasted, a perfectly timed soft-boiled egg, ripe, room-temperature cheeses, and house-smoked meats. When the weather allows, take this meal outside on the palm terrace.

How to get there: From San Francisco, drive north on Highway 101, 12 miles north of Santa Rosa; take the second Healdsburg exit; follow Healdsburg Avenue north to Mill Road, which becomes Westside Road. Inn is on the left. From the north, take Westside Road exit from Highway 101.

J: *What a beautiful place for a special celebration.*

olive Metcalf

Beazley House
Napa, California
94559

Innkeepers: Carol and Jim Beazley
Address/Telephone: 1910 First Street; (707) 257–1649
Rooms: 10 in main house; 5 with private bath. 5 in Carriage House; all
    with private Jacuzzi and fireplace. One room with wheelchair
    facilities.
Rates: $85 to $140, including full breakfast.
Open: All year.
Facilities and local attractions: Beautiful gardens. Jacuzzi tubs. Wine touring,
    hot mineral baths, ballooning, bicycling. Close to Napa shopping,
    restaurants. Facilities for weddings, small meetings.

    The blue-and-white striped awnings take your eye immedi-
ately. They give this shingled Colonial Revival the look of a grand
English vacation house. It is ☞ an old Napa landmark and sits on
half an acre of lawns and gardens within walking distance of the
town's shopping area.
    The solid-looking house is beautifully symmetrical, with an
especially wide staircase at its center. A beveled- and stained-glass
doorway opens to the entry and music room. To the right is a
formal dining room; to the left is a long, gracious living room with
polished, inlaid wood floors and large bay windows at either end,

one with a padded window seat. Brightly upholstered sofas and chairs are arranged in several groupings. There are a fireplace, bookcases, and a basket of Napa restaurant menus to peruse. A teacart arranged with china cups and saucers, tea, coffee, and sherry looks very civilized and Edwardian.

Halfway up the stairway is a window seat and a ☞ spectacular half-round stained-glass window. The bedrooms are pleasantly spacious. Carol has made most of the comforter covers herself in big, English floral prints with matching draperies. The Master Room, with a fireplace, and the Wine and Roses Room have private baths. They make a comfortable suite for couples traveling together.

At the back of the property, the old carriage house has been rebuilt from the ground up, modeled after the original barn. These rooms have fireplaces, high ceilings, and Jacuzzi tubs. The ☞ fresh scent of cedar comes from the bathrooms that are lined with tongue and groove cedar paneling.

The Beazleys set out a generous breakfast on the dining-room buffet for guests to help themselves and make return trips. Carol is proud that three of her muffin recipes are included in a recently published collection of country-inn recipes. A typical breakfast has large platters of sliced fresh fruit, yogurt, one of a variety of crustless quiches she makes, and homemade breads and muffins.

How to get there: From San Francisco, drive north on Highway 101 to 37 East, then north on 121 to 121 East; follow to Highway 29. Proceed north to the First Street/Central Napa exit. Follow exit all the way to the end; then turn left at Second Street. Continue ³⁄₁₀ mile to Warren Street. Turn left to the inn on corner of First and Warren.

J: *Jim or Carol Beazley will make arrangements for their guests to visit and taste at wineries that are not on the regular tourist routes. And they also know the best picnic spots in the valley.*

Country Garden Inn
Napa, California
94558

Innkeeper: Lisa Villiers
Address/Telephone: 1815 Silverado Trail; (707) 255–1197
Rooms: 6; all with private bath, including 3 with Jacuzzi. Air conditioning.
Rates: $75 to $130, December through March; $90 to $140, April through
November. Lowest rates Sunday through Thursday. Two-night min-
imum required weekends. Rates include full champagne breakfast
and early evening hors d'oeuvres and wine. Cannot accommodate
children or pets. No smoking.
Open: All year.
Facilities and local attractions: Gardens, deck, riverbank setting. Private
Jacuzzis. Winery tours, hiking, bicycling, hot-air ballooning, picnics,
mud baths. Fine restaurants all around.

Those English innkeepers, Janet and Geoffrey Villiers, have
struck again. Not resting on laurels garnered at their Old World
Inn near downtown Napa, they have opened another, more
pastoral inn on the famous Silverado Trail, with daughter Lisa in
charge.

The house was built in the 1850s as a coach stop, and it still
gives you a sense of "safe haven" when you pull off the road into
the acre-and-a-half wooded setting. It 🖝 sits right on the bank of

the Napa River, almost overrun with trees and what I call a typical British-style haphazard abundance of flora and fauna. There are pathways surrounding a shaded terrace, a deck overlooking the river, and a profusion of flowers and vines and cats. On this July day, fat roses in every imaginable color made a dazzling display from a formal circular rose garden.

The common rooms have a very English feeling with beamed ceilings and a handsome wood mantel over the fireplace. An assortment of easy chairs and chintz-covered sofas are arranged for conversation with ☛ British magazines and guide books on the tables.

This is a room to enjoy fair weather or foul. I like the idea of afternoon tea and cookies before the fire, or wine and a cheese board before going out to dinner. When you return, sweetmeats and dessert wines are set out. Those British! They do know how to pause and refresh, don't they?

These are romantically decorated bedrooms in soft colors with antiques, some canopied beds, and two have Jacuzzis. One large room has a sitting area between two walls of beveled-glass windows. One has a private deck right over the river.

Breakfast is served at tables covered with long chintz skirts and top cloths. Champagne or mimosas are poured while you have fruit and coffee cakes, eggs Benedict, or perhaps English bangers and omelets. In lovely weather—and since this is the Napa Valley, not England, there's plenty of it—you can eat on the deck if you like.

How to get there: From Highway 29 in Napa, take Trancas Street east to fork in the road. Bear right (signed 121 to Napa). The inn is 7/10 mile on the right.

olive Metcalf

La Residence
Napa, California
94558

Innkeepers: David Jackson and Craig Claussen
Address/Telephone: 4066 St. Helena Highway N.; (707) 253–0337
Rooms: 9 in Mansion, 7 with private bath, 11 rooms in the French barn; all with private bath. Air conditioning; wheelchair access.
Rates: $65 to $150, including full breakfast and afternoon wine social. No pets.
Open: All year.
Facilities and local attractions: Spa, heated pool. Elegant dining room available for parties, catered dinners. Wine tours, ballooning, bicycling. Close to fine restaurants, shopping. Concierge service for all area activities.

The two buildings that together are La Residence are different, but both are so delightful that it is hard to decide which to choose. The inn began with the Gothic Revival mansion Harry C. Parker built in 1870 when he moved to Napa County to farm. He was a river pilot from New Orleans, and the house shows a distinctive Southern character, with all the winning features of a fine Victorian home.

If you ever visited this picturesque farmhouse in earlier years, you should see why its new owners now call it "The Mansion."

The graceful architecture has been splendidly renovated and rooms inside ☞ elegantly decorated with American antiques, plantation shutters, the finest linens, and coordinated fabrics and wallcoverings. When you see period charm restored with this degree of taste and eye for comfort, you have something special. There are newly added private baths, fireplaces, and a small kitchen where you can keep your wine chilled.

Across the yard is a much newer building, a handsome shingled structure built in the style of a French barn. I say "barn," but I assure you the only animals roaming these elegant rooms are a few porcelain geese decorating the dining room. It's actually called "Cabernet Hall," probably a prudent move on the part of the innkeepers. Claussen, who is from Iowa, says he could imagine giving a telephone description of the accommodations and getting a response, "A barn? I'm not paying good money to sleep in a barn!" The eleven rooms here each have a sitting area, fireplace, and French doors opening onto a patio or balcony. Furnishings are English and French country pine, queen-sized beds, and Laura Ashley fabrics.

The two acres of beautiful grounds now have a ☞ Jacuzzi spa and a heated pool surrounded by brick patios, gazebos, trellis, and gardens, all shaded by 200-year-old oaks and acacias.

A beautifully presented full breakfast is served in the dining room of Cabernet Hall, sometimes before a blazing fire, and always with fresh flowers and the morning papers. This is an innkeeper production with David cooking (his wife is getting a Ph.D.—no kitchen time for her!) and Craig serving. First course is a fresh-fruit plate, followed by an egg entree with homebaked breads or cinnamon rolls.

How to get there: Take Highway 29 through Napa; pass Salvador Street and look for the inn sign on the right.

⤐

J: *When I heard this inn I admired had new owners and was enlarging, I feared another casualty of charming inn into slick corporate facililty. It's good to see La Residence being run with the warmth and personal attention that always separate innkeepers from strictly bottom-liners.*

Olive Metcalf

The Old World Inn
Napa, California
94559

Innkeepers: Janet and Geoffrey Villiers
Address/Telephone: 1301 Jefferson Street; (707) 257–0112
Rooms: 8; all with private bath, including 1 with Jacuzzi. Air conditioning.
Rates: $87 to $122, including substantial breakfast. Winter discounts. No
    pets or children; no smoking.
Open: All year.
Facilities and local attractions: Large Jacuzzi. Walk to Napa restaurants,
    shopping. Winery tours, ballooning, bicycling, picnics.

There are no better innkeepers than the British. Their impeccable manners, that wonderful sense of fun, the ever-ready cup of tea or glass of sherry all seem to project an atmosphere that says you're going to be well looked after. Or is it that confident accent? Before I ever saw The Old World Inn, I had only to hear Janet Villiers' crisp voice over the telephone telling me about her "letting rooms" to be won over.

If you prefer to tour the wine country from a base in the town of Napa rather than out in the countryside, this is an engaging choice. The handsome, old house is a mélange of wood shingles, wide shady porches, leaded and beveled glass, dormers, and bays. I wouldn't dream of putting a label on its architectural style; let us just say "eclectic."

238

In addition to its British innkeepers, the inn's outstanding feature is its ☛ lovely decor. The entire house has been decorated with gorgeous fabrics inspired by the Swedish artist Carl Larsson—French blue, French pink, soft peach, and green. Painted Victorian and antique furniture accent these fresh colors. The parlor invites you with plump upholstered furniture, a tile fireplace, and tall ceilings whimsically painted with sunny quotations.

The individually decorated bedrooms have ☛ full or half canopied queen-sized beds and coordinated linens. Fresh flowers are everywhere—that's another thing the British have a special flair for. Most of the private baths have a Victorian, claw-footed tub and a shower, and one room has a Jacuzzi.

At breakfast, a buffet is spread on a romantically draped table in the sunny Morning Room. Janet says, "Geoffrey really does the *most* beautiful fruit platters of six or more fruits." There is also a hot dish (perhaps a quiche) and homemade breakfast breads. Guests help themselves and sit at individual tables by a huge bay window.

In the early evening, wine is served and an ☛ international cheese board is offered in the Morning Room. The Villiers are well acquainted with reasonable restaurants you can easily walk to, and more lavish ones are only a short drive away. When you return to the inn, they will have homemade sweetmeats (their own almonds) and dessert wines waiting.

After dinner is when most guests like to use the large custom Jacuzzi. It is open to the stars but surrounded by vines and trees.

How to get there: From San Francisco, drive north on 101; exit onto 121 at Sears Point. Turn left on Highway 29; take Lincoln East exit in Napa, and turn right on Jefferson Street. Inn is on the right.

Olive Metcalf

Auberge du Soleil
Rutherford, California
94573

Innkeeper: Adair Borba-Thoms, general manager
Address/Telephone: 180 Rutherford Hill Road; (707) 963–1211
Rooms: 48; all with private bath, fireplace, television, deck or patio.
Rates: $210, double room, to $480 for 2-bedroom suites; rate includes
   continental breakfast and use of tennis, spa, and swimming facilities.
Open: All year. Lunch, dinner, bar. Reservations advised.
Facilities and local attractions: Swimming pool, Jacuzzi, masseuse, steam
   rooms, tennis courts, bikes for rent. Visit wineries, picnic; nearby hot
   springs, restaurants, shops.

First, there was the prestigious Auberge du Soleil Restaurant;
then it expanded into a chic, country inn comprised of ten
two-story and one three-story Mediterranean-style villas. The
entire resort is nestled into thirty-three acres of olive groves spread
over a hillside looking down on the Napa Valley.

The ☞ atmosphere here is quite simply . . . luxury. Oh, it
may be understated and unfussy, but this is *major* luxury. On each
level of the villas are two bedrooms, two baths, two fireplaces, and
a large living room with a ☞ stocked refrigerator—liquors,
champagne, wine, pâté, and aged cheeses. Each suite converts to
a one-bedroom unit and a one-bedroom suite keeping the amen-

ities. From each private deck is a perfect view of the Napa Valley with the Silverado Trail winding through.

The decor is a blend of European sophistication and California informality—sort of an ☞ earthy elegance. Floors are covered with Mexican tiles, and furniture is kept to a minimum, but much of it is bold, like Mexican pigskin chairs and concrete stone-roller lamps. Walls are the same rough, adobe-colored plaster as in the restaurant, with white framed, French glass doors and casement windows with heavy, white louvered doors and inside shutters. The only splash of color comes from fresh flowers and oversized pillows on sofas and chairs. Sheets are percale, towels the thickest; and bathrooms are big enough for small meetings.

One look at the elegant dining room and terrace overlooking the valley tells you this is *not* the place to order anything you ever cook at home . . . not that you're going to find meat loaf on the menu. Liberate your plastic card and wallow in the chic California cuisine. Try salad of ☞ duck with mangoes, curry-and-lemon linguine, or braised pheasant with crayfish and truffles. The wine list is a catalog of California's finest. Some of the grapes came from the very valley you look over.

Facilities for weddings or small business meetings are exceptional. A recent addition for private events is an intimate dining room with a skylight ceiling that accommodates up to thirty people.

How to get there: From San Francisco, take Highway 80 northeast to connect with Highway 37, then Highway 29. From Highway 29 in Napa Valley, follow any of the cross-valley roads west to the Silverado Trail; continue north to Rutherford. The inn sits above the trail. Fly-in: Napa County Airport.

Olive Metcalf

Rancho Caymus Inn
Rutherford, California
94573

Innkeeper: Dean R. Cook; owner, Mary Tilden Morton
Address/Telephone: Rutherford Road (mailing address: Box 78); (707)
 963–1777
Rooms: 26 suites, all with private bath, air conditioning, color television,
 wet bar, refrigerator; most with fireplace.
Rates: $95 to $250, including continental breakfast. Two-night minimum
 for weekends. No pets; children under 5 discouraged.
Open: All year. Breakfast, lunch.
Facilities and local attractions: Ideal location for wine touring; easy bicy-
 cling; hot-air ballooning. Interesting restaurants, shops close by.

This luxurious three-year-old inn with red tiled roofs and
rough stucco walls ☞ captures the feeling of early California. It's
a two-story building with colonnades and open balconies, shaped
around a central garden court in the Spanish style. Each room has
a sitting area with either a wet bar or a complete kitchen; bed and
bath are up two steps to another level. Most have fireplaces and
private patios or balconies. Hand-hewn beams and planking from
an old barn give the rooms a warm, western feeling.

The concept of a handcrafted hacienda was a five-year labor
of love for owner Mary Tilden Morton. She is a third-generation

Californian, a sculptor, and grape rancher who has spent most of her life in the arts. Morton also designed Rutherford Square, a dining-entertainment complex next door to the inn.

Morton has made the inn a showplace for artisans and carpenters. Sausalito artists made the ☞ hand-thrown stoneware basins that sit in counters made from slabs of black walnut. Parota-wood chairs and matching dressers were carved in Guadalajara. A Napa artist created the stained-glass-window murals behind the Jacuzzi tubs in the bathrooms of the five master suites.

Much of the inn's character comes from the ☞ hand-crafted furnishings and appointments done by Ecuadorian artists: hand-carved, black walnut queen-sized beds and wrought-iron lamps, vibrantly colored bedspreads, rugs, and wall hangings dyed and woven by South American Indians.

The Caymus Kitchen serves only breakfast and lunch. Continental breakfast of freshly baked breads and house-blend coffee can be served in your room or in the garden. For lunch there are excellent sandwiches (smoked turkey and avocado), fresh daily soup, Mexican specialties like quesadillas and chicken enchiladas, and changing chef's specials.

Sampling all the many superb dinner places in the valley is a gourmet adventure. One of them in Yountville is Mustard's, one of the great restaurants in the country—innovative, fresh, and fun! It's also popular, so be sure to ask the innkeeper to make your reservation.

How to get there: On Highway 29 through the Napa Valley, turn east at the crossroads of 29 and Highway 128, south of St. Helena. The inn is on the left, just past Rutherford Square complex.

Olive Metcalf

Wine Country Inn
St. Helena, California
94574

Innkeeper: Jim Smith
Address/Telephone: 1152 Lodi Lane; (707) 963–7077
Rooms: 25; all with private bath. Wheelchair access.
Rates: $93 to $161, including continental breakfast. No children under 12.
Open: All year.
Facilities and local attractions: Swimming pool. Walk country lanes. Close to
    tennis courts, hot-air balloon rides, mineral baths, many wineries,
    antique stores, restaurants.

The Wine Country Inn has grown the past dozen years, along
with the tremendous popularity of the Napa Valley. It has added
buildings, patios, and, most recently, a swimming pool and spa,
but it is still a family operation. You can hear Jim Smith describing
a room to a guest over the telephone, adding, "And my mother
made the quilt on the bed."

Unlike many inns in the area, this one was built new from the
ground up. The Smiths borrowed ideas from historic buildings in
the valley, making their three-story stone-and-wood inn look
right at home in the vineyards.

Each room is individually decorated, combining old and new.
There are fresh, pretty color combinations, floral wallpapers,

carpeting, and modern baths. Most rooms have a fireplace and vineyard view. Patios and intimate little balconies invite you to sit and appreciate the beautiful surrounding hills. Early on weekend mornings, you can usually see vividly colored hot-air balloons wafting their passengers over the vineyards.

Coffee is always ready in the large country-style common room. Make yourself at home in the comfortable sofa or wingback chairs beside an iron stove. Attractive books about wine and the area are all about, along with all the local restaurant menus. In St. Helena, Meadowood has elegant food at lunch and dinner in a beautiful hideaway setting. At Knickerbockers', within walking distance from the inn, you'll find a more casual menu and outdoor seating.

Guests gather at a long refectory table, or at individual tables throughout the room, for continental breakfast. Along with juice and fruit, the substantial fare includes two nut breads, several pastries, butter, and jams. French doors lead to a deck, which is the best breakfast spot of all with views of vineyards and hills. These are pleasant, relaxed mornings, always with friendly staff there to refill your coffee cup and help you with plans for your day.

How to get there: From Napa, take Highway 29 2 miles past St. Helena. Turn right on Lodi Lane. The inn is on the left.

✣

J: *Take your bikes to St. Helena. If you ride early in the morning on the lanes that wind through still-dewy vineyards, you will begin to understand how the wine country can become a passion.*

Olive Metcalf

Melitta Station Inn
Santa Rosa, California
95409

Innkeeper: Diane Jefferds
Address/Telephone: 5850 Melitta Road; (707) 538–7712
Rooms: 6; 5 with private bath; 1 shares bath with innkeeper.
Rates: $55 to $65, with full breakfast.
Open: All year.
Facilities and local attractions: Wine touring. Visit Jack London State
    Historical Monument, Annadel State Park. Spring Lake sailing,
    fishing. Hiking, bicycling, picnics.

Ever heard of the Valley of the Moon? There is such a place in
the rolling Sonoma countryside, and it is as poetically beautiful as
its name. Jack London called the area "my paradise" and built his
famous Wolf House here.

The Melitta Station has been a part of Sonoma's history since
the late 1800s as a stagecoach stop, then a railroad depot, a general
store, and post office. The Jefferds have converted the long
redwood barn into a homey inn. It has that ☞ winning country
charm that magazines love to photograph, but in this instance it is
less slick, more genuine, and ever so much more warm.

You step into the sitting room and find a large woodburning
stove, wood floor with colorful rugs, baskets of kindling, and

rough beams contrasting with white walls. Diane and a local artisan have stenciled a border of folk-art designs around the room.

Bundles of drying herbs hang from the rough-beamed high ceiling. A red-and-white quilt hangs on one wall. Furniture is American Country, featuring a mellow pine sideboard and a wicker sofa with bright print pillows. The cozy bedrooms are also furnished with antiques and collectibles, and all but one have private baths.

The Melitta's location wins my heart. It is rural and quiet, but with all the advantages of being in the very center of Sonoma County's abundant attractions. You are surrounded by outstanding wineries, close to the historic town of Sonoma, and near elegant Santa Rosa restaurants. John Ash is very hot at the moment and just a mile and a half from the inn. Specialties include *rillettes* of duck with bitter greens, California nut torte, and dinners featuring local wines and wine makers.

A hearty breakfast is the only meal served regularly, but everything is homemade, from quiches and tortes to baked apples and muffins. Diane also makes a big, puffy Dutch Baby topped with fruit. But this is a 🖝 very personal inn, and the Jefferds will arrange just about anything you want: unique luncheons, champagne tours, mud baths and massages, hot-air ballooning, or glider rides. Let the good times roll.

How to get there: From Highway 101, exit at Highway 12 exit and follow signs to Sonoma for 5½ miles. Cross Calistoga Road; turn right at Melitta Road, first road on the right. Continue about a mile to the inn.

Olive Metcalf

Vintners Inn
Santa Rosa, California
95401

Innkeepers: Francisca and John Duffy
Address/Telephone: 4350 Barnes Road; (707) 575–7350 or California only, (800) 421–2584
Rooms: 44, including 1- and 2-bedroom suites; all with private bath, television, radio, telephone. Facilities for the handicapped.
Rates: $88 to $155, including continental breakfast.
Open: All year. Restaurant serves lunch, dinner Tuesday through Sunday; Sunday brunch. Closed Mondays; lunch not served Saturdays.
Facilities and local attractions: John Ash & Company restaurant. Extensive conference facilities. Spa and sun deck. Ideal location for wine touring. Russian River water sports, fishing.

Four creamy-pink stucco buildings with red tiled roofs around a ☞ plaza complete with fountain comprise the splendid Vintners Inn. It rises in the ☞ center of a forty-five-acre vineyard (Chardonnay, Pinot Blanc, Sauvignon Blanc), the picture of a village (although a new one) in the South of France. Actually, it is just sixty miles north of San Francisco at the crossroads of the Sonoma County wine country.

The European concept was carefully planned by the Duffys when they determined that a luxury country inn was needed in the Sonoma and Alexander valleys. "We tried to design it to be the way we like things when we travel," says Francisca. They went to Europe, Francisca's original home, and studied Provence market-places, plazas and architectural details, then came home to re-create the feeling in the middle of their own vineyard.

The forty-four rooms were individually decorated in French Country fashion after a meticulous search for authentic details. Chairs at writing desks and in the dining room are from a factory in France; outdoor lamps and standards are from a foundry near Brussels that has been in business 200 years. ☞ The exceptional antique, European pine armoires and desks were collected in East Germany, refinished in Antwerp, and then shipped to the United States. The queen-sized pine beds are new, but they were designed by John from sketches made in France and custom made by a local craftsman.

There are ☞ no small rooms. Their airy spaciousness includes sitting areas, dressing rooms, and elegant bathrooms with brass and porcelain fixtures. Most have a fireplace. Provincial wallpapers with matching draperies decorate all the rooms. Pleasing tall arched windows look out at vineyards or the plaza.

A tiled library and a dining room, both with fireplaces and decorated with more Old World accents, are in the common building. Wine-bar receptions featuring local wines are often held here. This is also where a continental breakfast of fresh fruit and homebaked rolls is served.

The addition to the inn of the John Ash & Company res-taurant is another indication of the Duffys' concept of excellence. Ash is a highly acclaimed chef who blends classic European training with Califonia's bounty. He focuses on local foods—Somoma's famous cheeses, oysters from Tomales Bay, and pro-duce and chickens from Sonoma ranches. He serves a fixed-price dinner as well as a la carte.

How to get there: Just north of Santa Rosa, exit Highway 101 on River Road. Follow west to the corner of Barnes Road. Inn is on the left. Fly-in: Sonoma County Airport.

Olive Metcalf

Magliulo's Pensione and Restaurant
Sonoma, California
95476

Innkeepers: The Magliulo Family
Address/Telephone: 691 Broadway; (707) 996–1031
Rooms: 4; 2 with private bath. Wheelchair access.
Rates: $70 to $80, includes tax and continental breakfast. No children or
    pets; no smoking.
Open: All year. Lunch, dinner, bar.
Facilities and local attractions: Walk to Sonoma Plaza, the Mission, unique
    shops, galleries, restaurants. Winery tours, picnics, bicycling.

    Many Sonoma visitors will remember the Au Relais Res-
taurant. It was a favorite for many years, serving outstanding food
in handsome redwood surroundings. Its ☞ garden patio was
always my preference for dining on starry Sonoma nights. New
owners, the Magliulo family, now run both the restaurant and the
inn.
    The recently redecorated *pensione* is a charming 1880s Victo-
rian house just a few stepping stones from the restaurant. Besides
being an utterly delightful retreat, its location has some distinct
advantages: It is completely removed from the comings and goings

of restaurant patrons but close enough to have drinks and hors d'oeuvres available at your request. And when you're ready for company and a first-rate meal, you need only step next door. Not bad.

The entire inn, even the woodwork, is decorated in restful, soft shades of rose and peach with touches of a misty aqua. Relaxing by the fireside in the common sitting room, you feel wrapped in a rosy cocoon. Comfortable upholstered furniture and antiques accent the tranquil surroundings.

The bedrooms are all a generous size and are romantically decorated with pretty bed linen and tables draped in fabric and lace. Some have beautiful quilts hanging as wall accents, armoires, and brass beds. Ceiling fans have been added to every room. Dishes of potpourri are a nice touch.

The restaurant serves regional Italian cuisine featuring veal and chicken dishes and various pasta entrees. One of the most popular is Angelhair and Basilico. Full dinners include soup, salad, pasta, and vegetable along with coffee. The garden patio is still there and, with Sonoma's great weather, can be enjoyed much of the year.

Pensione guests step over to the restaurant for their complimentary breakfast consisting of fresh juice and fruits, muffins, croissants, and freshly ground coffee.

How to get there: From San Francisco, drive north on Highway 101 to 37 East, then 121 north to Sonoma. The highway becomes Broadway. The inn is on the left, just before the Sonoma Plaza.

☀

J: Remarks in a guest book can often tell the tale. This one was filled with sentiments like "The cuisine was only exceeded by the hospitality."

Olive Metcalf

Sonoma Hotel
Sonoma, California
95476

Innkeepers: John and Dorene Musilli
Address/Telephone: 110 West Spain Street; (707) 996–2996
Rooms: 17; 5 with private bath, 12 share baths at end of hallways.
Rates: $58 to $98, including continental breakfast.
Open: All year. Lunch, dinner, bar.
Facilities and local attractions: Located on Sonoma's historic plaza with
    Mission San Francisco de Solano, Sonoma Barracks, boutiques,
    restaurants, galleries.

My affection for this old hotel stems from the morning I was coming down the steps from my room and recognized (before I saw her) the unmistakably rich voice of Maya Angelou. She was lingering over conversation and coffee with the elderly man on duty at the desk and, as she told me with a smile, delaying the moment when she would have to climb the stairs and begin work in the tiny third-floor room she kept for writing. From that morning on, I've always thought of the colorful 1870s hotel as having an especially authentic, literary atmosphere. Indeed, Room No. 21 on the third floor is the Maya Angelou Room.

Sonoma is a delightful town to explore, with its history as a distant outpost of the Mexican empire, the northernmost of the

California missions, and General Vallejo's barracks and home. At the Sonoma Hotel, you are directly on the historic plaza and can walk to all the attractions in town.

John and Dorene Musilli have recently restored and refurnished the entire inn so that the ☞ authentic early California atmosphere is more fresh and comfortable than ever. Dorene says there is not a reproduction in the place. The furnishings came from private homes, antique stores, and loans from the Sonoma League for Historic Preservation. You can sleep in a carved rosewood bed from the Vallejo family, a unique, solid-oak bed inlaid with ebony, or in impressive brass beds.

Third floor rooms are smaller, lower in price, but still have some choice antiques.

A restaurant and long bar gleam with beveled glass and polished wood. Menus change weekly, and the cooking has been winning raves. A recent favorite was pork loin stuffed with pancetta, onions, and dry Vella Jack, the local cheese. Dessert specialties include a Queen Mother Torte, and—steady on, you chocoholics—a ☞ white-chocolate cheesecake.

Continental breakfast specialties—like French croissants— and superb bran muffins are baking while guests still sleep. A pleasant change of taste from excessively sweet breakfast breads, they are served along with fresh fruit, fresh juice, and coffee and tea.

How to get there: From San Francisco, take Highway 101 north to Ignacio; then take Highway 37 east to Highway 21, which leads to Sonoma Plaza. The hotel faces the plaza.

Olive Metcalf

The Inn at Valley Ford
Valley Ford, California
94972

Innkeepers: Sandra Nicholls and Nicholas Balashob
Address/Telephone: 14395 Highway 1 (mailing address: Box 439); (707) 876–3182
Rooms: 4 share 2 baths; the W. Somerset Maugham Cottage shares a bath.
Rates: $55 to $63, including tax, full breakfast, afternoon tea. No pets; no smoking.
Open: All year.
Facilities and local attractions: Bicycles, sun deck, good bird watching. Minutes from Bodega Bay fishing, boating, beach walking. Nearby historic towns, art galleries, antiques, restaurants.

In this age of specialization, here's an inn for lovers of literature. Innkeeper Sandra Nicholls is a romantic with an M.A. in English literature and an inn to indulge her fantasies.

Her guest rooms are named for Virginia Woolf, Colette, and Molly Bloom; the fourth is "a room for the muse." Each is decorated in a style that reflects the writer or character for whom it's named, and stocked with a 🖝 library of the lady's work or of the author who wrote about the character.

The house is late-1860s vintage and retains that era's feeling, even with the architectural changes that the innkeepers have made. Rooms are decorated with flair—beautiful fabrics, lace, big puffy comforters, and wicker. The two bathrooms—one with a claw-footed tub, the other with an ☞ enormous sunken shower— are as efficient as one could ask.

The wallpaper in the light-filled dining-room sitting area is wonderful. It has a black background with big colorful flowers blooming over it, reminiscent of a gaudy English chintz. You'll have a Sandra–style breakfast here: fruit compote, fresh juice, and just-ground coffee. You'll also see something made with the farm-fresh eggs she gets, and when it's berry time (as it was during our visit), she just *has* to do a "little something" with them . . . perhaps cobbler or coffeecake.

The cheerful dining room looks into a dream of a kitchen. Outside is an English–style flower garden, a broad deck (a sunny spot to read) that overlooks the Sonoma countryside, and a yard in the process of change. Most recently completed are a gazebo, an arbor, and a new accommodation called the W. Somerset Maugham Cottage. It is dedicated to travel, and in addition to Maugham's books, it includes a travel library.

Merely the address of Highway 1 tells you that this is ☞ beautiful, peaceful territory. A hundred years ago, Valley Ford had 126 people living here; 126 people live here today—reportedly not the same people. Only ten minutes away by car are restaurants and pubs in Bodega Bay.

How to get there: From San Francisco, follow Highway 1 north to Valley Ford, 5 miles past Tomales. The inn is on the left.

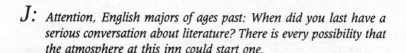

J: Attention, English majors of ages past: When did you last have a serious conversation about literature? There is every possibility that the atmosphere at this inn could start one.

Olive Metcalf

Magnolia Hotel
Yountville, California
94599

Innkeepers: Bruce and Bonnie Locken
Address/Telephone: 6529 Yount Street (mailing address: P.O. Drawer M);
(707) 944–2056
Rooms: 12; all with private bath.
Rates: $85 to $155, with full breakfast. No credit cards; no children under
16; no pets. No smoking.
Open: All year.
Facilities and local attractions: Swimming pool; Jacuzzi spa. Walk to all
Yountville shops, restaurants, galleries. Wine tours; hot-air balloon-
ing; picnics.

In the '70s, before the Napa Valley became a bigger tourist
attraction than Disneyland, "quaint lodgings" meant the Magnolia
Hotel. The first time I stayed there, our party booked the entire
hotel—all four rooms—for a birthday celebration. Some of us were
enchanted with the ☛ old stone building behind an iron gate
entwined with roses, but others in the party failed to see any
charm in small rooms and doors that didn't lock. The experience
was an early indication of which of us would become country inn
fans and which would settle only for efficiency.

The valley has grown, and so has the Magnolia, but the

outside appearance is as picturesque as ever. Now there are twelve antique-decorated rooms (the innkeepers want you to know that all their doors lock), ranging from tiny to spacious, all with a private bath, and some with fireplace, sitting area, and king-sized bed. Second- and third-floor rooms have views and access to several balconies and sun decks.

Only breakfast is served in the little dining room where once were served fine dinners. The innkeepers say that most people come to the valley looking forward to trying some of its famous restaurants; therefore, they would rather concentrate on feeding guests a good breakfast and then help them choose which restaurant to sample from among the riches. In Yountville, you can walk to half a dozen choices, including The Diner, Mama Nina's (Italian), or the elegant French Laundry.

Through the back courtyard, past the pool and spa, are several interesting shops—one almost impossible to ignore is a designer chocolate place.

The courtyard comes out on Washington Street and Vintage 1870, a brick complex of restaurants, unique shops, galleries, and a little theater you should visit. A beautiful fifteen-minute entertainment there is well worth your time. Photographer Keith Rosenthal captures the spirit and changing beauty of the valley's vineyards with a combination of dramatic music and spectacular photography, from spring's yellow mustard carpet to fall's harvest magenta.

How to get there: Follow Highway 29 through the Napa Valley to the Yountville exit. You will see the red brick and flags of Vintage 1870. The inn is opposite the complex, one street farther east on Yount Street.

J: *Attention all "Falcon Crest" junkies: The Rosenthal show includes an exclusive inside look at the Spring Mountain Vineyard mansion used on the show.*

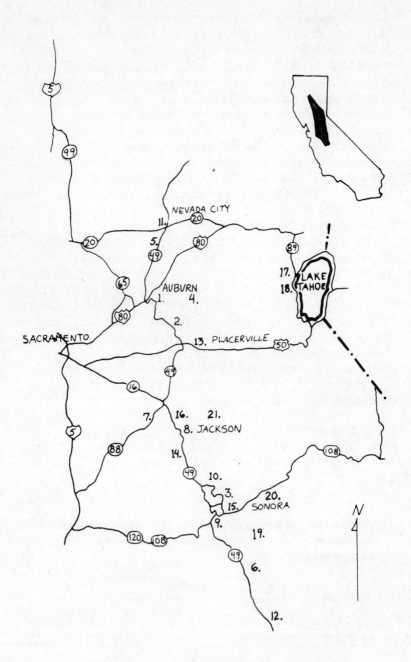

NEVADA CITY

AUBURN

SACRAMENTO

PLACERVILLE

JACKSON

SONORA

LAKE TAHOE

N

California: The Mother Lode and Sierras

Numbers on map refer to towns numbered below.

Olive Metcalf

Power's Mansion Inn
Auburn, California
95603

Innkeeper: Doreen Sanderson, resident manager
Address/Telephone: 164 Cleveland Avenue; (916) 885–1166
Rooms: 13; all with private bath, telephone, air conditioning. Wheelchair access.
Rates: $65 to $150 including full breakfast. No pets; smoking only in patio area.
Open: All year.
Facilities and local attractions: Half block to downtown Auburn restaurants, shops. Explore Old Town Historical area. Nearby hills offer facilities for fishing, boating, swimming, hiking, horseback riding, snow and water skiing.

The Power's Mansion is a rambling, impressive Victorian with landscaped grounds and fills a full city block. Yet a guest at the door making a return visit called, "Hi, Doreen! I'm home."

Is that any way to act in an imposing place like this? Apparently it's directly due to the kind of tender loving care you get at this local landmark, now home away from home for a lot of Auburn visitors. When we arrived on a drizzly April day, a fire was glowing in the parlor fireplace, fresh flowers were in every room, and a plate of homebaked cookies and coffee waited on the dining

260

room buffet for arriving guests in need of immediate sustenance.

The downstairs entry, parlor, and cozy sitting room (there's a television here) are elegantly decorated with fine Victorian pieces, including a beauty of an old pump organ that is in fine working order. Individual round tables are well spaced in the dining room, and a big sunny bay window makes it a cheerful place for breakfast.

The comfortable guest rooms are both on the main floor and upstairs. Six of them are actually in a new wing, built so cleverly you can scarcely tell they aren't the same vintage as the 1901 house. They're all pretty, with queen-sized beds and English antique furniture. The Anniversary Room and the Honeymoon Suite are both more lavishly decorated—one in pale lavender, one in peach—and have fireplaces. The Honeymoon Suite also has a major bathroom with a sunken, heart-shaped Jacuzzi tub for two.

There are eighteen historical landmarks in the Auburn area. And even though it has its quaint Old Town district, Auburn is not a sleepy gold-country town; it is the hub of busy recreational, tourist, and forestry businesses. Many travelers in town on business are finding the mansion a comfortable alternative to their usual motel, with an all-the-comforts-of-home atmosphere. Doreen cheerfully accommodates breakfast times, clears a dining room table for someone who wants to work there, lends an ironing board, and is always ready with a pot of tea and cookies to take to your room. Pretty nice treatment.

Breakfast menus vary, but a blender fruit drink, a fresh-fruit plate, homemade muffins, and a strata, quiche, or oven-baked French toast are typical items. Doreen recommends Butterworth's for dinner, a fine restaurant in a Victorian house nearby.

How to get there: From Highway I–80 exit on Elm; turn back toward Old Auburn. Turn right on High Street ½ block to Cleveland Avenue and the inn.

Olive Metcalf

Coloma Country Inn
Coloma, California
95613

Innkeepers: Alan and Cindi Ehrgott
Address/Telephone: 2 High Street; (mailing address: P.O. Box 502); (916) 622–6919
Rooms: 5; 1 with private bath, 4 share 2 baths.
Rates: $65 single to $75 double, including expanded continental breakfast. Package rates available for raft trips and ballooning. No smoking; no pets; no credit cards. Advance notice requested for children.
Open: All year.
Facilities and local attractions: Canoeing; walk about surrounding state park, historical Coloma, south fork of American River. Raft trips arranged. Hot-air ballooning available. Local events: Coloma Christmas celebration; spring Heritage Home Tour; wine tasting; fall apple picking. Facilities for weddings and small parties.

Here's Norman Rockwell charm. This old-fashioned house on a country road is so appealing I stopped before I even knew it was an inn. The spic-and-span, two-story yellow-and-white house sits on five green acres with a pond, big shade trees, flowers, white wicker on a long front porch, and a gazebo. Sounds almost too adorable?

To the innkeeper's credit, they've not overplayed their treasure of an 1852 house. The long beamed-ceiling living room is fresh and uncluttered. Colorful early American art objects stand out against white walls, old crocks flank the hearth, and a bright quilt hangs on the wall. A vivid oriental rug and easy furniture before the fireplace are inviting.

The Ehrgotts serve breakfast in the dining room, which has a view of the old pond in back. There is always a variety of fresh fruit, homebaked muffins, breads, and good coffee. You can also arrange for a picnic basket if you intend to ramble during the day.

Guest rooms are decorated with antique double beds and pretty quilts, touches of lace here, a stained-glass window there. Each has a sitting area and always fresh-cut flowers. Take a look at a wonderful Eastlake-style bedroom set in a room up the hand-stenciled stairway. By the time this goes to press there will be an additional private bath and separate Carriage House quarters offering two bedrooms, living room, kitchen, and bath.

Alan is a commercial hot-air balloon pilot and offers flights on request. He also arranges white-water rafting trips. The inn has bicycles, and down at the pond there are ducks to feed and a canoe. I vote for lemonade and a good book on the front porch.

Situated in the middle of the 300-acre Gold Discovery State Park, the inn is surrounded by history. Sutter's Mill in Coloma was the site of the first gold discovery in 1848, and there are many old structures and points of interest within easy walking distance.

How to get there: From Placerville, take Highway 49 north 8 miles to Gold Discovery State Park. Cross the intersection of 49 and Cold Springs Road and turn onto Church Street. One block down, turn right onto High Street. Inn is on the right.

J: *Dream on this: From a picturesque old church down the road, you arrive in a horse-drawn buggy at the inn for a reception around the gazebo. I'll bet someone would take a snapshot of that.*

Olive Metcalf

Vineyard House
Coloma, California
95613

Innkeepers: Gary, Frank, and Darlene Herrera, and David Van-Buskirk
Address/Telephone: Cold Springs Road (mailing address: Box 176); (916)
    622–2217
Rooms: 7 share 1 bath.
Rates: $54 to $64, double occupancy, continental breakfast included. No
    children under 16.
Open: All year. Breakfast, dinner, saloon, Sunday brunch. Closed Mon-
    day. Open 7 days a week May through September.
Facilities and local attractions: Gift shop; live entertainment in saloon
    weekends. Banquet and wedding facilities. White-water rafting,
    fishing; California State Gold Discovery Park, museums, antiques.
    Summer melodramas at Olde Coloma Theatre.

Naturally, there's a story behind a four-story house with a
ballroom (totaling 11,000 square feet) sitting in the rolling hills of
the gold country. Robert and Louisa Chalmers, vintners of fine
wines of the era, built the house in 1878. The wines and brandies
of Vineyard House pleased even that noted tippler, President
Ulysses S. Grant, who visited twice. When a blight wiped out
Robert's 500 acres of vines, the poor man went insane, finally
starving himself to death, and penniless Louisa opened Vineyard
House as a boarding house.

The present owners rescued the house in 1975 from total neglect. Stripping floors and walls, they completely refurbished the house. Today they have seven comfortably furnished bedrooms on the second floor, all with fine views of the mountains surrounding Coloma. Authenticity is maintained with one bathroom at the end of the hall.

This is a friendly, family operation marked by enthusiasm rather than elegance. Homemade and hearty describe most of the dining-room specialties: tureens of soup, big bowls of help-yourself-salad, freshly baked wheat bread, honey, and special desserts. The absolute favorite that keeps bringing the locals back is chicken and dumplings—slow-simmered chicken with a 2-inch topping of dumplings and gravy. A summertime Sunday brunch treat is waffles, piled high with fresh strawberries and whipped cream.

The old wine cellar downstairs is now a saloon. Cool brick walls make it an inviting retreat on a hot day. It also contains the remains of a late-nineteenth-century "stopover" jail. The parlor and a long veranda are two more spots where guests can relax.

Bay Area weekenders in gold country will appreciate a Sunday dinner that is served beginning at 4:00 P.M., allowing time to still drive home that night. River rafters often stop at Vineyard House before a trip and for a quiet recovery after the adventure.

How to get there: From Sacramento, take Route 50 to Placerville; exit at Highway 49; continue north to Coloma (Cold Springs Road). Watch for the Vineyard House sign on the left, just before Coloma.

✳

J: *An old graveyard across the road is fascinating for the story its markers tell about the days of gold fever.*

olive Metcalf

City Hotel
Columbia, California
95310

Innkeeper: Tom Bender
Address/Telephone: Box 1870; (209) 532–1479
Rooms: 9; all with private half-bath, share showers down the hall.
Rates: Balcony rooms $70; parlor and hall rooms $60 to $65, double occupancy. Theater and lodging packages. Ski package in season. Continental breakfast included. Children welcome.
Open: All year. Lunch, dinner, What Cheer Saloon. Saturday and Sunday brunch.
Facilities and local attractions: Stroll the town with its restored buildings, working weavers, blacksmith, harness, and saddle shops. Stagecoach rides. Fallon House Theatre. Special events: Fire Muster in May; old-fashioned Fourth of July Celebration; two-week Miners' Christmas Celebration.

Early one morning in Columbia, I walked alone down Main Street's boardwalk, passed a stagecoach and team standing by the Wells Fargo Office, saw a woman in pioneer costume opening her candy store, and listened to the barber outside his shop playing a tune on a harmonica. This is the heart of gold rush country, and no town captures that spirit better than Columbia.

In its gold-fever days, Columbia had forty saloons, 150

gambling houses, and eight hotels. Today the entire town is a state park, with tree-shaded Main Street barred to cars during the day to enhance the 1850–1870 atmosphere. But this is no static museum ghost town. Columbia is alive and bustling, and the jewel of the town is the City Hotel.

The two-story red-brick building has an upstairs parlor opening onto a wrought-iron balcony. A continental breakfast is served here each morning. Bedrooms are furnished with unusually impressive antiques, massive Victorian bedsteads, and marble-topped bureaus. Half-baths in each room are restoration additions, but showers down the hall are scarcely a hardship when you're provided with a wicker basket to tuck over your arm holding robe, slippers, and all the essentials.

The handsome, high-ceilinged dining room is an improbable surprise. Gold-rush-country explorers usually don't expect white linen, silver napkin rings, and haute cuisine. Try escargots or fresh bluepoint oysters while sipping a selection from the outstanding wine list. Then choose from twenty-four elegant entrees such as chicken braised in Madeira with morel mushrooms and walnuts. Complete your feast with a divine lemon soufflé that must be ordered ahead. That most necessary of mining-town establishments, the What Cheer Saloon, is the place for a nightcap and the local news.

How to get there: From San Francisco, take Highway 580 to Tracy, then 205 to Manteca. Take Highway 120 east, past Knights Ferry, to Highway 108 intersection. Continue on 108 east to Sonora; then Highway 49 to Columbia.

❋

J: *I know a man who insists that eating the lemon soufflé is like looking into the face of God. Understatement, apparently, is not his style.*

olive Metcalf

The American River Inn
Georgetown, California
95634

Innkeepers: Will and Maria Collin, Neal and Carol La Morte
Address/Telephone: Orleans Street at Main (mailing address: Box 43);
　　(916) 333–4499
Rooms: 18; 5 with private bath, 7 additional baths shared. 7 suites, all with
　　private bath. Queen Anne House separate from main inn, with 5
　　bedrooms, bath, living room, and kitchen. Facilities for the handi-
　　capped.
Rates: $61 to $71; suites $80. Full breakfast included.
Open: All year.
Facilities and local attractions: Pool, Jacuzzi, croquet, badminton, horse-
　　shoes, table tennis. Bicycles provided. Explore the gold country.
　　Rafting, kayaking, fishing on American River. Hot-air ballooning.
　　Antique/gift shop.

　　This is upscale, beautiful lodging for the gold country. But
that's only fitting for a town that in 1853 estimated it had mined
two million dollars in gold since the discovery in 1848. Once-rich,
booming Georgetown, which then enjoyed the more picturesque
name of Growlersburg, is now the setting of an ☞ impressive inn.
There's no escaping the fact that a lot of money has been spent
restoring the original American Hotel, but the four young innkeep-

ers have also lavished love, hard work, and attention to detail on the effort.

Antiques, polished pine floors, and bright provincial fabrics invite you into the attractive common rooms. In the late afternoon, the innkeepers serve local wines and hors d'oeuvres in the tasteful parlor. They'll also tell you about restaurants you can stroll to for dinner, or others a short drive away. Tall, handsomely draped windows, and antique tables and chairs are in the light-filled dining room. Breakfast here is a full production: fresh fruit (from the inn's own garden), juice, quiche or other egg dishes, Canadian bacon, berry muffins, and freshly ground coffee.

The spacious bedrooms have each been individually decorated and have luxurious bathrooms with thoughtful touches like robes. Rooms that open onto porches are especially pleasant. On a mid-week visit, when the town is quiet, these are delightful spots for reading in a comfortable wicker chair.

Besides the fresh mountain air and the clear rivers and lakes, history's footprints are everywhere in these foothills of the Sierra Nevada. ☞ Georgetown, itself, is well worth your time. It's a pleasure to see some of the stately homes built in the '70s and '80s, surrounded by well-tended gardens. Georgetown is one of those gold towns with charm but few tourists . . . always a winning combination.

If you're looking for adventure, the innkeepers will arrange hot-air ballooning, rafting, or kayak trips down the American River. They'll even provide the bicycles and pack you a luxury picnic basket to take along while you explore, and you keep the basket for future trips. But a look at the beautiful ☞ natural stone swimming pool or the Jacuzzi could easily persuade you that relaxing right here has a lot of merit.

How to get there: From Sacramento, take I–50 or I–80 to Highway 49 to Highway 193. Follow the signs to Georgetown. The inn is 2 short blocks from the junction of California 193 and Main Street. Fly-in: Georgetown Airport.

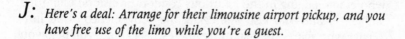

J: *Here's a deal: Arrange for their limousine airport pickup, and you have free use of the limo while you're a guest.*

Olive Metcalf

Murphy's Inn
Grass Valley, California
95945

Innkeeper: Marc Murphy
Address/Telephone: 318 Neal Street; (916) 273–6873
Rooms: 9; 7 with private bath, 4 with fireplace. Air conditioning.
Rates: $48 to $118 with full breakfast.
Open: All year.
Facilities and local attractions: Swim-spa; sun deck. Airport shuttle. Located in the heart of Grass Valley's historic district; walk to restaurants, unique shops, saloons, historic landmarks. Arrangements made for sporting activities; many performing arts events. Minutes from Nevada City.

The Sierra foothills are ☞ a sportsman's paradise—fish one day, ski the next. You can golf, pan for gold, go white-water rafting, and hike beautiful trails.

Marc Murphy is an avid participant in all these sports, and he also happens to have an inn. It's a great combination for those who enjoy lodging in the luxurious comfort of historic California ambience, but who also appreciate the convenience of an innkeeper who shares their sporting interests. ☞ Marc will help you fit it all in, make the arrangements, even shuttle you there if you wish.

Murphy's Inn is an elegant 1866 home built by one of the gold barons, Edward Coleman, owner of the North Star and Idaho mines. It's immaculately maintained, from the manicured, topiary ivy baskets hanging on the wide veranda, to the handsome sitting rooms with fireplaces and sparkling decanters of sherry set out for guests.

Beautiful pine, oak, and mahogany antiques are in every room. Four of the bedrooms have fireplaces, some have private entrances. There are large bathrooms, some with skylights and double shower heads. Two suites across the street in The Donation Day House are the latest Murphy refurbishment. Each consists of a king-sized bed, sitting room, fireplace, television, and private bath.

A big, cheerful kitchen and dining area has been added to the house. Marc can chat with guests while he makes "innkeeper's choice" breakfasts. There's always freshly squeezed juice, fruit, home-baked breads, and then whatever inspires him, maybe eggs Benedict, or sausage and hash browns. The house special is Belgian waffles.

Strangers are pleasantly surprised to hear about the many fine local restaurants. Right in Grass Valley, the Main Street Café and the Café Pomme de Terre (with a California Culinary Academy chef) are two of the best.

Any jet setter's opportunities for good entertainment and fun pale with the calendar of special events around here. The acclaimed Music in the Mountains series, theater, art shows, dogsled races, house and garden tours, Christmas Fairs—the choice is amazing. But staying at this pleasant inn and lolling on the sun deck or in the swimming pool–Jacuzzi spa isn't a bad choice either.

How to get there: From Highway 49, exit on Colfax (Highway 174), turn left at first stop sign. Turn left at second (two are close together) stop*light* on Neal Street. Proceed 3 blocks to inn on right corner of School Street. Fly-in: Nevada County Airport.

⚬⁊⚬

J: *The Grass Valley area is rich in gold-country lore. A few of the old residences remain, among them the frame house of the notorious Lola Montez.*

olive Metcalf

Hotel Charlotte
Groveland, California
95321

Innkeepers: Ruth and Jim Kraenzel
Address/Telephone: Highway 120 (mailing address: Box 787); (209) 962–6455
Rooms: 12; 2 with private bath, 4 bathrooms in hallway; 2 suites have bath in between; sinks in rooms.
Rates: $35 to $55, double occupancy, including continental breakfast. Ask about special package rates. Children welcome.
Open: All year. Breakfast, lunch, dinner. Dining room closed Tuesdays.
Facilities and local attractions: Private dining room available for parties. Explore historic town, old mine shafts. Close to Pine Mountain Lake 18-hole golf course; rafting launch point. Airport pickup available. Direct route (25 miles) to Yosemite entrance; road open all year.

Garrote was the name of Groveland back in gold rush days, when town names told a story. A horse thief was hanged here, and the descriptive name hung on for twenty years. When the western-looking Charlotte Hotel was built here in 1918, more civilizing influences had arrived. As "Groveland," the town had a second boom; it became the construction site for work on the Hetch Hetchy Dam, the system that brings water from the Sierras to San Francisco. When that flurry of activity ended, the town was deserted again.

Among the good reasons to seek out Groveland now is the Hotel Charlotte. Highway 120 through town is the 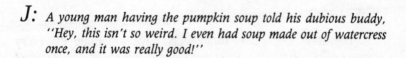 most scenic and direct route to Yosemite from the Bay Area, and the hotel's fresh, homey guest rooms are a comfortable stop on your way to the park.

The lobby has white wicker furniture, books, and games, and it also serves as the waiting room for the hotel dining room. Upstairs with the bedrooms is another sitting room. It's the kind of place you'll find comfortable when traveling with children. They can explore the hotel and the town on their own.

I arrived at lunch time on a beautiful, warm Halloween Day, which accounted for the creamy pumpkin soup on the menu. I tried and enjoyed. But the kitchen also turns out homemade biscuits, "beefalo" steaks, and a great Sierra-burger and fries. A continental breakfast is provided for hotel guests, but if you want to order from the menu, the popular favorite is Scramble of the Day: eggs with the chef's choice of additions.

Just a few miles away is the starting point for one of the great Sierra adventures—rafting the South Fork of the Tuolumne River. I hear that on an international scale of eight for rafting rivers, this trip gets a five—a white-water thriller.

Pine Mountain Lake is another attraction, only two and a half miles away. Its championship golf course has incredible views, and the air is wonderful.

How to get there: From Highway 120 or Sonora on Highway 49, follow signs to Groveland; drive into the town's one main street. Hotel faces the street. Fly-in: Pine Mountain Lake Airport. Hotel pickup in a '65 white Mercedes.

J: *A young man having the pumpkin soup told his dubious buddy, "Hey, this isn't so weird. I even had soup made out of watercress once, and it was really good!"*

273

Olive Metcalf

The Heirloom Inn
Ione, California
95640

Innkeepers: Patricia Cross and Melisande Hubbs
Address/Telephone: 214 Shakeley Lane (mailing address: Box 322); (209) 274–4468
Rooms: 6; 4 with private bath.
Rates: $50 to $85, including generous breakfast. No credit cards; no pets or small children.
Open: All year.
Facilities and local attractions: Beautiful setting for receptions. Bicycles available. Walking tour of Ione, antiquing. Explore surrounding Mother Lode area, Amador County wineries. Good restaurants nearby.

The Heirloom's two innkeepers have a handle on every nuance of hospitality . . . and they dispense it with 🖝 graciousness so genuine you'll know you've come across the real thing. Their thoughtful touches remain fresh and spontaneous—like appearing with a cold bottle of local white zinfandel and a couple of glasses while you're reading in the garden, or tucking a hot-water bottle in the foot of the bed on a cold night.

Their 🖝 antebellum brick house with classic, white Greek columns sits among towering old trees. It's filled with the innkeepers' personal furniture, china, silver, and antiques, including a splendid rosewood piano, said to have belonged to Lola Montez. The atmosphere is grand enough to be special, but so comfortable that perfect strangers feel quite at ease sitting in robes before the fire in the living room, sipping a late evening port.

Fireplaces, balconies, and private or shared baths are available in the four bedrooms in the house. In the springtime, we've often enjoyed the room with that name, with its private balcony surrounded by wisteria and magnolia.

A unique cottage with two accommodations is separate from the house. Its rammed-earth construction is as old as the Great Wall of China and as contemporary as environmental concern. All the earth scraped away to make room for the foundation makes up the walls and the sod roof. From the outside, the adobe house blends into its surroundings as if camouflaged. Cedar and redwood left in their natural finishes, skylights, wood-burning stoves, and handcrafted accessories give the inside a warm, tasteful ambience.

Breakfast is the leisurely, elegantly presented event that makes an inn visit memorable. Melisande and Pat, dressed in long skirts and pretty blouses, always look wonderful. They serve on beautiful china and pour from silver pots, and whatever the menu, the food is outstanding. There is always a fresh-fruit plate, homemade breads, muffins, and jams. The main dish might be soufflés, a quiche, or tender crepes filled with cream cheese and topped with fresh strawberries. To breakfast on a summer morning under a huge shade tree in this lovely yard is my idea of inn-heaven.

How to get there: All highways into Ione lead to Main Street. One block north of Main on Highway 104, turn down Shakeley Lane to the Heirloom sign on the left.

J: *Nobody does it better!*

Olive Metcalf

Gate House Inn
Jackson, California
95642

Innkeepers: Frank and Ursel Walker
Address/Telephone: 1330 Jackson Gate Road; (209) 223–3500
Rooms: 5; all with private bath.
Rates: $58 to $80 weekdays; $75 to $105 weekends, two-night stay tied
　　to Saturdays. Breakfast included. No credit cards; no children or pets.
Open: All year.
Facilities and local attractions: Swimming pool, screened-in barbecue room.
　　Walking tour of Amador County Museum, Jackson's historic houses,
　　churches, antique shops, restaurants. Explore nearby gold-rush
　　towns, wineries. Skiing at Kirkwood.

No really good innkeeper would bad-mouth another, but
lavish praise is not carelessly tossed around either. The Gate House
Inn is an exception. All around the Mother Lode, people speak of
the handsome house, elegant decor, and the "good job" the
Walkers do.

The buttercup-yellow Victorian mansion lives up to its reputation. It epitomizes Victorian charm, with peaked roofs, spacious
lawns, rose gardens, and a wisteria-covered pavilion. The summertime pool and 🖝 quiet grounds look out on the romantic
rolling terrain of gold country—380 acres of it owned by the
mansion's original family.

276

Through a beveled-glass front door is ☞ an interior grandeur matching that of the exterior. The original solid-oak parquet floors, Italian marble and tile fireplaces, an oak staircase, and many of the superb original wallpapers are in mint condition.

The Walkers have ☞ more than a hundred museum-quality antique clocks displayed throughout the house. The collection includes two rare grandfather clocks: one, with handpainted roses on the face, dates back to the 1700s; another, crafted of walnut burl, was created for Kaiser Wilhelm. More of their collection is at the Walkers' restaurant, The Sutter Creek Palace, in nearby Sutter Creek.

All five accommodations have queen-sized beds, private baths, and sitting areas, with antiques and fresh flowers. The Woodhaven Suite, formerly a nursery, is especially winning. It's lined from ceiling to floor with pine and furnished with a brass bed. A bank of windows looks out over the garden.

In the garden, a grape arbor leads to the fifth suite, the Summerhouse, with a cast-iron, wood-burning stove and an immense ☞ cedar-paneled bathroom with stained-glass windows from the Comstock mansion in Virginia City. Across the lawn is a barbecue area you are welcome to use if you tire of Jackson's Italian restaurants.

☞ Breakfast is served on lace and linen, with Royal Albert china that Ursel acquired as a child in Canada. A typical menu includes fresh fruits, yogurt, freshly baked muffins, pastries, and coddled egg. In spring, a camellia is on each napkin; in summer, it's a rose.

How to get there: Turn off Highway 49 onto Jackson Gate Road, just north of the intersection with Highway 88 from Stockton. Follow to the inn on the left.

Olive Metcalf

The Wedgewood Inn
Jackson, California
95642

Innkeepers: Vic and Jeannine Beltz
Address/Telephone: 11941 Narcissus Road; (209) 296–4300
Rooms: 4; all with private bath, tub, and shower.
Rates: $65 to $85, including full breakfast. Cannot accommodate children.
    No pets; no smoking.
Open: All year.
Facilities and local attractions: Walking trails through surrounding wooded
    area. Centrally located for shopping, sightseeing, dining, and special
    events in nearby Sierra foothill towns.

Vic and Jeannine Beltz are "nestors," collectors, and antique lovers, crazy for crafts, enthusiastic about their hobbies, and devoted to people. In other words—they *had* to become innkeepers. Their newly built Wedgewood Inn is the culmination of everything they like to do.

When Vic took an early retirement from IBM, he and Jeannine searched for a country property and built their dream house, a finely constructed, Victorian replica. Nestled on five wooded acres just six miles from Jackson, you nevertheless feel far from the bustle that goes with many foothill towns. As Vic says, "The only thing you hear are pine needles kissing in the wind."

Beginning at the front door's stained-glass inserts made by Vic, the house reflects the couple's many interests: the ambitious gardening he's begun, the grand piano from Austria that Jeannine plays, the Victorian lamp shades she makes (one has portions of heirloom lace from her wedding dress), her cross-stitch pictures and tapestry, and a collection of more than fifty dolls. Furniture and antiques collected for many years decorate the inn. There are spinning wheels from various countries, European tapestries hanging in the dining room, and accents from their travels around the world.

Whether you appreciate antiques or not, you will find these spacious bedrooms especially comfortable. Since the house is new, old-fashioned appointments like a wood-burning stove, a claw-footed tub, or a pull-chain toilet can be enjoyed without sacrificing a whit of comfort. I found the washstands Vic has made by inserting elegant sinks into antique dressers and chests especially attractive.

Antique car buffs will find a kindred soul in Vic. He'll show you "Henry," his 1921 Model T Ford that resides in the Carriage House.

When you arrive at The Wedgewood, cheese and a beverage refreshment are served in the parlor. Here is where guests who wish to can enjoy evenings of conversation, games, or singing around the piano. Morning brings coffee, ready and waiting for early risers. Later, a full breakfast will typically include Jeannine's homemade muffins, coffee, or poppyseed cake along with fruit compote, and an egg and meat entree. It's all served on bone china.

How to get there: Take Highway 88 east from Jackson 6 miles to 2,000-ft elevation sign. Turn right on Irishtown/Clinton roads. Immediately turn right on Clinton Road; go 0.6 mile to Narcissus Road. Turn left and go ¼ mile to the inn on the left.

olive Metcalf

Jamestown Hotel
Jamestown, California
95327

Innkeepers: Marcia and Mike Walsh
Address/Telephone: Main Street (mailing address: P.O. Box 539); (209)
  984–3902
Rooms: 8, including 7 suites with sitting area; all with private bath with
  tub and shower. King-, queen- and double-sized beds.
Rates: $45 to $95 double occupancy. Continental breakfast included.
Open: All year. Lunch, dinner, Sunday brunch, full bar.
Facilities and local attractions: Outdoor sundeck pleasant for weddings,
  private parties. Walk historic Jamestown; shops, antiques. Mother
  Lode exploring, gold prospecting tours. Ride Sierra Railroad.

Old West buffs come to Jamestown to walk picturesque Main
Street and to ride the Sierra Railroad's steam-powered locomotives
that pull tourists through the Sierra foothills. The Jamestown
Hotel is still another attraction, an absolutely ☞ smashing restoration accomplishment.

The Walshes have completely redone the hotel, from the old
brick exterior to the flamboyant gold-rush-style interior. A tidy
lobby, dining room, and inviting cocktail lounge are on the first
floor. Upstairs are eight antique-decorated bedrooms, all named
for personalities associated with the area's past—Jenny Lind, Lotta
Crabtree, Black Bart, Joaquin Murietta.

These are quaint Victorian-style rooms (seven are suites with sitting areas) with the distinct advantage of not *smelling* old. They're comfortable and immaculate, qualities that were, until recently, hard to find in the Mother Lode. Marcia has chosen colorful wallpapers as backgrounds for antique furnishings. Black Bart's floral bouquets on black and a black, claw-footed bathtub look particularly Victorian. I liked, too, the big portrait of "our next president," William McKinley, a Victrola, and an old eyeglass-salesman's case, complete with all the glasses.

The handsome dining room's wall covering is a fresh floral print on ivory with matching balloon draperies. Fresh linen, plants, and touches of etched glass fill the room with light at lunch time; during candle-lit dinners, the atmosphere is romantic. The dining room opens onto an attractive lattice-covered patio used for summer dining and special parties.

The hotel's kitchen has earned justly high praise. We started lunch with a basket of hot, puffy sopapillas. (*Try* eating just one!) Seafood salads, fresh, poached red snapper in white wine sauce, and spinach pasta with linquica and garlic sauce were the specialties the day I visited.

While this small hotel doesn't have quite the personal touch of an innkeeper's home, the staff is particularly friendly. A small plant-filled sitting room at the end of the upstairs hall opens onto a deck area with umbrellas and tables. This is a pleasant place to sit and sip on a summer evening while watching shadows on the foothills.

How to get there: From the San Francisco Bay Area, take Highway 580 to Manteca turnoff. Continue on Highway 108 30 miles past Oakdale to Jamestown. The hotel is on the right in the center of town.

✳

J: *As you gaze at the foothills surrounding Jamestown, remember: There are those who claim there's still "gold in them thar hills!"*

olive Metcalf

The National Hotel
Jamestown, California
95327

Innkeeper: Steve Willey

Address/Telephone: Main Street (mailing address: Box 502); (209) 984–3446

Rooms: 11; 5 with private bath, 6 with antique washbasins share 2 bathrooms. Rollaways, televisions available.

Rates: $45 to $55, including generous continental breakfast. Ask about lower mid-week and winter rates. Children under 10 by arrangement only.

Open: All year. Lunch, dinner, Sunday brunch; full bar.

Facilities and local attractions: Outdoor patio dining. Explore old gold-rush town, antique stores; home of steam-operated Sierra Railroad, Railtown 1897 State Park. Near cross-country skiing, backpacking trail heads. Forty-five minutes to Yosemite National Park entrance.

When you reach Jamestown, you get the 🐾 full flavor of what a Victorian-era gold-rush town was like. It was one of the boom towns, swarming with a sudden population bent on quick riches. If it looks familiar to you, it's because it's been used in hundreds of feature films, including *High Noon* and *Butch Cassidy and the Sundance Kid*. Our romantic attraction to those old towns continues, partly because of the picturesque buildings that remain and partly because of the natural loveliness of the Sierra foothills.

Like all gold towns, Jamestown has burned countless times, but the National Hotel is one of its survivors, operating since 1859. The Willey brothers have been working on its gradual restoration for over a decade, matching the façade to photos from the 1800s. Happily, it still looks much like the typical Old West hotel we've seen in movies—two stories with a balcony overlooking Main Street and a wooden sidewalk.

Inside is a ☞ massive, long bar (the original) with a brass rail and a splendid 1882 cash register; two dining rooms, and a stairway up to the bedrooms. The rooms are clean and cheerful with quilts, brass beds, and other antique furnishings. The atmosphere is a combination of nineteenth-century charm—pull-chain toilets—with twentieth-century comfort—modern stall showers.

The dining room serves lunch and dinner to the public—a classical cuisine ranging from escargots and gazpacho to steaks, veal saltimbocca, and lamb chops Dijon. The wine list is California with an emphasis on Gold Country vintages. A continental breakfast—fruit, breads, coffee, and tea—is for guests only. Photographs of the hotel and Jamestown's earlier days decorate the walls. Slow-moving brass fans, lace curtains, candlelight, and fresh flowers add still more to an inviting atmosphere. Adjacent to the dining room is ☞ a hundred-year-old grape arbor, a pleasant place for breakfast or for enjoying a bottle of wine after a day of exploring.

How to get there: From the San Francisco Bay area, take Highway 580 to the Manteca turnoff. Continue on Highway 108 past Oakdale 30 miles to Jamestown. You enter on Main Street. Hotel is on the right. Fly-in: Columbia Airport; hotel pickup service by arrangement.

olive Metcalf

The Palm Hotel
Jamestown, California
95327

Innkeeper: Jacob Barendregt
Address/Telephone: 10382 Willow Street; (209) 984–3429
Rooms: 9; 5 with private bath, 4 with sink in room share a large bath plus
    half-bath. Wheelchair access.
Rates: $55 to $100, including breakfast. Package rates for Sierra Repertory
    Theatre. No smoking preferred.
Open: All year.
Facilities and local attractions: Small seminars, weddings arranged and
    catered. Explore Jamestown, antique shops, Railtown 1897 State
    Historic Park. Ride Sierra Steam Train; gold-prospecting trips from
    livery stable. Near ski areas. Seven miles to Columbia State Park.

This old private home and one-time rooming house, situated
a block off Jamestown's historic Main Street, is completely remodeled and newly decorated. It's had the happy fate of being rescued
by Jacob Barendregt, a young innkeeper who has lived all his life
in this most western of gold-rush towns, but whose taste in decor
runs beyond that narrow trough into more cosmopolitan pastures.

Try to picture a dusty miner riding up Main Street past the
balconied buildings and heading for some R and R at The Palm. He
bellys up to the elegant marble bar in the reception room and
growls, "Espresso, please."

Maybe in a "spaghetti western," but surely not in old "Jimtown" . . . not in the "Gateway to the Gold Country"! But where is it written that you have to put up with nineteenth-century comforts just to explore the picturesque charms of an old town? The Palm is an attractive option for travelers who take their lodging seriously.

The inn's architectural flourishes give it an interesting exterior and an expansive, light-filled interior. The attractive lobby room (yes, there really is a marble bar and an espresso machine) is also where continental breakfast is set out. Two bedrooms are on this floor.

Up a broad, handsome stairway are the other seven bedrooms. Four of them have washbasins and share ☞ an elegant marble shower. ☞ A Thai canoe hangs over the stairwell like an enormous mobile. The rooms are attractively decorated with some wonderful antiques, and most have a sitting area. Amenities in the larger rooms include a television and a small refrigerator. The innkeeper's keenness for marble is seen again in the palatial bathrooms.

Intriguingly different windows are a feature of the restoration design. Small ones in various shapes are placed unexpectedly; large, tall arched ones have a stunning visual impact.

Jacob has lots of irons in the fire—he's opening a restaurant soon on Jamestown's main street, and he's running for local office, to name two—so he's not a hovering innkeeper. He serves a satisfying breakfast buffet that he maintains is continental, but conversation reveals he's a pushover and usually cooks whatever people ask for. He's also exceptionally knowledgeable about the Mother Lode scene and has dining, touring, and recreation suggestions.

How to get there: On State Highway 49, 3 miles south of Sonora. From Main Street, turn up Willow Street 1 block to inn on your left.

Olive Metcalf

Murphys Hotel
Murphys, California
95247

Innkeeper: Robert Walker
Address/Telephone: (mailing address: Box 329); (209) 728–3454
Rooms: 9 historical rooms share 4 baths; 20 separate motel units with
    private baths.
Rates: $37 to $55; continental breakfast included in historical-room rate.
Open: All year. Breakfast, lunch, dinner, full bar.
Facilities and local attractions: Walk the town; visit its museum. Explore
    surrounding historical towns, Mercer Caves, Calaveras Big Trees,
    Columbia State Historic Park. Many local wineries.

On a cold December morning, a fire burned cheerily in the
pot-bellied stove in Murphys Victorian lobby. A Christmas tree
filled the room with the fresh aroma of pine. In the dining room,
platters of sausage and hot bowls of oatmeal were bustled to the
tables as waitresses and locals bantered about weather and horses,
dogs, pickup trucks, and foaling mares.

On crisp, clear winter days like this, when tourists are back in
the city, old gold-rush towns show their true character. If authenticity is your delight, then ☞ quiet, little Murphys, "Queen of the
Mother Lode," is a must. It was once a major stagecoach route. A
few old stone buildings survive and stand near the hotel in the

center of town. Winding roads leading out to Angels Camp and Sheep Ranch are ☞ beautiful mountain drives.

But historic lodgings aren't for everyone. You have to be amused with floors that slant; tolerant of shared facilities; fascinated with walls of old photographs; and prefer stick-to-the-ribs fare instead of California cuisine. The picturesque hotel looks very little different today from the way it did when Ulysses S. Grant, Samuel Clemens, Horatio Alger, Henry Ward Beecher, and Black Bart were guests.

Grandest of all the historic bedrooms is the General Grant Room, with a splendid antique bed and a square piano that has been there as long as anyone can remember. The other bedrooms are smaller and are simply furnished with antique beds, dressers, and quilts.

The saloon and dining room on the main floor remain much as they were originally. A new chef, Marc Kirby, has expanded the no-nonsense menu of prime rib, steaks, liver and onions, and fried chicken to include pasta, a spinach salad, and several fresh fish choices. A continental breakfast delivered to guests (along with the morning paper) in the old historic rooms consists of coffee or tea, juice, and a homemade cinnamon roll.

The Mark Twain Ballroom upstairs opens onto a balcony with the original cast-iron railing. The Victorian room, with flamboyant cranberry red chandeliers, was decorated this day for a Christmas party.

A longtime citizen of the town, Elizabeth Kaler, wrote about the hotel in *Memories of Murphys:* "I think ☞ the balcony was the most charming. It has an old world air to it that has helped to make Murphys different. It was a rendezvous for friends both far and near."

How to get there: From Highway 49 east of Stockton, take Highway 4 east at Angels Camp to Murphys.

Olive Metcalf

The National Hotel
Nevada City, California
95959

Innkeeper: Tom Coleman
Address/Telephone: 211 Broad Street; (916) 265–4551
Rooms: 43; 30 with private bath. Air conditioning.
Rates: $39 to $95; EP.
Open: All year. Breakfast, lunch, dinner, full bar.
Facilities and local attractions: Swimming pool. Live music Saturday,
Sunday nights in bar. Walk Nevada City, shops, restaurants, antiques,
American Victorian Museum. Cross-country skiing nearby. Horse-
drawn carriage rides.

The old National Hotel is the centerpiece of the town. The ☞
broad veranda across the front of the building is the place to be for
gala celebrations and parades on the Fourth of July and Constitution Day. Sitting out here in the summer under an umbrella with
a cool drink is the perfect cat-bird seat for watching the passing
scene.

Nevada City was originally called Nevada before the state
came along and took possession of the name. Then the outnumbered citizens of the gold town had to add "City" to their town's
name. It still has much of the ☞ character of an 1850s mining
town with many old buildings and picturesque gas lamps along
Broad Street, the town's main street.

The atmosphere in the Victorian Dining Room and bar is decidedly Gold Rush—chandeliers, period floral wallpapers, velvet and satin love seats and chairs. The ornate bar was originally part of the dining room buffet in the San Francisco Spreckels mansion. In the old days, gold dust was the medium of exchange in the bar. It could be traded for tokens, some of which can be seen in the lobby and hallways along with other artifacts from the era.

The menu includes seafood dishes, as well as prime rib, steaks, and lobster tail. Pork specialties are a current kitchen interest. One they're proud of is roast pork with a fresh apricot and brandy sauce. At dinner your table is lighted by attractive coal oil lamps.

You'll be pleasantly surprised at the size of some of the suites—big bordering on huge—with a few of the bathrooms as large as an ordinary bedroom. There are small rooms, too, but plans are afoot to combine and enlarge most of them. These are not luxury rooms, but they do have a sense of history. Massive antique beds and armoires, floral wallpapers, and chandeliers give the rooms a Victorian feeling. As befitting the large rooms, some fairly sizable projects have been hatched in them, too: Pacific Gas and Electric (PG&E) was organized in suite 74.

Recent additions to room appointments are direct-dial telephones and televisions. Although some people feel that they detract from the old-fashioned ambience, Tom says there's a vocal guest list that feels shockingly deprived if they're absent.

How to get there: Follow Gold Rush Highway 49 north past Grass Valley. Take Sacramento Street off ramp to downtown Nevada City. The National is on the left.

☀

J: *Nobody asked me . . . but isn't there something contradictory about seeking out historic lodgings with authentic antique charm, and then wanting a television beside the marble fireplace or dear little Victorian settee?*

Olive Metcalf

The Red Castle Inn
Nevada City, California
95959

Innkeepers: Mary Louise and Conley Weaver
Address/Telephone: 109 Prospect; (916) 265–5135
Rooms: 8; 6 with private bath.
Rates: $65 to $95, including full breakfast and afternoon tea. No credit
    cards; not suitable for children or pets.
Open: All year.
Facilities and local attractions: Walking path to downtown shops, restau-
    rants, antiques in Nevada City. Local theater, musical events. Walk to
    mountain creek for swimming; cross-country skiing twenty minutes
    away; picnic baskets on request.

Almost eighteen years ago, a San Francisco architect and his
wife visited Nevada City and stayed at the Red Castle Inn. She fell
in love with the Victorian red-brick mansion, and they continued
to visit it through the years. The thought of ever owning it was
mere fantasy, but now that the Weavers have bought it from the
former innkeepers, Mary Louise says it is a case of a dream coming
true.

Hanging on a hillside nestled among dense trees, The Red
Castle is an ☛ impressive sight from many places around Nevada
City. The Gothic-revival mansion is wrapped in rows of white,

painted verandas and lavished with gingerbread trim at roofline and gables. From the driveway, walk around a veranda, with stylish canvas draperies tied back at each pillar, to the front of the house, where you can survey the historic mining town's rooftops and church steeples.

Since it was built in 1857, the castle has had a succession of caring owners who have maintained it without compromising its elegant period character. The Weavers have brought not only their respective professional skills in architecture and design but also some 🖝 impressive art, including several Bufano sculpture pieces, and fine furniture. Eight guest rooms range over the four floors, each one of them a vibrantly decorated, tasteful delight. Most furnishings are Victorian, but not fragile or frilly. An explosion of color from wallpapers, fabrics, and rugs has an engaging effect in combination with the dramatic architecture. Two garret rooms on the top floor share a sitting room, bath, and balcony. It was from here that the original owner's son used to serenade the town with impromptu trumpet concerts.

A cozy sitting room off the entry hall has cushy upholstered sofas, wingback chairs, and an inviting collection of art books. We helped ourselves to an elegant tea spread here and took it outside. Three small terraced gardens, one with a fountain and pond, are idyllic sitting and strolling areas. A path through cascading vines leads down to Nevada City's main street.

The Weavers are proud of their vintage inn and are enthusiastic about Nevada City. They'll arrange a horse-drawn buggy tour of the town, and they always have good suggestions for restaurants and local events. We had an outstanding dinner at The Country Rose Cafe.

The 🖝 lavish breakfast buffet is a splendid sight—all of it homemade. Ours was typical, but the menu varies everyday: juice, poached pears, glazed fresh strawberries, a baked egg curry with pear chutney, cheese croissants, banana bread, jams, Mary Louise's Grandmother's bread pudding (what a treat!) with a pitcher of cream, and, of course, great coffee.

How to get there: From Highway 49 at Nevada City, take Sacramento Street exit to the Exxon Station; turn right and immediately left onto Prospect Street. The driveway takes you to the back of the house. Walk around the veranda to the front door.

Olive Metcalf

Ye Olde South Fork Inn
North Fork, California
93643

Innkeepers: Virginia and Darrel Cochran
Address/Telephone: 57665 Road 225 (mailing address: Box 731); (209) 877–7025
Rooms: 9 share 3 bathrooms. Cribs available.
Rates: $49 to $85 for family room that sleeps seven; includes expanded continental breakfast. No pets; smoking outside only. Children welcome.
Open: All year.
Facilities and local attractions: Eight miles to Bass Lake with all recreational facilities; 28 miles to Yosemite gate. Loggers Jamboree first weekend of July; Indian Fair first weekend of August.

You may well wonder where on earth you are when you wind your way into this out-of-the-way village, but Virginia Cochran can tell you precisely. "We're in the exact center of California," she says. "People sometimes think we're gold-rush country, but we're not. This is the ☞ gateway to Yosemite and the Ansel Adams Wilderness Area."

The inn that she and husband Darrel have in this remote area is a dandy place to stop over before you head on to Yosemite Park. Or if you've been out camping for a few days, this is a convenient place to regroup, shower, and have a good night's sleep in a clean, comfortable bed.

By all means, bring the children—this is their kind of relaxed, easy place. The living room has a television and opens into a large common room. When it's not being used for breakfast, all the tables and chairs are handy for games. A piano is here, too, and boxes of toys.

The nine bedrooms accommodate flexible sleeping arrangements for families, with daybeds and cribs. The rooms are simple and fresh, with country antiques and ceiling fans.

There's not an acorn-ful of pretension here. It's western-style comfort, where the beautiful scenery at hand overrides indoor decor. You're not going to find Ye Olde South Fork Inn in *House Beautiful,* but you will find comfortable beds and warm hospitality.

The Cochrans (Darrel is retired Navy) have lived in this foothill community for sixteen years. They know the area well and are helpful in directing you to mountain attractions you might otherwise miss.

This Sierra foothill community, like so many others, does quite happily without shops or chic, but the local events are rousing. The two biggies are the Loggers Jamboree in July and the Indian Fair in August. Ask Virginia, also, about dates for the Mountain Peddler's Flea Market.

How to get there: From Highway 99 at Madera, follow Highway 145 to Route 41. From Fresno on Highway 99, take Highway 41 immediately. Continue north toward Yosemite about 30 miles to O'Neals. Follow signs to North Fork. Proceed through village to South Fork. Inn is on the left.

✳

J: *Virginia sells her knitting to boutiques. If you arrive just before she sends off a shipment, as I did, you'll get first pick of some fine handmade sweaters.*

Olive Metcalf

The Chichester House
Placerville, California
95667

Innkeeper: Nan Carson
Address/Telephone: 800 Spring Street; (916) 626–1882
Rooms: 3; all with half-bath and share bathroom with tub. Air conditioning; no smoking.
Rates: $60 to $65, double occupancy. Full breakfast included. No credit cards.
Open: All year.
Facilities and local attractions: Elegant library and parlor for relaxing. Historic Placerville, Gold Bug Park, and Gold Bug Mine and Park. Short jaunt to Sutter's Mill, foothill wineries. Antiques, shops, and restaurants.

"Woody and I want to have an inn where people want to come back" and "I don't like to sit someone down with a croissant and call it breakfast." Nan Carson says that these are her and her husband's two philosophies of innkeeping. You just *know* you're going to be well taken care of when you hear sentiments like these.

The Carsons' 🐕 handsome Victorian home was built in 1882 to be the finest residence in Placerville. It's believed to have been the first house in town with built-in plumbing. Some grand houses of this vintage are interesting but a little musty and dusty. Not Chichester House. The antiques are the real McCoy, and they, like the house, are beautifully restored and well maintained.

The Yellow Rose Room is the largest of the three and has a half-bath. There's a wonderful old Pullman car fold-up sink that Woody has polished within an inch of its life. A sunny sitting area in the bay window, in a corner a dressmaker dummy in vintage costume, great robes to relax in, and little touches that delight the eye are everywhere in the room. On the blazing hot day of our visit, we had no quarrel with a departure from authenticity by way of air conditioning.

As for that breakfast *sans* croissant, it begins with freshly brewed, especially aromatic coffee and tea on the dining room buffet at 7 A.M. The room's fresh flowers and gleaming silver enhance the bounty to be served a little later. Maybe it will be a beautiful fresh-fruit plate, eggs Benedict so good they make you remember why they became popular, and Nan's county-fair blue-ribbon prize muffins.

For dinner, the Carsons will help you choose from a variety of restaurants. They highly recommend Zachary Jacks, a French restaurant just five miles away in Diamond Springs. We tried Mama D. Carlo's, within walking distance, where we had good pasta. As Woody says, Placerville is not a gourmet capital, but the food is hearty. "The trick is to find someplace that serves small portions."

Back at Chichester House, enjoy the library and parlor. When you retire, you'll find that Nan has turned down your bed. You never get that kind of attention at Motel Six.

How to get there: From Sacramento, take Highway 50 to Placerville. Exit at Highway 49 North (Spring Street). Make the next 3 right turns on Coloma, High, and Wood streets to parking behind the house.

✳

J: *Nan hangs "little surprises" everywhere around the house or tucks them in drawers to amuse you when you explore—like a dainty old-fashioned, batiste romper suit with drop-seat.*

Olive Metcalf

The Combellack-Blair House
Placerville, California
95667

Innkeepers: Jim and Cec Mazzuchi
Address/Telephone: 3059 Cedar Ravine; (916) 622–3764
Rooms: 2 share 1 bath.
Rates: $70.20 (tax included) double; $64.80 single. Full breakfast included. No credit cards or smoking. Not convenient for children.
Open: All year except Thanksgiving and Christmas weeks. Closed Monday and Tuesday.
Facilities and local attractions: Relax on the porch swing and appreciate this house. Walk to town with parks, shops, and restaurants. Visit nearby Gold Discovery Park, foothill wineries.

This ☛ elaborate, late Victorian, Queen Anne home is too special to miss if you are in the area. Do two guest rooms make an inn? Perhaps not, and even Cec Mazzuchi herself says, "This is more a home than a business. But I didn't want to get too commercial. If I only use two rooms for guests, I can take care of everybody the way I like to."

The Combellack-Blair House was just recently placed in the ☛ Register of National Historic Houses, and it is a jewel. The

296

Mazzuchis have lived here fifteen years but have been innkeeping for only the past four.

Naturally, there are antiques throughout the house. The owners are completely aware of the responsibility of living in a masterpiece and have chosen the decor with care and taste. The two guest rooms have everything necessary for comfort, starting with good beds and pretty linen.

The full breakfast Cec serves features freshly ground coffee, juice, fresh fruit, and blueberry muffins with honey butter. Then there is bacon or sausage and sourdough pancakes made from her own starter. She also does a baked egg dish. Cec is so serious about authenticity that she even grinds her own flour for her home-baked breads.

Looking at a house like this seems always to bring Christmas to mind. Last year a local theater group decorated the house and did a Christmas program. It would be an especially pleasant time to visit.

How to get there: From downtown Placerville, follow Cedar Ravine Street north to the house on the left.

☀

J: *Placerville started out as Dry Diggings and descended to Hangtown for awhile. The El Dorado County Historical Museum has some interesting exhibits of gold-rush times.*

Olive Metcalf

Fleming Jones Homestead
Placerville, California
95667

Innkeeper: Janice Condit
Address/Telephone: 3170 Newton Road; (916) 626–5840
Rooms: 6; 4 with private bath, 2 share 1 bath. Wheelchair access.
Rates: $60 to $80; singles $5 less; 3 nights for price of 2 Sunday through
  Thursday, September 1 to June 1. Includes full breakfast. Smoking
  only on decks and balconies. Children by arrangement. No credit
  cards.
Open: All year.
Facilities and local attractions: Enjoy porch swing, garden, animals, and
  shaded woods. Convenient base for day trips to gold-rush towns,
  foothill wineries, Apple Hill fruit orchards. "Picnic supper in a
  basket" available by arrangement. Garden weddings, receptions,
  business meetings accommodated. Good local restaurants. Spanish
  spoken.

When you have a yen to leave big city woes behind you and
return to the simple satisfactions of rural life, this 1883 farmhouse
in the Sierra foothills is a satisfying place to try. It was under a
cloudless blue August sky that we drove up the lane to the back
garden. An American flag flapped in the breeze from an upstairs
porch; flowers, fruit trees, and vegetables were growing in an

amiable hodge-podge; and a dozen or so exotic chickens roamed the yard. The aroma of honeysuckle, roses, and green grass was pure summer.

Innkeeper Janice Condit and Rocky, the "fetchin' dog," greeted us. She is a rural whirlwind, very much the capable 1980s woman, and proof that all female entrepreneurs aren't in offices wearing dress-for-success suits. Besides running her inn and an expanding catalog business for her farm's products, she grows vintage roses, organizes an annual tour of some of the Mother Lode's most beautiful gardens, nurtures her fancy-breed chickens, and plays cello for the Sierra Symphony. Just your average down-home farm girl.

You enter through the back door to the kitchen that looks and smells like a country boutique. Rows of county fair blue-ribbon preserves and jellies gleam on counters and cupboards in addition to potpourri (some packaged and some drying in bowls), herbal vinegars, and fresh farm eggs—all for sale; all Janice's enterprises.

As you pass through into the dining room and parlor, you'll notice that not all the animals are outside. Dozens of stuffed ones have seats of honor and hidden perches throughout the house. The parlor also has a 1917 Steinway grand that Janice invites guests to try. She is a trained concert pianist and especially likes to have guests bring instruments with them to play along with her.

We had the large room upstairs with windows on two sides, an extra single bed to use as a sofa, and a door out to the upstairs porch. This shaded, plant-decorated porch has squeaky old wicker chairs and is an inviting vantage place for dozing or surveying the farm.

Breakfast was particularly relaxed around the oak dining room table. Most guests had already been out to watch the chickens and ponies have their morning nosh; really participatory guests even help with the feeding. I preferred the porch swing and the morning paper, but aromas from the kitchen were too good to dawdle when the call for breakfast came. You feel you're honestly back to basics, knowing ☞ the eggs, fresh fruit, and preserves for the homemade muffins all came from the farm where you slept.

How to get there: From Sacramento take Highway 50 east to Placerville. Continue through the town. Exit right at Newton Road. At the end of exit road jog right to a stop sign. Turn left onto Broadway. It becomes Newton Road. Continue 1.4 miles to the inn's driveway on the right.

olive Metcalf

River Rock Inn
Placerville, California
95667

Innkeeper: Dorothy Irvin
Address/Telephone: 1756 Georgetown Drive; (916) 622–7640
Rooms: 4, including 1 suite; 2 with private bath; 2 with half-bath share a
full bath and stall shower. Television, air conditioning.
Rates: $65 to $80, single or double occupancy. Full breakfast included.
Children welcome; pets discouraged. No credit cards.
Open: All year.
Facilities and local attractions: VCR. Hot tub on deck. Rafting, fishing;
touring gold country, Marshall State Park, antique stores, wineries,
restaurants.

Some people might *tell* you their inn is on a river, when you
can see it from only an upstairs bathroom window; Dorothy Irvin
really *means* it. Her contemporary house is situated smack-dab on
a glorious section of the American River. And this is ☛ central-
casting river: sparkling, white water rushing over rocks and
roaring in your ears. It's understandable that TV film companies
like using it, most recently for a commercial.

Three bedrooms and the large deck are on ☛ eye level with
the river, perfect for uninterrupted viewing. Once down the
driveway, gate closed, you'll feel totally removed from the bustle

of Placerville tourists. Ease into a large, beautiful hot tub on the deck, or walk down the expansive yard and put your feet into the water.

This is a comfortable, unpretentious house. Rooms are pleasant and nicely furnished, but if you aren't out watching the river, the hub of activity is the kitchen and living room. Some freshly baked treat is usually sitting there tempting you. The living room has a large fireplace, sofa and chairs to snuggle into, books, games, and a TV if you're at wits' end.

Breakfast here definitely falls into the category called "full." Dorothy calls it a ☞ gold-country breakfast. Typically, it might include fresh juice, apple crepes, eggs Benedict, Dorothy's own baked rolls or baking powder biscuits, homemade jams, and fresh fruit. (Lunch, anyone?) This is served on the deck or in a glassed-in breakfast room that looks out at the river.

If you can tear yourself away from enjoying the river from the deck, Dorothy will help you arrange for one- or two-day raft trips with qualified guides. She'll also prepare a dinner or picnic lunch for you, by special arrangement.

It's not surprising that most of Dorothy's guests are repeaters. Some of them settle in for a week or two, leaving only for dinner at one of the nearby restaurants.

How to get there: From Placerville, take Highway 49 (Coloma Road) north to intersection of Highway 193 (Georgetown Road) leading to Chili Bar. Cross the American River and turn left immediately on first road, which leads to the inn.

☙

J: *A stack of books, the American River, and thou.*

Olive Metcalf

The Robins Nest
San Andreas, California
95249

Innkeeper: Robin Brooks
Address/Telephone: Highway 49 (mailing address: Box 1408); (209) 754–1076
Rooms: 8; all with private bath.
Rates: $55 to $95; mid-week winter rate $55 for any room available. Extended breakfast, evening wine and snacks included. Cash or personal checks. No pets. Children over 12 welcome.
Open: All year.
Facilities and local attractions: Luncheons and dinners arranged for parties of six or more. Wedding and small seminar facilities. Mystery and Western weekend parties arranged by reservation.Central location for exploring entire Mother Lode. Year-round local events. Gold-panning tours; skiing, good restaurants nearby.

When Robin Brooks finished restoring this Queen Anne Victorian, she had the original builder's ninety-year-old daughter as her first guest and put her in the very same room in which the woman had been born. The old lady recognized the elegant old bathtub but insisted that the pull-chain toilet must have been a recent addition. "Mother said that there are *some* things you just don't do in the house!"

By those genteel standards, Robin made an aesthetic mistake when she added all the new bathrooms; by any other measure, Robins Nest is an outstanding addition to gold-rush lodgings.

Robin left the world of Los Angeles real estate to turn the 1895 house—vacant for forty years—into a colorfully decorated inn. In the sitting room, she has mixed comfortable furniture with antiques, including a grand piano that gets frequent workouts.

Three bedrooms on the main floor and five new ones upstairs each have a unique decorating theme—a mode of transportation in California at the turn of the century. The carriage, balloon, bicycle, and train are all remembered with wall hangings, prints, and artifacts. The rooms are cheerful and spacious, with gabled ceilings and expansive views. The Steamship Room looks out at an old windmill on the property. In addition to the modern bathrooms, all rooms also have delightful brass lavatories, faithfully polished to a warm sheen.

Robin is an enthusiastic innkeeper brimming with ideas and a dash of the unexpected. Her breakfast buffet will almost always introduce you to something new. How about fresh plum juice for a change, or a frittata of apples and Monterey Jack cheese? She also makes a variety of homemade breads, quiches, and crepes.

Evening wine in the sitting room is the time to look through Robin's collection of local restaurant menus for dinner suggestions. When you return to the inn, she'll have brandy waiting, a turned-down bed, and candy on your pillow. You're invited to find your own snacks in the kitchen if hunger strikes at odd hours.

How to get there: San Andreas is on Highway 49 between Angel's Camp and Jackson. The inn is on the west side of the highway at the north end of town; parking in back. Fly-in: Calaveras County Airport.

❋

J: *Robin distributes a bimonthly newsletter keeping guests up to date on all the area's activities—and they're legion! Craft fairs, fiddle festivals, jumping frog contests, and Black Bart Day are just a few.*

olive Metcalf

Gunn House
Sonora, California
95370

Innkeeper: Peggy Schoell
Address/Telephone: 286 South Washington Street; (209) 532–3421
Rooms: 25; all with private bath, television, air conditioning.
Rates: $40 to $65, tax included, with continental breakfast, bar snacks.
Children welcome.
Open: All year. Full bar.
Facilities and local attractions: Swimming pool. Walking tour of town's heritage buildings, Tuolumne County Museum and Jail. Five miles to Columbia State Park, theater; 3 miles to Sierra Railroad in Jamestown. Fishing, boating, backpacking, antiquing, panning for gold.

Gunn House is one of the relics of Sonora's past when it was "Queen of the Southern Mines." It was the first two-story adobe structure in town, built in 1850 by an enthusiastic newspaper editor, Dr. Lewis C. Gunn.

But Sonora is not a sleepy gold-rush town. It's a hub of commerce and the county seat of Tuolumne County. The busy crossroads lead to the Mother Lode, the recreational wonderlands of Sonora Pass, and Yosemite National Park over Tioga Pass.

The house was restored by owner Margaret Dienelt in the

early '60s. This was before antique stores dotted the countryside, and she had to scour the area for the antiques and accessories that now decorate the Victorian rooms. She acquired some handsome period pieces—settees, carved chairs, marble-topped tables—and has combined them with the practical comforts of air conditioning, televisions, and private baths.

Gunn House is on heavily trafficked Washington Street, but being on a steep hill gives it several levels of 🖝 covered verandas and patios in back. It is quieter here. There is no sitting room, but tables and chairs are on these verandas and around the oval swimming pool.

The Josephine Room is a small barroom with marble-topped tables. In the morning you'll find a continental breakfast here—coffee, fruit, and rolls. When full bar service opens in the afternoon, the public, as well as inn guests, drop by.

Up and down Washington Street are a variety of restaurants, but making the biggest noise currently is 🖝 Hemingway's, just a block east of the inn. It has an intimate, attractive decor featuring photographs of the author, and an ambitious San Francisco–style menu. While I attacked an excellent carpaccio, the waiter assured me solemnly that the recipe was directly from Harry's Bar in Venice, "one of Papa's favorite hangouts." I felt more literary with every swallow.

How to get there: Take Highway 120 from Manteca east to join Highway 49, the Gold Rush Highway. Follow into the center of town. Turn right at stoplight (Washington Street). Inn is 2 blocks down on the right.

Olive Metcalf

Jameson's
Sonora, California
95370

Innkeepers: Virg and Jean Birdsall
Address/Telephone: 22157 Feather River Drive; (209) 532–1248
Rooms: 4 share 2 adjoining baths.
Rates: $45 to $60; breakfast included. Ask about special winter package rates including dinner and theater; mid-week skiing package at Dodge Ridge. No credit cards; smoking on outside decks only; no pets.
Open: All year.
Facilities and local attractions: Extensive in-house library, games, pool table. Close to boating, fishing, skiing, riding. Gold panning; Mother Lode exploring; colorful local events.

Although Sonora is Jameson's mailing address, the inn is actually located ten miles east of town and a hundred miles away in atmosphere. Jameson's is a beautiful contemporary house that nestles into its ☞ wilderness setting so perfectly that it almost disappears.

It was built over a creek among enormous granite boulders, waterfalls, and centuries-old oak trees. Large expanses of glass and deck give every room the effect of being outdoors. Bedrooms open to decks where the ☞ sound of the waterfalls, both front and rear, can be enjoyed in the tranquil environment.

The atmosphere inside is utter comfort, tasteful and relaxed. This is a smoothly run operation by charming innkeepers with antennae alert to their guest's desires. They'll drive to meet you if you're concerned about navigating the back roads. They're brimming with ideas for exploring the Mother Lode or just good conversation if it's company you want. But if it's a quiet haven you're seeking, they'll leave you with good music, books, refreshment, and solitude to absorb the natural beauty all around you.

Jean puts a note in your room so that you can specify when and where you will take breakfast. The back deck looking at the waterfalls is a lovely spot, but when the trees are touched with snow, you'll welcome a spot by the fireside indoors.

Each of the guest rooms is beautifully appointed and completely different from one another. One is decorated in sunny yellow and greens for an Irish flavor; Charmaine has French touches; Maria Elena, in bold reds and beige, overlooks the deck and creek. Scheherazade is the ☛ enchanting bridal suite decorated in an exotic paisley print with canopied bed, beaded screen, brass, and even a few peacock feathers. Robes that match the decor are in each room.

The entire house is so inviting and conducive to nestling in, it's perfect for an anniversary or occasion when you don't have to leave first thing in the morning. Besides, Jean's home-baked breakfast muffins, coffee cakes, and breads ("I've never had to fall back on a bakery yet!") are reason enough to linger.

How to get there: From traffic light in central Sonora, follow Highway 108 south for 7.6 miles. At Mono Vista/Soulsbyville exit turn left across Highway 108 for 0.2 mile. At Longeway Drive turn right for 0.7 mile. At Chrystal Falls Drive turn left; follow 1.4 mile to stables. Turn right onto Feather River Drive for 0.6 mile. Watch for mailbox on left (22157); turn up driveway on right. Fly-in: Columbia Airport.

olive Metcalf

Lavender Hill
Sonora, California
95370

Innkeeper: Alice Byrnes
Address/Telephone: 683 South Barretta; (209) 532–9024
Rooms: 3; 1 with private bath, 2 share 1 large bath.
Rates: $50 to $60, including full breakfast. No credit cards.
Open: All year.
Facilities and local attractions: Walking distance to downtown Sonora restaurants, shops. Explore surrounding historic gold-rush towns; Columbia State Park. Dodge Ridge ski area; good stop for Yosemite trip.

The gold country has long lured California history buffs to explore its beautiful countryside and colorful towns. You could always find lodgings rich with authentic ambience and history—qualities less sentimental travelers call dusty, musty, and old. But something new is happening on the scene. Inns are now opening that are often still in charming old buildings, but they're being architecturally restored and freshly decorated for comfort.

The Lavender Hill is a premier example of the new trend. It sits on one of Sonoma's quiet streets above the town, as pretty and appealing as a sedate Victorian lady. A soft shade of dove gray covers its turn-of-the-century lines, and an immaculate newly planted yard, flowers, and trees surround it.

Inside is period charm with polished wood floors, spacious rooms, and tall ceilings, but all newly restored and clean. The attractive entryway has a captivating ☞ working, white iron stove. Opening from here are two elegant parlors and a sunny dining room, all furnished comfortably rather than in prim, hard Victorian. Guests are invited to make themselves at home.

A handsome stairway leads up to the bedrooms. At present, Alice uses only three of them for guests. The largest is the ☞ Lavender Room, named for its luscious carpet color. A few judiciously chosen antiques and colorful linens make an appealing room.

Breakfast is generous here—fresh fruit, perhaps scrambled eggs, and always, says Alice, something fresh from the oven like whole-wheat bread or cinnamon rolls. For other meals, Sonora has a range of restaurants from hearty Italian to the continental Hemingway's. You can walk to many of them.

The house is a lovely setting for a wedding. When I visited, Alice was looking forward to hosting members of the Northern California Inn Association. When they see this quiet, elegant inn above the bustle of Sonora, they'll be glad they came.

How to get there: From downtown Sonora, take Highway 108 east out of town. At Safeway Store on right, get in center lane; make first left onto South Barretta. Inn is on the right.

Olive Metcalf

La Casa Inglesa
Sonora, California
95370

Innkeepers: Mary and John Monser
Address/Telephone: 18047 Lime Kiln Road; (209) 532–5822
Rooms: 5, including 1 suite with whirlpool tub; all with private bath, queen-sized bed.
Rates: $55 to $80 Sunday through Thursday; $70 to $95 weekends and holidays, taxes included. No credit cards. Full breakfast included. No smoking indoors. Cannot accommodate children or pets.
Open: All year, except Christmas.
Facilities and local attractions: Hot tub; pond on grounds. Old gold mine area to explore. Nearby gold-rush towns, antique shops, restaurants. Close to fishing, golf, water sports. Dodge Ridge skiing 30 miles.

What a surprise to see a grand English-style country house in the wooded foothills of the Sierras. La Casa Inglesa is one of the Mother Lode's newest inns and is on its way to becoming one of the most elegant. Mary Monser's Hispanic background accounts for the inn's name and its unique blending of two cultures.

The Monsers built their home on the Kincaid Flat, the site of the former Kincaid Gold Mine. The old mine shaft lies sunken near the center of a two-acre pond on the property. The day we arrived gardeners were planting a large flower garden in the front lawn;

Mary says it will be the variegated English kind. Another lower garden is down by the pond.

I like the feeling of the fine oak paneling in the entryway and throughout the formal dining room. It's impressive but still welcoming. A large, comfortable but somewhat formal living room with a fireplace is for guests to use.

The spacious guest rooms upstairs embrace you with the charm of pitched ceilings. Decorated with appealing wallpapers and quality fabrics, they're fresh and airy and have queen-sized beds and wonderful bathrooms. The grand suite is the largest and has an opulent bath with a whirlpool-spa. I was smitten with another room that looked very English to me. It might be the white-and-green floral wallpaper, or maybe the iron bed, but it's probably the ☞ grand oak bathtub sitting in a bay that stroked my Anglophile tendencies. For one mad moment, I fantasized Alistair Cooke soaking there. A patio and hot tub are on this upper level of the house.

You don't go B&Bing to hang around someone else's kitchen, but this one will knock your socks off. Mary says people do tend to wander in . . . and stay. Brick and blue tiles are the background and accent color for all the finest culinary appointments, the star being a handsome ☞ wood-burning cook-stove in an arched brick enclosure. And if kitchens don't turn you on, the gourmet breakfast that comes out of it will: fresh fruits of the season, a variety of Mary's homemade breads and jams, and a main course specialty.

How to get there: Take Highway 49 south through Sonora. At the intersection with Highway 108 just before the Safeway Store, veer right onto Lime Kiln Road. Continue 2½ miles to the inn on the left. Fly-in: Tuolumne County Airport 4 miles north of Sonora.

olive Metcalf

The Foxes
Sutter Creek, California
95685

Innkeepers: Pete and Min Fox
Address/Telephone: 77 Main Street (mailing address: Box 159); (209) 267–5882
Rooms: 6 large suites, all with private bath and queen-sized bed; 3 with cable television, 3 with fireplace. Air conditioning; covered parking.
Rates: $70 to $115, with bountiful breakfast. Singles deduct $5. No children or pets. Smoking outside only.
Open: All year.
Facilities and local attractions: Walking tour of Sutter Creek historic buildings; restaurants, antiques, specialty stores, art galleries.

The six elegantly decorated suites at The Foxes are the ☞ zenith of Mother Lode luxury. When they bought this historic house, Realtor Pete Fox and his wife, Min, an antique dealer, thought they would simply combine their businesses under one roof. But Min's flair for creating beautiful settings meant "goodby antique store, hello innkeeping." Pete keeps his office on the first floor, but Min spends all her time pampering guests and making every room a picture.

Their name was an easy handle for a symbol. You'll see ☞ foxes—fluffy, stuffed, patched, toy, ceramic, funny, and artistic—

312

throughout the house. But Min's lavish decorating goes far beyond a cute theme. Her handsome house is the background for outstanding antiques and her knack for putting things together with great taste.

Three spacious rooms are in the main house, and three are in the carriage house. You can't go wrong with any choice since every room is not just elegant but comfortable. If you enjoy beautiful rooms, you should try arriving before all guests check in for a chance to see more of them.

The Honeymoon Suite is the only downstairs room and has a private entry. It is an opulent setting, with a large brick fireplace, a latticed-front Austrian armoire, and a demi-canopied bed with a Victorian burled walnut headboard. Fabrics are sumptuous in a creamy blue and camel. A crystal chandelier sparkles in the adjoining bathroom with matching wallpaper and balloon window draperies.

Upstairs are Victorian and Anniversary suites. A Louis XIV tapestry in rich burgundy and cream sets the color scheme for the first suite. There's also a 9-foot Victorian headboard and matching dresser, an adjoining room as your breakfast chamber. The Anniversary Room has a cathedral ceiling, a massive Viennese walnut armoire deeply carved in a rose motif and an old-fashioned tub.

Breakfast is "cooked to order," says Min, so they can cater to any special dietary restrictions. She takes your order the previous night, and Pete turns out beautiful fruit compotes, eggs any style, bacon or ham, sourdough toast, and jams. Whatever the menu, it arrives on an impressive silver service and is arranged on the elegantly appointed table in the sitting area of each room. It does feel posh to lounge in your "jamies," pouring coffee from a silver pot and scanning the morning paper that's been delivered to your door.

How to get there: Sutter Creek is on Highway 49, which becomes Main Street in the center of town. The inn is on the west side of the street.

J: Don't rush it. The longer you're here, the more elegant touches you'll see.

Olive Metcalf

The Hanford House
Sutter Creek, California
95685

Innkeepers: Lucille and Jim Jacobus

Address/Telephone: 61 Hanford Street (mailing address: Box 1450); (209) 267–0747

Rooms: 9; all with private bath, queen-sized bed, air conditioning. Access for the handicapped and special facilities in one room.

Rates: $55 to $100, including extended continental breakfast. No-smoking; no pets.

Open: All year.

Facilities and local attractions: Innkeeper knows American sign language for the deaf. Mid-week small groups and meetings welcomed. Take walking tour of Sutter Creek, historic houses, antique shops, art galleries, restaurants. Golfing, skiing nearby. Many local wineries.

Modern comfort in California country ambience is the atmosphere at the Hanford House. A 1930 cottage is at the core of a handsome two-story brick building with ample off-street parking in front. Jim Jacobus calls it "old ☞ San Francisco warehouse style," but you must understand that there are some very chic warehouses in that city.

The interior of the cottage at the nucleus of the inn has a Spanish feeling, with soaring whitewashed beams. It consists of a delightful parlor, with brightly slip-covered sofas, antique pine tables, magazines and plants, and some of the many teddy bears that hibernate at the inn.

The new brick wing has guest rooms with luxurious baths, and they are furnished in a captivating mélange of California country, early American, and nineteenth century pieces. Jacobus bought the inn from antique dealer Ron Van Anda (who also designed and constructed Hanford House)—collection and all.

On the top floor is a large suite with a fireplace. A 🖝 common deck up here overlooks the rooftops of Sutter Creek and the foothills. It's a choice spot to take your morning coffee—ready at 7:30 A.M. along with a newspaper.

Breakfast is a relaxed affair served at separate tables between 8:30 and 9:30 A.M. in the dining area. Juice, fresh fruit, and a selection of cheeses, muffins, or sweet rolls make up the continental fare, with your choice of hot beverage.

Jim's past experience as a Bay Area stockbroker and Lucille's former position in a mental-health agency seem remote from life in the Sierra foothills, but now they're both enthusiastic converts to country life. They're eager for guests to know about points of interest and good restaurants around Sutter Creek. Right next door is the 🖝 Pelargonium Restaurant and Gallery, which serves elegant California cuisine. Around the corner is The Palace, whose reviews get better and better.

How to get there: Highway 49 runs through the center of Sutter Creek. At the north end of town where the Highway divides, turn left. Immediately on your left is the inn.

Olive Metcalf

Sutter Creek Inn
Sutter Creek, California
95685

Innkeeper: Jane Way
Address/Telephone: 75 Main Street (mailing address: Box 385); (209) 267–5606
Rooms: 18; all with private bath, electric blankets, and air conditioning.
Rates: $45 to $100, full breakfast included. Children discouraged. Two-day minimum on weekends. No credit cards; no pets.
Open: Closed Thanksgiving and the day before, Christmas Eve, and Christmas Day.
Facilities and local attractions: Handwriting analysis by appointment. Enjoy inn's gardens, hammocks, library, and games. A good town for walking: art galleries, antiques, historic houses, restaurants.

When the subject is California inns, the talk invariably goes to the Sutter Creek Inn and Jane Way. ☞ Jane started the phenomenon of country inns in this state twenty years ago. In fact, she's become a legend in her own time. Former guests like to swap stories about what she did while *they* were there: Jane captivating her guests with tales of the house ghost; Jane doing handwriting analysis; Jane ladling brandy into your before-breakfast coffee; Jane and the famous swinging beds. Her boundless energy and flair have made the Sutter Creek a prototype for country inns.

On a busy street of shops, restaurants, and overhanging balconies, the Sutter Creek Inn is a charming New England–style residence surrounded by a green lawn, trees, and flower beds. Some bedrooms are in the main house, others in outbuildings in back that Jane has extensively remodeled and decorated with great ingenuity. Their names recall Sutter Creek's gold-rush history—Wood Shed, Lower Wash House, Tool Shed, Miner's Cabin.

Each room is completely different. Nine have fireplaces, some Franklin stoves, some private patios; others open onto the garden. And there are the ☞ swinging beds—an idea Jane discovered in Mexico—but not to worry, they can be stabilized if you wish. Room appointments are cozy and comfortable, right down to the selection of magazines and books. During the winter months, guests are welcomed with hot spiced cider and homemade cookies; in summer it's fresh lemonade.

Gathering in the beautiful living room for coffee before breakfast is the quintessential inn experience. Jane holds court, introducing guests and overseeing breakfast. When the breakfast bell rings, you move to four polished pine tables in the large cheerful kitchen.

The meal might include eggs a la Sutter Creek (baked in cream cheese sauce and served on an English muffin) or pancakes full of chopped apples and nuts, served with blackberry syrup and ham. Hot biscuits or muffins and fresh fruit and juice put you in a benign glow for the day. Or is it Jane's coffee?

How to get there: Sutter Creek is 4 miles north of Jackson on Highway 49, which runs through the center of town. The inn is on the west side of the street.

❀

J: *Pick up a copy of the* Stroller's Guide to Sutter Creek *at any store along Main Street. It will lead you to the back streets of older buildings and interesting stores.*

Olive Metcalf

Mayfield House
Tahoe City, California
95730

Innkeeper: Janie Kay
Address/Telephone: 236 Grove Street (mailing address: Box 5999); (916) 583–1001
Rooms: 6 share 3 baths. King-, queen-, and twin-sized beds.
Rates: $65 to $100, including 1 suite. Continental breakfast and complimentary wine. No children; no pets. Wheelchair access.
Open: All year.
Facilities and local attractions: Walking distance to shops, restaurants, tennis courts. Free buses to Squaw Valley and Alpine Meadows skiing 10 miles away. Hiking, bicycling, boating; all the attractions of Lake Tahoe.

Mayfield House is an agreeable alternative to motel or condo digs while you enjoy the mountain air of Lake Tahoe. The house is a fine example of 🖙 old Tahoe architecture. It was built in 1932 by Norman Mayfield, one of Lake Tahoe's pioneer contractors. Refurbished in 1979, it is comfortable and traditional in atmosphere, serene rather than chic. It's the kind of place to read and relax in.

All the bedrooms have down pillows, down comforters, and robes. They each have a sitting area, very cozy if you like breakfast served in your room. In the '30s, one room, now called Julia's Room, was always reserved for Julia Morgan, the architect of San Simeon and a personal friend of the owners'. It's a surprisingly feminine, simple room in contrast to many of her projects. She designed several estates along the west shore of Tahoe for which Mayfield was the contractor. Much of her work was done here at his home.

The Mayfield Room is the master suite upstairs. It has a sitting area, dining area, and king-sized bed. One of the bathrooms up here features a 6-foot-long tub installed by the tall owner who evidently liked to stretch out while he soaked.

On the main floor, the wood-paneled former office of Norman Mayfield is decorated in brown, beige, and rust plaid. With its outside door, it offers easy access for a wheelchair.

The Margaret Carpenter originals on the walls and fresh flowers lend a pleasant feeling to the large living room. With its fireplace and snuggly sofas, it's a cozy place to read and enjoy your complimentary wine in the afternoon.

Continental breakfast is served in the dining room, unless you choose the quiet of your bedroom or the patio. There are juice, seasonal fresh fruit, cheeses, and homemade pastries along with coffee and teas.

How to get there: From San Francisco, take Highway 80 to Truckee; turn south on Highway 89 to Tahoe City. Turn north on Highway 28 to Grove Street; turn left.

$$*$$

J: *One of the most talked-about restaurants in northern California is here in Tahoe City. Wolfdale's has a small, sophisticated menu of exceptional cuisine that changes frequently. Try a summertime lunch on the deck overlooking the lake.*

Olive Metcalf

Alpenhaus
Tahoma, California
95733

Innkeepers: Pat and Vern Lucas
Address/Telephone: 6945 West Lake Boulevard (mailing address: Box 262);
 (916) 525–5000
Rooms: 9; 7 with private bath; 6 housekeeping cottages.
Rates: $55 to $85; $12 per extra person. Winter ski package. Full breakfast
 included. Children welcome.
Open: All year.
Facilities and local attractions: Restaurant; full bar. Swimming, hiking,
 biking, tennis, Ping-Pong, horseshoes. Nearby Lake Tahoe attractions.
 Two miles from downhill skiing at Homewood; one-quarter mile
 from Sugar Pine Point State Park for cross-country. Basque nights
 (accordion music) Wednesdays.

The fresh invigorating air of this beautiful area can be
downright inspiring. Some people claim it even caused them to
give up smoking. Tahoma, situated on the west shore of Lake
Tahoe, is known for a little more quiet beauty than other parts of
the lake. You can quickly get to the nightspots and gambling if the
fever strikes, but Alpenhaus seems to lure skiers and hikers to its
more country-like atmosphere in the trees.

Most guests were enjoying the pool the hot day I visited, but the inn's Swiss Alpine look is especially appropriate with snow on the roof—and they get plenty of it. Skiers are only minutes away from both ☞ Alpine and Nordic skiing.

The cheerful dining room has a rich green carpet, and pictures and objects reveal a European touch. It's the scene of three meals a day—big breakfasts, light lunches, and robust dinners. Swiss and German specialties are featured—hearty soups, sauerbraten with spätzli, fondues, and raclette.

☞ Basque night is a popular Wednesday night event that really brings people in. Typical, authentic Basque food is served family style in big bowls accompanied with much toasting, accordion music, and—before you know it—singing. You don't leave Basque night a stranger.

The entire inn was refurbished just a few years ago. Now a small lounge area with a stone fireplace and a bar provides a place for guests to get acquainted. It's casual, with a friendly atmosphere you'll feel the minute you walk in. Upstairs, the bedrooms are plain and neat, with hand-painted wood furniture and thick comforters for cold mountain nights.

The cottages with living room, fireplace, and kitchen are a good bargain for families. There's nothing like fixing a few of your own meals to make a vacation more affordable. These are well equipped and cozy.

How to get there: From Sacramento, take Highway 80 to Truckee and Highway 89; continue south to Tahoma. Inn is on the right of the highway.

Olive Metcalf

Oak Hill Ranch
Tuolumne, California
95379

Innkeepers: Sanford and Jane Grover
Address/Telephone: 18550 Connally Lane (mailing address: Box 307);
 (209) 928–4717
Rooms: 4; 2 with private bath and queen-sized bed; 2 with double
 bed share 1 bath. 1 cottage (sleeps 5) with private bath, kitchen,
 fireplace.
Rates: $55 to $75, double or single; $15 per extra adult. Full breakfast
 included. No children; no pets; no smoking. No credit cards; personal
 checks okay.
Open: All year.
Facilities and local attractions: Walk beautiful countryside. Explore southern
 Mother Lode. Near Dodge Ridge skiing; 63 miles to Yosemite. Sonora
 restaurants.

 Discovering Tuolumne is a delightful experience, but the
capper is to follow a country back road another mile past town,
then up the lane to this gracious ranch home. The Grovers say
their 🖝 Ranch Victorian was completed in 1980, but it's actually
110 years old. Since they began collecting Victorian building
materials and furniture more than twenty-five years ago, the
house has been their dream.

It was designed by their architect son in the '70s, but years of stripping old wood (and an understanding contractor) were required before the dream came to life. The result is the period ambience of tall ceilings, wide hallways, and authentic wood detailings in an immaculate background of modern kitchen, plumbing, and heating. If you're from condo-land, the generous size of the house alone is a pleasure.

The 🖝 setting is spectacular, on a wooded hill overlooking miles of rolling terrain with the Sierra range in the distance. On a crisp October morning, the Grovers, 🖝 in period costume, welcomed me into an inviting living room with a fire burning in the fireplace, fresh flowers, and refreshment. It was downright pastoral ensnarement.

A wonderful floral carpet sets the tone of stylish, uncluttered, Victorian charm. The upstairs and downstairs bedrooms have fetching decors, one with a canopied bed, another opening to a balcony that overlooks pastures and ponds.

Your hosts (retired educators) are naturally hospitable, and they're adamant about always putting their best foot forward. They'll help you choose restaurants in the area and point out some beautiful drives to take.

Many innkeepers endeavor to make breakfast a special treat, but the Grovers know that it's not just a lot of food that makes the occasion special, it's serving it with style. When guests gather for an Oak Hill breakfast in the impressive dining room (it must be more than 20 feet long), Jane, in long skirt and ruffled cap, and Sandy in crisp shirt and arm bands, make the morning memorable. The menu may feature quiche, baked eggs, or French toast, always freshly made in their large farm kitchen and engagingly served.

How to get there: From Sonora, take Highway 108 to Tuolumne Road; follow to center of Tuolumne. Turn south on Carter Street to the schoolyard, left onto Elm Street, and right on Madrone Street, which turns into Apple Colony Road. Follow to Oak Hill sign on left. Fly-in: Columbia Airport; inn pickup.

olive Metcalf

Twain Harte's Bed and Breakfast
Twain Harte, California
95383

Innkeepers: El and Pat Pantaleoni
Address/Telephone: 18864 Manzanita Drive (mailing address: Box 1718);
  (209) 586–3311
Rooms: 6; 2 with private bath, 4 with sink in room share 2 baths.
Rates: $40 to $65 double occupancy, includes full breakfast. Ask about ski
  and theater packages. Children welcome.
Open: All year.
Facilities and local attractions: Pool table, television. Walk to downtown
  Twain Harte. Hike surrounding woods; fishing, hunting, boating,
  water skiing. Close to Yosemite; Dodge Ridge Ski Resort (cross-
  country and downhill).

Mark Twain lived and wrote around this area, and Bret Harte
lived here for a time. It's beautiful country just to walk in and
enjoy quietly, but the variety of recreational activities in the area
make Twain Harte an 🖝 exceptional headquarters for family
vacations.

This rambling inn welcomes children and makes it convenient
for parents to bring them. An unpretentious living room with a

fireplace opens to a spacious recreation room complete with a pool table, games, and television. A family suite upstairs can sleep six. It has a large living room and kitchen with a microwave oven for fixing your own snacks.

A big sun porch upstairs is a sunny place to play. El says several people have had winter weddings up here. In summer, the outdoor decks are perfect places for a mountain wedding.

Newly expanded skiing facilities at Dodge Ridge make lodging at Twain Harte all the more interesting. Families who used to ski all day and then face a long drive home will enjoy coming back to Twain Harte for dinner at one of the good restaurants nearby, then a cozy evening at the inn. After a comfortable sleep and a hearty breakfast, you can be off to ski again.

A long glassed-in front porch is the breakfast room. The entire house is heated with wood, and a huge farmer's boiler in here serves as a unique and efficient stove. The morning menu is usually a fruit combination, eggs poached or scrambled, bacon or sausage, and muffins.

The gold-rush town of Columbia is only fifteen miles away with many attractions, including a theater company. One of the inn's promotions is a package that includes dinner at Twain Harte's Villa D'Oro Restaurant, theater tickets to the Columbia Actors Repertory, and a night and breakfast at the Twain Harte, all for $95 per couple.

How to get there: From Sonora, take Highway 108 to Twain Harte. Just past the town center, look for Manzanita Drive; turn right. Inn is on the left, across from schoolyard. Guest parking behind.

olive Metcalf

Saint George Hotel
Volcano, California
95689

Innkeepers: Marlene and Charles Inman

Address/Telephone: 2 Main Street (mailing address: Box 9); (209) 296–4458

Rooms: 20; 14 on two floors in hotel share a bath and a half-bath on each floor; 6 separate motel units, all with private bath.

Rates: Rooms start at $38, breakfasts $6. Weekend MAP, approximately $45 per person including dinner and breakfast.

Open: Closed Monday and Tuesday and first six weeks of year. Dinner Wednesday through Sunday by reservation; breakfast weekdays if requested. Full bar.

Facilities and local attractions: Facilities for meetings; luncheons arranged for 20 or more. Walk every square inch of Volcano; visit original jail, stone ruins of Wells Fargo, "Old Abe." Close to other historic gold towns, shopping, antiques, restaurants. Indian Grinding Rock State Park.

Volcano is a ☞ highlight of any Mother Lode tour, the most picturesque of all the gold-rush towns. Its enduring charm is that it doesn't change. Located a few miles off Highway 49, it has somehow remained aloof from gentrification, beautification, supermarkets, gas stations, neon, and boutiques!

During its heyday, more than ninety million dollars in gold was taken from the hills and gulches around Volcano and poured into the United States Treasury. It was during the Civil War, and the issue of whether the gold would go to the north or the south was decided by virtue of the abolitionists in town having "Old Abe." The ancient cannon (which would have been more of a threat had there been any cannonballs to go with it) was never tested. The abolitionists prepared by gathering stones from the riverbed for ammunition, but the outnumbered southern sympathizers retired from the fray.

The Saint George Hotel is *the* can't-miss landmark on Main Street. The modest three-story structure is admittedly crumbling, but vine-covered balconies give it an Old West appeal I can't resist. From them, you can look out over the quiet town (population eighty-five) and the rolling hills of the beautiful countryside. The spring wild flower display on nearby Daffodil Hill is one of the wonders of the Gold Country.

The two upstairs floors contain simple bedrooms, some of them quite large, with shared baths at the end of the hall. Each is decorated with antiques and crocheted bedspreads. A modern annex is available with private baths, but only the hotel has the old-time flavor. On the main floor are the dining room and the lounge, notable for a floor-to-ceiling mirror cracked by what everyone chooses to believe is a bullet hole.

Dinners on weekends offer a single entree: prime ribs of beef on Saturday and spring chicken on Sunday. Hearty soups, breads, and desserts are made at the hotel.

How to get there: Five county roads lead into Volcano, each a winding route through the foothills. Try the road east from Jackson on Highway 88 to Pine Grove, then north on Volcano–Pine Grove Road to Volcano. Beautiful.

❋

J: *Volcano is not exactly life in the fast lane, as evidenced by the posted business hours of the Outhouse Antiques: "Mon. Tues. Wed. Thurs. closed. Fri. Sat. & Sun. open 12–3."*

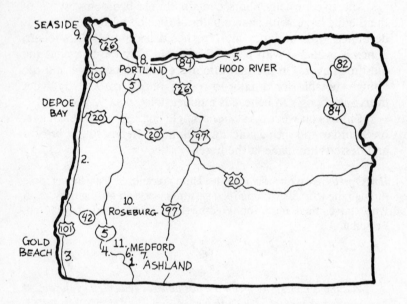

N

SEASIDE
9.

26

8.
PORTLAND

84

5.
HOOD RIVER

82

101

5

26

DEPOE
BAY

20

20

97

84

2.

20

42
ROSEBURG

10.

97

GOLD
BEACH

101

5

11.
4. 6. 7.
1.

MEDFORD

ASHLAND

3.

Oregon

Numbers on map refer to towns numbered below.

Olive Metcalf

Chanticleer Bed and Breakfast Inn
Ashland, Oregon
97520

Innkeepers: Jim and Nancy Beaver
Address/Telephone: 120 Gresham Street; (503) 482–1919
Rooms: 7, including a suite with kitchen; all with private bath and direct-dial telephone.
Rates: $70 to $130, includes full breakfast.
Open: All year.
Facilities and local attractions: Walk to Ashland theaters, restaurants, Lithia Park, shops. Convenient to Rogue River white-water rafting, Mt. Ashland skiing. Facilities for small business conferences.

With the success of its Shakespearean festival, Ashland has become a mecca for bed and breakfast inns. In the past year I've collected a file of clippings about them, mostly letters written to travel editors from past visitors singing the praises of one particular inn—the Chanticleer. Now that I've been there too, I can appreciate the enthusiastic chorus. It's undoubtedly one of the most attractive, romantic inns in Ashland.

The name comes from Chaucer's tale of Chanticleer and the fox, a European barnyard fable. That's the feeling here—cozy and

European. The country living room has a warm appeal with its blue rug, rock fireplace and hearth. Comfortable, cushy furniture, books, and an ever-welcome tray of sherry complete the picture. I'm always favorably predisposed toward *any* room that includes these amenities.

Everything about you looks freshly painted and is immaculate. If you're not off to a matinee, it's a pleasure to spend your day at this inn. Some of the rooms overlook Bear Creek Valley and Cascade foothills; others open onto a brick patio and a perfectly lovely rock garden.

The seven cheerful bedrooms are engagingly decorated with crisp linens, cotton slipcovers on puffy goose-down comforters, wallpapers, and fresh flowers. Complimentary toiletries and thick towels appoint your private bath. Several of these rooms accommodate a family of four nicely.

Jim and Nancy think of many ways to be obliging. They're endlessly helpful in choosing where to have dinner, and what to see in the area. But most thoughtful, I think, is having in your room copies of all the current plays running in Ashland's three theaters. Wonderful for resolving after-the-play discussions.

Everyone who stays here raves about the breakfasts, and with good cause. Even the orange juice and fresh fruit seem tastier than when you prepare them at home. Maybe it's Jim and Nancy's solicitude for everyone's comfort, or perhaps it's the lively conversation with other guests that accounts for this. Of course, the baked pears with orange sauce, blintzes, quiche, or shirred eggs with cream, the hot breads and blueberry muffins, the superb coffee and teas have something to do with it, too.

How to get there: Driving north to Ashland on I-5, take exit 11; proceed along Siskiyou to Iowa Street, and turn left. At Gresham Street, turn right. Inn is on your right.

❋

J: *The Beavers are professionals in a business with a lot of willing amateurs. They give highly regarded workshops on the how-tos of innkeeping.*

Olive Metcalf

Hersey House
Ashland, Oregon
97520

Innkeepers: Gail E. Orell and K. Lynn Savage
Address/Telephone: 451 North Main Street; (503) 482–4563
Rooms: 4; all with private bath and air conditioning.
Rates: $65 single to $90 for three persons; full breakfast included. No
   credit cards; children over 12 welcome. Smoking on the porches.
Open: All year except October to mid-April.
Facilities and local attractions: Walk to Ashland theaters, shops, restaurants,
   Lithia Park. Explore nearby historical mining town of Jacksonville.
   Biking, golf, tennis, fishing, water sports available locally.

   No car; no hassle. Those are two great advantages of Hersey
House. It is open almost exclusively for the Ashland theater
season, and you couldn't choose a more comfortable or convenient
place to nestle in while you see it all.
   Ashland's beautiful theaters—including the experimental and
conventional as well as the outdoor Elizabethan Stagehouse—are
as highly regarded as the talent they draw. But what makes
Ashland pure pleasure for theater lovers is the ☛ low-key
atmosphere and the easy way you can take it all in. A few days of
first-rate theater in the beautiful setting of the Rogue Valley can
easily diminish the allure of more high-powered, metropolitan
theater seasons.

At graceful Hersey House, you can have afternoon wine or tea while the innkeepers tell you about the enticing range of restaurants you might try for dinner, and all of them are just a stroll from your inn and the theaters.

The house was built in 1906, and five generations of the Hersey family lived there. When the present owners converted it into an inn, they were careful to keep the Victorian charm while they entirely updated and refurbished it. They evidently succeeded, even in the eyes of Hersey family members, who have lent the inn some ☞ grand family portraits of the first Herseys to live in the house. The portraits now hang in the stairway.

There are only four guest rooms, but each one is a beauty, tastefully decorated in airy floral prints, several with matching wallpaper, a queen-sized bed and tiled bath. The Sunshine Terrace Room has a private balcony and a view overlooking the Cascade foothills; the Eastlake Room has a view of Mt. Ashland.

Breakfast in a theater town inn is especially congenial because the conversation has an immediate hook: What did you see? . . . What did you think of it? . . . Where did you have dinner? The innkeepers stoke the talk with freshly brewed coffee and herbal teas, fresh juice and fruit, and home-cooked delights that change daily, like orange nut bread and Eggs Hersey.

How to get there: From I-5, take exit 11 into Ashland. Proceed north along Siskiyou, which becomes Lithia Way, then North Main Street. Inn is on the left.

olive Metcalf

The Morical House
Ashland, Oregon
97520

Innkeepers: Joe and Phyllis Morical
Address/Telephone: 668 North Main Street; (503) 482–2254
Rooms: 5; all with private bath and air conditioning.
Rates: $70, double occupancy, $5 less for single. Weekday discount when
  outdoor theater is closed. Winter rates, November through February,
  $55. All rates include full breakfast.
Open: All year.
Facilities and local attractions: Walk to Ashland theaters, restaurants, shops.
  Skiing at Mt. Ashland.

Theater is the main reason people from all over the world
flock to Ashland. The Oregon Shakespearean Festival performs a
three-play repertory from June through September in the outdoor
Elizabethan Stagehouse and a season from late February through
October in the two other theaters.

But gorgeous scenery has always been Oregon's primary
attraction for travelers, and Morical House offers some of the best.
The 1880s house is surrounded by an acre of lawns, rocks, shrubs,
and more than a hundred varieties of trees, and it looks out on a
panoramic view of Bear Creek Valley and the Cascade Mountains.

When the Moricals decided to quit their California government jobs and become innkeepers, they visited a number of cities before choosing Ashland and this house. It is only a fifteen-minute walk to the theaters and a wide range of restaurants, but all of Ashland is a delightful walking town.

They have restored the house as a comfortable country inn with tasteful attention to its period charms such as stained-glass windows and detailed woodwork. The traditional nineteenth-century house has undergone many additions during the years in a way that makes the downstairs floor plan unconventional but entirely pleasing. Several light-filled sitting rooms, with comfortable sofas and chairs and well-stocked bookshelves, call you in to enjoy them. A kitchen you're invited to use for a quick snack, an ice machine, and a ready tea kettle all make this an inviting house to nestle in.

To fully take advantage of the inn's vista, the Moricals added a glassed-in porch across the back of the house. Eating one of the house breakfast treats, like Dutch pancakes, here, with the sweeping view before you, is a splendid beginning to the day.

Beautifully decorated bedrooms are upstairs, with mountain views and non-Victorian comforts of private baths, air conditioning, and soundproofed walls. The very private third-floor room is a favorite. What bliss to soak in a grand old claw-footed tub and read a play you'll see performed that night.

How to get there: Driving north on Highway 5, take exit 19 at Ashland. Follow to the inn on the left.

∽✿⌁

J: Real *Ashland theater buffs go to both matinee and evening performances. But this pleasant inn gives you a ticket to such a scene-stealing panorama of sky and land that it could easily become your matinee performance choice.*

Olive Metcalf

Mt. Ashland Inn
Ashland, Oregon
97520

Innkeepers: Jerry and Elaine Shanafelt
Address/Telephone: 550 Mt. Ashland Road (mailing address: Box 944);
  (503) 482–8707
Rooms: 4; all with private bath, queen-sized bed, and individual thermo-
  stat.
Rates: $60 to $70, including full breakfast, afternoon snacks, and beverages. No smoking; no pets. Special rates at Christmas and during
  theater season.
Open: All year.
Facilities and local attractions: Hearty snacks available when arranged
  ahead. Hiking, nature walks. Cross country, downhill skiing. Ashland Shakespeare Festival February through October.

A late April snow was falling as I drove up the road to Mt.
Ashland, making the passing scenery all the more breathtaking. At
5,500 feet, just two miles from the summit, the beautiful Mt.
Ashland Inn sits nestled in the Siskiyou Mountains 16 miles south
of Ashland, a snug haven of 🖝 outstanding craftmanship and
hospitality.

The cedar log structure was hand-crafted by the Shanafelts
from lumber cut and milled on the surrounding property. But

336

don't picture a cottage in the woods improvised by a couple with some land and a chain saw. Jerry's remarkable design and woodworking skills are apparent everywhere your eyes rest—in hand-carved mountain scenes on the doors, the decorative deck railing, log archways, stained-glass windows, and a ☛ unique log-slab circular staircase. Most amazing to me were the twelve Windsor chairs he made one winter, each one a smooth, perfect piece of art.

The peeled log walls of a common room draw you in with the warmth of cushy furniture, brilliant oriental rugs, mellowed antiques, and a stone fireplace. Can you imagine how the fire, music playing softly, and hot mulled wine hit me on this cold afternoon? Right. It was sleepy time in the mountains.

Each of the four guest rooms upstairs has a ☛ view toward Mt. Shasta, Mt. McLaughlin, or some part of the Cascades. When I looked out the window in the morning, the fir trees were thickly frosted with snow, and I felt like Heidi in Oregon. But pretending I was roughing it in the wilderness just wouldn't fly in the face of all the comforts: big chairs with reading lights by the windows, a queen-sized bed topped with a handmade quilt, and the woodsy aroma of cedar filling the air.

Breakfast in the dining room was fresh juice and fruit and a tasty entree of puffy orange French toast. Daffodils on the table were picked that morning as they popped through the snow.

If you must stir from this comforting cocoon, a cross-country skiing path that ties into old logging roads is out the back door. Two miles up the road, Mt. Ashland offers fairly demanding downhill skiing. For hikers, the Pacific Crest trail passes right through the property. The premier attractions in the area are the Ashland theaters, about a 25-minute drive (to good restaurants, also) from here.

A bonus of being up the mountain is that when Ashland is covered in clouds and fog, you're often in a pocket of sunshine here.

How to get there: North on Highway 5 take Mt. Ashland exit 5, turn right under the highway. At stop sign turn left, parallel highway ½ mile. Turn right on Mt. Ashland Road to ski area. Inn is 6 miles from the highway.

olive Metcalf

The Winchester Inn
Ashland, Oregon
97520

Innkeepers: Michael and Laurie Gibbs
Address/Telephone: 35 South Second Street; (503) 488–1113
Rooms: 7; all with private bath.
Rates: $59 to $89, depending on the season, double occupancy; breakfast
   included. Winter packages available. No pets.
Open: All year. Dinner, Sunday brunch.
Facilities and local attractions: Two blocks from Ashland theaters, Lithia
   Park; one block from shops, restaurants. Convenient for river rafting,
   skiing. Dickens Christmas Feast; special wine-maker dinners. Winter
   murder mystery weekends.

West Coast inns that offer meals are few and far between. The
Winchester Inn is the 🖙 only one in Ashland that serves dinner
to the public as well as to inn guests.

This inn is a graceful Queen Anne Victorian in Ashland's
downtown historic district. It was first a private home; then it was
Oregon's first hospital. White and stately, with a broad front
porch, it looks engaging from the outside, and once you enter the
handsome double doors, you'll not be disappointed inside, either.
Pale-rose carpeting runs from the entry, through the impressive
parlor with leaded-glass windows, and up the stairs to the
bedrooms.

I was there for Sunday brunch and thoroughly enjoyed the atmosphere in the glassed-in dining room. A Vivaldi tape was being played in the background, and my view of the colorful terraced gardens provided a delightful setting. Warm-weather breakfasts are served on an inviting patio decorated with clusters of potted flowers, where you can sit at umbrella tables under the trees.

Champagne, orange juice, and a coffee cup kept refilled soothe you while studying the menu. As you sip away enjoying the music and flowers, you're served ☞ hot scones with the house nut-butter and marmalade.

Entree choices that morning were eggs Benedict, sausage omelet, or stir-fried fresh vegetables and chicken. Attacks of desire for California-style cuisine grip me periodically when I get out of state, and this fresh stir-fry filled the bill.

Upstairs are the fresh, attractive bedrooms with high ceilings, antique beds, and green plants. Each one is decorated in a different pastel color—pale raspberry, lavender, blue—with comforters to match. Room treats cover all tastes—fresh flowers for the sentimental guest, a different chocolate treat each day for the sweets lover, and a crystal decanter of Spanish sherry for philosophers.

For theatergoers—and almost every visitor to Ashland is one—the Winchester's location is a great convenience. From the patio, you can hear the trumpets summoning players and audience to the outdoor Shakespearean theater. Forsooth . . . take thine umbrella.

How to get there: On I-5 driving north, take the first Ashland exit; it becomes Main Street. Continue to center of town; turn left at Second Street, and go 2 blocks. The inn is on the right corner of Hargadine Street.

Olive Metcalf

The Johnson House
Florence, Oregon
97439

Innkeepers: Jayne and Ronald Fraese
Address/Telephone: 216 Maple Street (mailing address: Box 1892); (503) 997–8000
Rooms: 5; 1 with private bath.
Rates: $45 to $75, including afternoon refreshment and full breakfast.
Open: All year.
Facilities and local attractions: Walk to waterfront of Siuslaw River; shops, restaurants, antiques in Old Town Florence. Lake fishing. Oregon Dunes Recreation Area; clamming, crabbing, beachcombing, bird watching.

The coastal town of Florence could be one of your most enjoyable discoveries on a driving trip from California to Vancouver, B.C. It is the halfway point from San Francisco, just off Highway 101 and situated on the northern edge of the National Sand Dunes Recreation Area. This fabulous stretch of coast has beige-colored dunes higher than those of the Sahara, their contours constantly changing by sand washed ashore and by the wind. They are wonderful to drive along or walk. Sometimes the coast lupines, strawberries, sand verbenas, and monkey flowers will be in bloom on the fore-dunes or on the open sand.

The historic community nestles at the mouth of the wide Suislaw River. The Johnson House is the oldest house in town, and Jayne and Ronald have restored it with an eye for original structure and details that give every room the atmosphere of warm Oregon coast living a century ago.

From its snow-white outside appearance to the beautiful bed linens and puffy comforters, everything here looks fresh, clean, and light. It is a homey, comfortable atmosphere without frills. There are sinks in the rooms that share baths, tall ceilings, antiques, and lace curtains. A living room and a cozy sitting area at the stairway landing are inviting places to curl up in or to browse through the book collection.

Count on a hearty breakfast that varies daily. Menus include a variety of soufflés, omelettes aux fine herbes, and crepes with fresh salmon. For other meals, there is no need to get back in the car.

A walk one block to the waterfront of Old Town Florence will introduce you to a colorful pioneer fishing village with small restaurants and coffee shops. The village is an appealing blend of old and new, with a small fishing fleet, antique shops, and boutiques. Stop in the Siuslaw Pioneer Museum to see the logging and sailing artifacts from the glory days of the sailing schooners.

How to get there: From Highway 101, Florence is 1½ blocks east. The inn is on the left.

olive Metcalf

Tu Tú Tun Lodge
Gold Beach, Oregon
97444

Innkeepers: Dirk and Laurie Van Zante
Address/Telephone: 96550 North Bank Rogue; (503) 247–6664
Rooms: 16, including 2 suites each accommodating 6; all with private bath.
Rates: $93, double occupancy, EP. $6 each additional person. Daily rate for two, including breakfast and dinner, $143.
Open: May 1 to November 1. Breakfast, lunch, dinner for guests, or by reservation only. Full bar.
Facilities and local attractions: Swimming pool, four-hole putting green; jet boat white-water Rogue River trips; salmon and steelhead fishing, seasoned guides available. Scenic flights over Siskiyou Mountains. Hiking, beachcombing, scenic drives. Legalized gambling in Gold Beach.

In case you have the mistaken notion that the Northwest consists of only fir trees and lumberjacks, consider the motto of Tu Tú Tun Lodge: "Casual elegance in the wilderness on the famous Rogue River."

That's summing it up modestly, for this is a very ☞ special blend of sophistication and an outdoor-lover's paradise. Top-notch accommodations and superb food are those of a classy resort, but the young owners create a friendly atmosphere that's more like that of a country inn.

Guest rooms are situated in a two-story building adjacent to the lodge. Each has comfortable easy chairs, extra-long beds, a dressing area, and a bath with tub and shower. Special touches that make wilderness life civilized aren't forgotten—fresh flowers, good reading lamps, and up-to-date magazines. No telephone or television intrudes as you watch the changing colors of the Rogue's waters at sunset from your private balcony or patio.

A bell at 6:30 P.M. calls guests to the lodge for cocktails and hors d'oeuvres. Dirk and Laurie introduce everyone, and by the time they seat you for dinner at round tables set for eight, you'll feel you're dining with friends. The single-menu dinner they serve is outstanding, and it always features regional specialties. Fresh Chinook salmon, a soup, crisp salad made from locally grown greens, freshly baked bread or rolls, and a raspberry sorbet is a typical dinner.

After dinner, guests usually gather around the two fireplaces on the terrace overlooking the river. There's much to talk about as you share ideas for the next day's plans. If those plans call for an early-morning rising for fishing, a river trip, or hiking, breakfast and lunch baskets are available.

One adventure almost every visitor to the lodge tries is the exciting 104-mile white-water round trip up (and down) the river. Jet boats stop at the lodge's dock to pick up passengers in the morning.

How to get there: Driving north on Highway 101, pass through Gold Beach, cross bridge, and watch for signs on right to Rogue River Tavern. Turn right and drive 4 miles to tavern; follow signs another 3 miles to lodge on the right.

✳

J: *The name comes from the Tu Tú Tun Indians who lived in a village on the very site of the Lodge. "Tunne" meant "people"; "Tu Tú Tunne" were "people close to the river."*

Olive Metcalf

Paradise Ranch Inn
Grants Pass, Oregon
97526

Innkeepers: Oliver and Mattie Raymond
Address/Telephone: 7000 Monument Drive; (503) 479–4333
Rooms: 14, including a 2-bedroom Gardener's Cottage; all with private bath.
Rates: Beginning at $49.50 winter rate (October through May 15) and $79 summer, for two, including continental breakfast. $10 each additional person in winter, $20 summer. Ask about package rates including dinners; special honeymoon package.
Open: All year. Sunday breakfast, dinners open to public. Winter dinners served only Thursday through Sunday. Full bar.
Facilities and local attractions: Swimming pool, hot tub, golf, bicycles, tennis, volleyball, boats, fishing, jogging trails. Recreation center with billiards, television, table tennis. Arrangements made for white-water Rogue River trips; one-day scenic fishing trips. Facilities for weddings, parties, business meetings.

Once I saw the Paradise Ranch Inn I had two immediate thoughts: 1) its name is right on the button, and 2) how *could* I have missed it all these years? The mini-resort has been operating for almost twenty years, but major renovations have brought it to a very classy status for an inn that 🖝 dares to welcome children and pets.

344

It's only 3 miles from Interstate 5 and an hour from Ashland, but this is a little world of its own that pushes every button for rural getaway fantasies. Everywhere you look over the 300-acre ranch the natural beauty of Oregon is inspiring. But the ranch has gilded that lily even further. There are three ponds, a lake, miles of white fences, an elegant barn, jogging trails through the woods, a triangle golf course, tennis courts, and a swimming pool.

All the recreation facilities are included in your room rate, and you don't even have to bring equipment with you. Fishing gear, tennis rackets, bicycles, and golf clubs are all for loan with a deposit. This is a wonderful opportunity to borrow a rod and fish on a 🖛 willow-lined pond stocked with rainbow trout.

A new 🖛 triangle golf course is an experience you just might find even more fun than the real thing. Each hole has three tees, so it plays like a nine-hole course. You play at your own pace—use all your clubs—and lose your fear of water.

The atmosphere around the ranch seems to emphasize opportunities for enjoying the quiet pleasures, too, in this beautiful setting. Watch the black swans and Canada geese, or row out on the lake and gaze at the awesome Cascades.

The fourteen guest rooms are in a long, low white building, one side facing the pond and the other facing the barn and green grounds. They are unpretentious, completely comfortable rooms, simply decorated in Ethan Allen–style furniture.

You won't find any straw on the floor in this barn. It's an attractive, carpeted recreation area, a place to have a quiet glass of wine, watch television, or enjoy the fire. On the upper level are billiard tables, Ping-Pong, another television, and games.

Great food, the kind that brings the locals out for dinner and summer Sunday brunch, is a major ingredient in this blend of sophistication and dude ranch. Oregon Quilcene oysters on the half shell, sauteed wild mushrooms, and deep-fried Oregon cheddar cheese are among the appetizer specials. Fresh Oregon coast seafood and local lamb are elegantly prepared along with beef and pork entrees.

How to get there: Driving south on I–5, take Hugo exit; turn right and follow Monument Drive 3.9 miles to the inn. Driving north on I–5, take the Merlin exit; continue left 1.9 miles. Fly-in: Josephine County Airport. Free shuttle to the inn.

Olive Metcalf

Columbia Gorge Hotel
Hood River, Oregon
97031

Innkeeper: Lynne La Fountaine
Address/Telephone: 4000 Westcliff Drive; (1-800) 345–1921
Rooms: 46, including 2 fireplaced suites; all with private bath. Wheelchair
  access.
Rates: $95 to $175, including enormous farm breakfast. $25 for each
  additional person in room. Ask about special package rates during
  winter months.
Open: All year. Breakfast, lunch, dinner served daily.
Facilities and local attractions: Beautiful grounds and gardens. The Valentino Lounge, piano music. Two nearby golf courses. Scenic drives
  along the Columbia Gorge. Maryhill Museum. Rafting on the White
  Salmon River. Skiing at Mt. Hood. Hiking. Sternwheel excursion
  trips on the Columbia River. Facilities and all arrangements made for
  weddings, business meetings.

When you're imposing, venerable, and have the word "hotel"
in your title, you're not exactly a country inn, but the Columbia
Gorge Hotel is too spectacular a setting to miss. Besides, they serve
☞ one of the all-time great breakfasts *anywhere*, included in your
room rate.

Many people fondly remember the famous breakfast that

originated at Snoqualmie Falls Lodge more than twenty-five years ago. I'll never forget the wide-eyed wonder of three little boys when the honey was swirled and poured with a flourish from high above the table. The whole happening has been transplanted to the more grand surroundings of the Columbia Gorge Hotel with all the important elements still in place. You'll read with astonishment a menu that warns, "It's not a choice; you'll get it all." And get it you do: fruits and apple fritters, old-fashioned oatmeal, sausages, pancakes, eggs, and the *pièce de résistance,* baking powder biscuits with apple blossom honey "poured from the sky." It's show biz—but so good!

Just an hour east of Portland, the red tile-roofed hotel sits high above the mighty Columbia on the edge of a deep canyon with ☞ sweeping vistas of Mount Hood and Wah-Gwin-Gwin Falls, a 206-foot cascade that tumbles into the river just behind the hotel. It was built in 1921 by timber baron Simon Benson. The elegantly appointed large public rooms, massive plastered beams, and decor still have a nostalgic '20s feeling, even though everything has recently been redecorated and modernized. Valentino and Clara Bow are two Jazz Era names who supposedly were guests. The Valentino Cocktail Lounge off the lobby (containing a fireplace and grand piano) is named for him.

Only two rooms have a fireplace, but each room is individually decorated, simply and comfortably. You can have garden or river views. About thirteen acres surround the hotel, grounds that have most visitors walking among the gardens with a camera in hand. From April to mid-November, it's a picture of thousands of blooming plants.

Celebrities are common among guests here, not surprisingly. Doc Severinson and Robert Goulet were among the recent crop. You should know also that the hotel is frequently the location for business meetings, where participants hold meetings and wear name tags.

How to get there: Driving east along the Oregon side of Columbia River, take Exit 62, I–84 in Hood River. Fly-in: Hood River County Airport just minutes away.

Olive Metcalf

Jacksonville Inn
Jacksonville, Oregon
97530

Innkeepers: Jerry and Linda Evans
Address/Telephone: 175 East California Street; (503) 899–1900
Rooms: 8; all with private bath and air conditioning.
Rates: $58 to $66, including full breakfast.
Open: All year. Restaurant, bar every night. Sunday brunch.
Facilities and local attractions: Wine and gift shop. Walk, explore Jacksonville: museum, art galleries, restored homes, antiques, shops. Britt Music and Art Festival in August; bluegrass, jazz, and dance festivals June and July. Fifteen-mile drive to Ashland theaters.

☛ Jacksonville is a wonderful discovery, the oldest town in southern Oregon. It began in 1851 with the discovery of gold in Rich Gulch, but, unlike so many mining boomtowns, it didn't become a ghost town when the gold ran out; quartz mining was to follow.

Exploring an old mining town is always a history of tragedies, and Jacksonville has survived its share. A smallpox epidemic in 1868 killed many of the original settlers; a flood in 1869 swept tons of mud and rock through the center of town; and fires destroyed most of the town's original frame buildings.

The inn is one of Jacksonville's early permanent structures—a two-story brick building erected in 1863. The walls of the dining room and lounge were built of sandstone quarried locally, and specks of gold are visible in the mortar. The eight bedrooms over the restaurant, lounge, and gift shop are up a stairway at the side of the building. They are not large, but each has a private bath and is individually decorated. The look is refreshingly uncluttered, attractively furnished rooms with antiques from the area: brass beds, rockers, and oak highboys with beveled mirrors.

A full breakfast is served between 8 and 10 A.M. in the dining room: fresh-fruit plate followed by quiche or perhaps Belgian waffle. Dinner offerings are pasta, prime rib, veal, and specialties such as fresh salmon and razor clams in season. The Evans are proud of their cellar of more than 500 wines.

This old town abounds with things for the tourist to do. They range from soaking up historical atmosphere in the cemetery (any fancier of headstone inscriptions will relish some of them here, like "Hanged for a killing") to a banquet of cultural events and attractions in the area. The ☞ Britt Music Festival in August is an outstanding music series featuring international musicians giving nightly concerts in the beautiful setting of the Britt Gardens. To enjoy the full flavor of a concert under the stars, ask the inn to prepare a picnic basket for you, then walk up the street to the Gardens. This is what summer nights are made for.

How to get there: From Highway 5 between Phoenix and Grants Pass take any of these roads west into town: South Stage Road, Highway 238, or Hanley Road; take Applegate Road or Old Stage Road leading south into town. All roads lead to the town's main street, California, and the inn.

olive Metcalf

Under the Greenwood Tree
Medford, Oregon
97501

Innkeeper: Renate Ellam
Address/Telephone: 3045 Bellinger Lane; (503) 776–0000
Rooms: 4; all with private bath with tub and hand-held shower.
Rates: $65 to $85, including lavish breakfast and high tea. Single rate $5
  less. Smoking on porches. No pets.
Open: All year.
Facilites and local attractions: Accommodates weddings and private parties.
  Convenient for visiting historic Jacksonville, Britt Music Festival
  July–September. Ashland Shakespearean Festival; Mt. Ashland ski-
  ing. Rogue River rafting. Antiquing in Medford. Short trips to Crater
  Lake, Oregon Caves National Monument. Paddock facilities.

No matter how delicious the food at an inn may be, sometimes
you have to speak first of the innkeeper. So it is at Under the
Greenwood Tree, owned, inspired, cherished, decorated, and
directed by Renate Ellam and indelibly stamped with her ebullient
personality.

   She brings an abundance of experience (she was a San
Francisco designer) and skills ☛ (she's a Cordon Bleu graduate

cook) to the art of innkeeping. And art is what Ellam makes it. If that sounds like grandiose praise for a four-room bed-and-breakfast inn, try it before you judge.

Her 125-year-old farmhouse sits on ten acres with old apple, pear, cedar, and black walnut trees. Some of the oaks are 300 years old. Renate was directing the construction of a unique gazebo when I arrived, and she pointed out sixty-five recently planted rose bushes. There is enormous, ☞ nostalgic appeal to this land and old farm buildings, some dating from 1861; the granary is the oldest weigh station in Oregon, and the barn and antique farm implements are of the vintage artists love to paint.

In the house, a first glance tells you it's been decorated by a professional; a second look tells you the rugs are real Persian; the ☞ quilts museum quality; and fabrics, wallpaper, antiques, and art objects are quite special. But is it comfortable, you ask? True, the rooms are not large, but with lovely decor, a private bath, top-of-the-line mattresses, and elegant linens, you don't belong at an inn if you have a complaint here.

The heart of Ms. Ellam's style is the joy she seems to get from nurturing people. It begins with a warm welcome and a 4:30 P.M. ☞ high tea. At night she turns down the bed and leaves a handmade European truffle with a copy of the lines about the Greenwood tree from *As You Like It*. Nothing pleases her more than doing something special for an anniversary or celebration. One season she noticed guests returning downcast from performances of *Macbeth* in Ashland and decided a dessert repast was needed to send them off to bed more cheerfully.

Renate serves a full gourmet breakfast by an old parlor stove. The scene may be country charm, but the table service is sterling silver and Rosenthal china, the tables are hand-carved, and the chairs upholstered in velvet. The menu springs fresh every day from the best local ingredients available and Ellam's inspiration. This day there were raspberries picked that morning, homemade muffins and nut bread, white grape and cranberry juices, a soufflé with Oregon cheese, and a dessert course extravaganza.

How to get there: From I–5 driving north, exit at ramp 27, Barnett Road, turn left onto overpass; at first signal turn left on Stewart. Follow approximately 3 miles until it becomes Hull. Continue 1 block; turn right on Bellinger Lane. Inn is on the left.

Olive Metcalf

General Hooker's House
Portland, Oregon
97201

Innkeeper: Lori Hall
Address/Telephone: 125 SW Hooker; (503) 222–4435
Rooms: 3; 1 with private bath; all with air conditioning, cable television, and VCR.
Rates: $45 to $60; $75 for suite made by combining 2 rooms. $20 extra person. Continental breakfast included and afternoon beverage.
Open: All year.
Facilities and local attractions: Library; 🖝 extensive taped movie collection for VCRs. Pleasant old neighborhood for walking. Excellent YMCA facilities a block away. Public track, parks, tennis courts in the neighborhood. Walk or public transportation to Pioneer Courthouse Square, PSU, Performing Arts Center, Waterfront Park, shops, restaurants.

With its gingerbread trim painted prettily, this dainty Victorian house seen from the outside predicts an interior you won't find. Lori Hall has been cheerfully unauthentic in restoring the house in a tree-lined neighborhood at the edge of Portland's downtown. Inside you find an atmosphere that is not nineteenth-century at all; the feeling is light, open, and contemporary. Lori calls it "neo-Victorian." I call it comfortable.

She has blended a few massive antique pieces with her 🖙 fascinating collection of modern art and books and set it all against a background of white, touches of navy and tan, and neutral-color textured fabrics. What were once two small parlors are now opened out and combined to make a spacious, interesting sitting area.

On the landing of the stairway up to the bedrooms is an impressive mirror, old and enormous. At the top of the steps in the hallway is a refrigerator stocked with wine and soft drinks. My room was the Iris. It has a private entry via a roof deck with a glamorous view at night of downtown Portland. The room was sleek and cheerful: a comfortable day bed extended to double bed size, a desk, a built-in buffet for wine glasses, books, television, VCR, and a shelf full of films. (The main collection is downstairs.) The Victorian element was a handsome armoire. Combined with the Daisy, these two rooms make a suite for three or four with private bath and entry.

The largest room is the Rose with a 7-foot-long bed or two twins. This room, too, has access to the roof deck. Colors are bone white, navy, a beautiful batik patchwork comforter, and touches of rattan.

It wasn't surprising to meet a young woman, another guest, traveling alone on business. This is just the kind of 🖙 secure, relaxed atmosphere that increasing numbers of businesswomen are discovering as an alternative to a confining motel room. We talked around the breakfast table in the morning, enjoying the fresh fruit, homemade granola, hot muffins, and good coffee. Lori Hall is a fourth-generation Portlander who really knows and loves her city.

I know you're bored with tales of ubiquitous inn cats, but mention must be made of the Hooker House cat. She's named Happy, of course. This velvety Abyssinian thinks she is a dog and races up and down the steps playing fetch. Hilarious? Maybe you have to be there.

How to get there: Hooker Street is in the downtown area between SW 1st and 2nd Avenue, 1½ blocks east of Barbur Boulevard. Coming from downtown, get on 1st Avenue at the Marriott Hotel and go south for ¾ mile to Hooker. Turn right to the inn with its lamppost on the right side.

Olive Metcalf

Portland's White House
Portland, Oregon
97212

Innkeepers: Larry and Mary Hough
Address/Telephone: 1914 N.E. 22nd Avenue; (503) 287–7131
Rooms: 6; 4 with private bath, 2 share 1 bath.
Rates: $47 to $75, including full breakfast. No pets; no smoking. Children under 12 discouraged.
Open: All year.
Facilities and local attractions: Grand setting and facilities for weddings, receptions, private parties, business meetings. Explore Portland's shops, Saturday Market, restored waterfront area, restaurants.

How do you feel about The White House as a B&B? When you go to Portland, you'll have a chance to try an inn that looks remarkably similar to the Washington, D.C., lodging.

At the Portland White House, stately Greek columns, circular driveway, fountains, and landscaped grounds are a pleasant alternative to big-city accommodations. What's more, the rates are less than a downtown hotel, and you have the advantages of staying in a pleasant area to walk, with plenty of free parking and a full breakfast elegantly served.

This big white house in a quiet residential neighborhood is what you would expect of a lumber baron's home: pretty impressive. Through the mahogany front doors is a large entry hall with its original hand-painted murals and oak inlaid floors. At one side is a formal parlor, its French windows draped in lace, which is quite inviting as a sitting room for guests. At the other end of the hall, the formal dining room is a blend of mahogany, crystal chandeliers, and a lace-covered dining table. This is where a hearty full breakfast is served.

A sweeping central staircase leads to six guest rooms on the second floor. They are sweetly old-fashioned with a mixture of antiques and old favorites. Some have queen-sized beds (one is a canopy bed), and the others are double-sized. The Balcony Room affords the opportunity to fantasize about the roaring crowds below yelling for your victory . . . or maybe your neck.

When you watch Larry and Mary Hough work together as afternoon guests begin arriving, you would have to agree they're a perfect team. "We've found our niche," says Mary. Her mother ran a boarding house in England, so she comes from a legacy of innkeeping. Mary, who is Irish, used to buy and sell antiques, but taking on this 1912 mansion (with forty-three leaks in the roof) was a big leap. They seem to thrive on it.

The Houghs make a strong bid for hosting special events. The house ☛ lends itself well to weddings, parties, and business meetings. If the word I hear is correct, that cocktail parties are coming back into fashion, this would be a grand place to have one.

No one who lives here agreed with me, but I found Portland confusing and difficult to drive around. In addition to the directions below, get some back-up detail from the Houghs when you make your reservation.

How to get there: Driving north on I–5 take the Lloyd Center–Coliseum exit to the second stoplight. Turn left on Wilder. Continue to 22nd Street and turn left to the inn. Driving south on I–5, take the Lloyd Center exit to the first stoplight. Turn right on Wilder and continue as above.

❁

J: *The doorbell doesn't play "Hail To the Chief" (personally, I think it would be a nice touch), but the Houghs do keep George Washington and Ronald Reagan in a cage. They're the house birds.*

olive Metcalf

The Boarding House
Seaside, Oregon
97138

Innkeepers: Dick and Barb Edwards
Address/Telephone: 208 North Holladay Drive; (503) 738–9055
Rooms: 6, plus a cottage; all with private bath, television.
Rates: $45 to $75 for cottage, including breakfast. Deduct $5 for single;
  add $5 for each additional person. Children under 3 are free.
Open: All year.
Facilities and local attractions: Beach walks, clam digging, swimming;
  fishing on Necanicum River. Stroll to downtown shops, restaurants.

"This old house serves comfort" is the motto posted at the door. The rustic, 1898 Victorian boarding house keeps that promise, and at a refreshingly modest price. Built entirely of fir tongue-and-groove lumber, with beamed ceilings and paneling throughout, the house has recently been completely restored. New comforts include private baths, color TVs, and a private side entrance. Brass and white iron beds, down quilts, antiques, and wicker add a country touch.

There is a delightful paneled parlor for relaxing with a piano, comfortable sofa and chairs, and a window seat. One feature sure to please those intrepid souls who travel with children is that ☛ this inn actually welcomes little ones. Barb Edwards says "This is

356

a family-oriented inn, so we have it fairly child-proof. We also have high chairs, playpens, and daybeds."

Behind the house is a 100-year-old cottage sitting right on the river. It has been renovated and is a wonderful family accommodation sleeping six. Children will love the sleeping loft. Parents will appreciate that it is self-contained with a microwave. The river is also great for entertainment, watching the ducks and heron, or taking out one of the paddle boats available for rent.

Breakfast is served in a sunny, paneled dining room with beamed ceilings, a built-in buffet, touches of stained glass, and another big window seat. Tables are covered to the floor with blue and white cloths. You can also take your breakfast outside to a wrap-around porch.

The Edwards' menu is a full one with juices, lots of fresh fruit, and something like a fancy French toast with fresh berry sauce and whipped cream, or a special egg dish and rich coffee cake as typical entrees.

The town of Seaside is in the extreme northwest corner of Oregon in an area called the North Coast. This marks the end of the Lewis and Clark Trail and encompasses the oldest settlement in the West: Astoria.

One of the joys of being in a quaint seaside town is to forget the car and walk to all the attractions. From the Boarding House, you are four blocks from the ocean and two blocks from downtown. The nearly two-mile beach promenade is lined with charming old houses. You can rent horses, or dig for clams, or surf fish. The resort-atmosphere town has small shops and a variety of restaurants. Carole and Dick will point you in the direction of your interest.

How to get there: Exit Highway 101 at Seaside and follow signs to City Center; the street becomes Holladay Drive. Inn is on the right.

✹

J: *In February, Seaside hosts the highly regarded Trail's End Marathon—one of the country's top road runs.*

olive Metcalf

Steamboat Inn
Steamboat Springs, Oregon
97447

Innkeepers: Sharon and Jim Van Loan; Patricia Lee, manager
Address/Telephone: Highway 138 (mailing address: P.O. Box 36); (503)
    496–3495/498–2411
Rooms: 8 cabins; all with private bath. 4 new cottages; all with fireplace,
    living room, mini-kitchen, soaking tub.
Rates: $65, single or double, $15 each additional adult; cottages $95. EP.
    Dinner $22. No smoking in restaurant.
Open: All year. Breakfast, lunch, dinner daily; special Fisherman's Dinner
    for guests or by reservation. Weekends only during winter season;
    wine and beer bar.
Facilities and local attractions: Steelhead fishing, swimming, nature trails.
    Drive to downhill and cross-country skiing. Near several vineyards.

After a twisting 38-mile drive along the North Umpqua River,
in a downpour that never slowed, the welcome at Steamboat Inn
was underwhelming. I was looking for a cup of coffee and good
cheer. Instead, I entered a room pungent with gloom. Seated
morosely around a 20-foot-long pine table were a dozen fishermen, angling fanatics from all over the world who feel very
proprietary about this extraordinary ☞ 39-mile stretch of white
water reserved strictly for fly fishing.

They eyed the intruder sourly and went back to staring bleakly out the windows or stomping about the stone floor of the common room, waiting for the storm to slow down to merely a hard rain. Only destiny and the inn's gastronomical reputation had brought us together.

Pat Lee, who doubles as chef and angling guide, rescued me with coffee and a tour that was cheering. This may indeed be "the ☞ greatest stretch of summer steelhead water in the United States," as Jack Hemingway says, but it's also an idyllic spot for readers and loafers.

The rustic main room with a huge rock fireplace opens onto a glass-enclosed sun porch where meals are served. Beyond the flowers and trees are eight cabins sitting right on the river, connected by a long deck. You needn't be a fisherman to have a visceral reponse to the ☞ majestic setting of tall fir trees and white water tumbling past. The cabins are unexpectedly well appointed: paneled and carpeted, furnished comfortably, all with modern baths, good beds, and reading lights. And each room opens onto the deck.

All day, the kitchen serves hearty breakfasts, fast lunches, and early dinners to distracted anglers. But come evening, the restaurant closes, and the inn assumes a different identity. Out come linens, silver, candles, and it's ☞ haute cuisine on the North Umpqua: The Fisherman's Dinner.

In deference to fishermen who can't quit until dark, wine is poured and hors d'oeuvres are set out half an hour *after* sunset. Sharon Van Loan and Pat do the classy cooking that has won compliments from *Fly Fisherman* to *Gourmet* magazines. A typical entree might be a pork loin in lemon-basil marinade, sauced with a tomato, thyme, and applejack combination; perfectly braised carrots with hints of mustard and mint; then, a watercress salad with hazelnuts, followed by freshly ground coffee and perhaps a Bavarian chocolate torte.

Do real fishermen deserve less?

How to get there: From Roseburg, take Highway 138 east for ☞ 38 scenic miles along the Umpqua River. Inn is on the right.

olive Metcalf

Wolf Creek Tavern
Wolf Creek, Oregon
97497

Innkeepers: Joy and Sam Angelos
Address/Telephone: P.O. Box 97; (503) 866–2474
Rooms: 8; all with private bath.
Rates: $30 single, $36 double; Parlor Chamber $42; EP.
Open: All year; closed Christmas Day, first two weeks in January.
Breakfast, lunch, dinner, Sunday brunch; wine and beer bar.
Facilities and local attractions: Historic waystop; no town. Twenty miles to
Grants Pass headquarters for Rogue River fishing and boating guides;
U.S. Forest Service Office for maps, information about 40-mile Rogue
hiking trail. Small seminar and wedding facilities.

Looking for all the world just like a stagecoach stop ought to
look, the Wolf Creek Tavern looms up unexpectedly among dense
trees along Highway Five. The imposing two-story white building
was once ☞ a way station for stages that stopped on the six-day
trip between Portland and Sacramento.

Wolf Creek Tavern's history is surrounded by legendary
romantic—and largely unauthenticated—events, but records indi-
cate that it was built around 1857. The State Parks and Recreation
Division acquired it in 1975 and leases it to the Angeloses to
operate as an inn.

360

Today the tavern is providing good food and beverage, comfortable beds, and old-fashioned hospitality for the traveling public, but with some modern conveniences. They include heating, air conditioning, and a bath for every room. These are unpretentious rooms, clean, plain, and simple. Furnishings in the first floor rooms represent pieces from the early 1900s to the 1930s, but one of the rooms upstairs has been furnished as an 1870s chamber. Another special bit of history preserved upstairs is a tiny room with a single bed where Jack London used to stay.

On the first floor, a central stair and hallway divide the ladies' parlor from the men's sitting room—the tap room. Original paint colors were researched and have been reproduced on walls, woodwork, and chimneys. The tavern and dining room have pine floors and rustic tables with burgundy and blue cloths. ☞ Waitresses dress in period costume.

At dinner, as I listened to the banter between the staff and familiar locals who had stopped in for the innkeepers' good cooking, I wondered where they had come from. Driving in a few hours earlier, it seemed as though this was practically a wilderness, and now the sounds of friendly travelers having a good time filled the tavern.

Entree choices included Athenian Scampi, scallops in sauce suisse, and weekend tavern specialties such as prime rib. I planned ahead for the night's special dessert: fresh peach-and-apple crisp . . . a la mode. Good thinking. Homey old dishes like this made with fresh fruit from the garden are so soul-satisfying.

How to get there: Leave I–5 about 20 miles north of Grants Pass at exit 76. Follow the signs to Wolf Creek.

৵৶

J: *This remote stop gives you a feeling for what it must have meant to earlier travelers to find good cheer and hospitality after hours of bouncing in a stagecoach.*

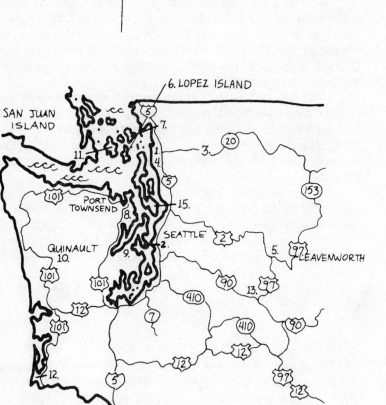

N

6. LOPEZ ISLAND

SAN JUAN
ISLAND

5
7.

3. 20

11. 1.
4.
5 153

101
PORT
TOWNSEND 15.
8.
SEATTLE 2
QUINAULT 2. 5. 97
10. LEAVENWORTH

9.
101 90
101 13. 97

12
410

7
410 90

101
12
12

12. 97
5 12

14.

Washington

Numbers on map refer to towns numbered below.

Olive Metcalf

The Channel House
Anacortes, Washington
98221

Innkeepers: Pat and Dennis McIntyre
Address/Telephone: 2902 Oakes Avenue; (206) 293–9382
Rooms: 4 share 2 large baths.
Rates: $55 to $65, breakfast and evening snack included. Children over 12
    welcome. No smoking.
Open: All year.
Facilities and local attractions: Hot tub. Bicycle rentals. Minutes from ferry
    docks leading to San Juan Islands, British Columbia. Explore Decep-
    tion Pass, Washington Park, Mt. Erie.

A bedroom off the library was mine when I stayed in this
1902 Victorian. It's a pretty room with a brass bed, a log-cabin
quilt made by Dennis's mother, and other antique appointments.
But what won my heart was the view from a wicker rocker in front
of a 🖝 window looking out at the Guemes Channel and the San
Juan Islands. A tray of tea and cookies sweetened the scene while
I rocked away in absolute contentment.

The library itself is a fine place to spend time—a good stereo,
comfortable furniture, and interesting books and magazines. Making yourself at home for an evening among another person's books
is almost as personal as moving into his or her bedroom. In the

case of the McIntyres, the library reflects Pat's English background, a love of spy novels, mysteries, current fiction, and the history and biography that Dennis reads.

Pat's decorating is fun—not an all-Victorian theme or mood, but rather a collection of interesting pieces: an elegant antique here, a romantic chaise there, enlivened with something amusing like stuffed sheep (on the stairs) she brought back from Scotland.

Two bedrooms upstairs have the best view in the house—from the claw-footed tub in the common bathroom. An elegant dining room with French doors going out to the garden is downstairs from the living room. Breakfast here consists of especially fine coffee (made from a blend of fresh beans), fresh fruit, a variety of hot entrees, like stuffed French toast, and homemade muffins with several spreads.

"Doing" the islands is one of the main reasons one comes to Anacortes, but trying to figure out the least expensive route while stopping at all the towns you want to see can loom as a complex undertaking. The McIntyres are thoughtful hosts who will help you make sense of the ferry schedule and even volunteer breakfast at a time convenient to the ferry you want to catch. This is the kind of ☞ treatment that gives innkeeping a good name.

How to get there: From Seattle, take I–5 north to junction with State 20 past Mt. Vernon. Follow 20 west to Anacortes. Remain on 20 through town. The name changes to Commercial, then Oakes. Inn is on the right. Fly-in: Anacortes airport.

❁

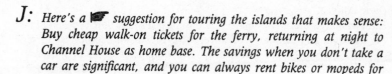

J: *Here's a* ☞ *suggestion for touring the islands that makes sense: Buy cheap walk-on tickets for the ferry, returning at night to Channel House as home base. The savings when you don't take a car are significant, and you can always rent bikes or mopeds for exploring during the day.*

Olive Metcalf

The Bombay House
Bainbridge Island, Washington
98110

Innkeepers: Bunny Cameron and Robert Kanchuk
Address/Telephone: 8490 N.E. Beck Road; (206) 842–3926
Rooms: 5, including 1 suite; suite and 2 on first floor with private bath, 2
   on second floor share a bath. Air conditioning.
Rates: $50 to $78, expanded continental breakfast included. Children
   welcome weekdays; no pets. American Express or checks preferred.
   Smoking restricted.
Open: All year.
Facilities and local attractions: An island to bicycle. Visit Fort Worden State
   Park, Eagle Harbor Waterfront Park, Indian battlegrounds. Picnic
   areas, tennis courts, golf nearby. Shopping, restaurants in Winslow.

At Bombay House, you can sit at the breakfast table enjoying
muffins, homemade granola, and fresh fruits and 🖝 watch the big
white ferries gliding through Rich Passage. All the ships bound for
the Bremerton Navy Yards go through, too. In the daytime, it is
endlessly fascinating; at night, the lighted ferries look like ocean
liners in the dark waters.

"Unlikely" is the way the big house strikes me. Part Victorian,
part nautical, and part just the independent ideas of the master
shipbuilder who built it in 1907. The house sits on a half acre of

green lawn, a hilltop location with marine views and wonderful unstructured gardens. It's a delightful place for a country-style wedding—there is even a rustic, rough cedar gazebo. During my May visit, a big American flag was flapping in the breeze, the flowers were glorious, and twisted old apple trees looked romantic.

If you have visited the inn before, you will surely remember the unexpected sight of a full-size rabbit named James Brown snoozing on the brick open-hearth fireplace. It seems he began to add electrical cords to his diet, and now poor James no longer has the run of the house. He still thrives, but outdoors.

The bedrooms are all roomy, except for the cozy Crows Nest, which has one of the best views from the house—but you have to be in bed to see it. The Captain's Suite is the spacious master bedroom upstairs. You have good views from here, a sitting area with a wood stove, small refrigerator, game table, and sleeper couch. The bathroom facilities are a claw-footed tub and a shower. The first-floor King Room has a unique, blue-tin soaking tub in the room. The Red Room has a brass bed, a sitting area, and a tub and hand-shower across the hall.

This is an informal house with a casual kind of atmosphere. The morning meal is served in the kitchen, not a formal dining room, and the innkeepers have a young child. Bunny says that at Christmas they have custom decorations that are great.

How to get there: From Seattle, take Winslow Ferry to Bainbridge. Proceed left on Winslow Way, right on Madison, left on Wyatt. Turn right at the "Y" in the road. Past the elementary school on your left, veer to the right down the hill. Turn right on Beck. The inn is on the corner. Free ferry pick-up available.

J: *On a scale of one to ten, the thirty-minute ferry ride from Seattle Harbor to Bainbridge Island rates a ten: a glorious panorama of that city's skyline and the romantic fun of heading for an island!*

olive Metcalf

Cascade Mountain Inn
Birdsview-Concrete, Washington
98237

Innkeepers: Ingrid and Gerhard Meyer
Address/Telephone: 3840 Pioneer Lane; (206) 826–4333
Rooms: 6; all with private bath.
Rates: $52 to $78, full breakfast included. No smoking.
Open: All year.
Facilities and local attractions: Spectacular setting. Nature hikes, biking, fishing. Skagit River boat launch. Dinners arranged if one party books entire inn.

Snoqualmie, Snohomish, Klickitat, Quinault. Colorful place names are indigenous to Washington state, so why my enthusiasm for a placed called Concrete? Merely because it's a region of such ☞ startling natural beauty it leaves you tongue-tied; a little-known area of rich green meadows, deep river valleys, lush forests, and, towering over all, the amazing, always snowcapped Cascade Range. Besides, the town name has recently acquired a hyphenated upgrade to Birdsview-Concrete.

Sitting on ten acres of meadowland bordered by the North Cascades is the handsomely designed, new (1985) Cascade Mountain Inn. The Meyers had been coming here for years with their sons to fish. When Gerhard Meyer retired after thirty years of international corporate life, he and his wife, Ingrid, chose this remote spot to build an inn from Ingrid's design.

Having been all over the world, the Meyers's collection of furniture and art from each place they lived now makes their inn ☞ a kind of international house. Eiderdown quilts and pillows, furniture, and porcelain plates decorate the German room. Bamboo, shells, lace, and oil paintings from the Philippines depict that region. The Peruvian room in warm brown has hand-woven bedspreads, a duo of handsome leather chairs, and smaller Peruvian articles like hats, calabasas, and money bags. American and Scottish rooms are also in the main house. In addition to their interesting decor, these are spacious rooms, comfortable and immaculately maintained. The sixth room is a large studio over the garage decorated with tiles and wall hangings from the Meyers' hometown, Bremen. With a separate entrance, mini-kitchen, and nonstop views, this is a very private snuggery.

Ingrid gives a ☞ European flavor to her efficient kitchen style. She makes and serves six different kinds of bread and jam. There's her European granola (muesli) and yogurt mixed with fresh fruit or, in winter, blueberries and raspberries she has frozen. This and more keep guests happy at breakfast while she does the hot dish, maybe quiche or German pancakes, served at a big table in a cheerful glassed-in breakfast room looking out at the meadow or on the patio.

Few people are familiar with this scenic region, but the Meyers are, and they take great delight in sharing suggestions for activities at every time of year. Day-trip possibilities abound. They'll pack and label breakfast and lunch for hikers who want to start out early. They know where to point you when the salmon and steelhead are running, or what programs or classes might be available from the North Cascades Institute. In the winter you're welcome to sit around the fireplace in the living room (a television is here), and in summer, there's often a campfire outside. Warm hospitality is a part of the package with the Meyers . . . it's their natural way.

How to get there: From I–5 north of Burlington, drive 24 miles east on Highway 20 to a sign reading "Lodging, next right." Turn right on Wild Road ¼ mile to Pioneer Lane. Turn right.

Olive Metcalf

Downey House
La Conner, Washington
98257

Innkeepers: Jim and Kay Frey
Address/Telephone: 1880 Chilberg Road; (206) 466–3207
Rooms: 5; 2 with private bath, 3 share 1 bath.
Rates: $50 to $70, including full breakfast. No pets; no smoking.
Open: All year.
Facilities and local attractions: Hot tub. Minutes from La Conner's unique
  shops, restaurants, waterfront. April tulip festival.

Downey House is a big, beautiful, 1904 farmhouse sitting on
the outskirts of one of Washington's most picturesque towns. It
has the kind of 🖝 roadside appeal that people pull off the road to
photograph—broad green lawn, flower beds, and old trees. When
I visited the last week of April, acres of tulips were ablaze in the
surrounding countryside, and Mount Baker loomed majestically
over the valley.

This is a house of memories and roots deep in the Skagit
Valley. The Freys acquired and moved the house (surprising for a
house this large) to this site more than twenty-four years ago. They
raised their family here and only in 1986 began sharing it as an
inn.

If you love the history of families who remained together and part of the land through several generations, the old photographs here will delight you. A few lucky guests with roots in the area have picked out relatives in some of the threshing scenes and old school groups.

The good news for all guests is that nostalgia and antiques are dished out in updated comfort. There's not a whit of musty-dusty atmosphere. These personal objects collected from both Kay and Jim's families are refinished, polished, and lovingly cared for—treasures like the pump organ, a china cupboard, and a huge old-fashioned dining room table where breakfast is served.

The bedrooms are roomy and decorated with fresh, light fabrics and handsome Victorian pieces—an elegant chair here, a fine old chest there, and several big walnut beds. The fifth bedroom is separate from the house: the Downey Room, a suite with its own bath. It's a warm contemporary room in rich green and beige—even the ceiling beams are green—and decorated with a collection of David Hagerbaumer's watercolors of wildlife scenes.

Kay and Jim are innkeepers who genuinely enjoy their guests. You're welcome in the big country kitchen, and, after breakfast is served, they like to join everyone at the table with a cup of coffee. That breakfast often includes their own potato sausage, and always fruit, juice, and an egg dish or crepes.

How to get there: Driving south on I–5, take exit 230 to La Conner. Turn left at Best Road, which becomes Chilberg Road. Inn is on the right. Driving north, take exit 221 to La Conner and Conway. Continue on Fir Island Road west, crossing a bridge. Road becomes Chilberg Road. After crossing a second bridge, the inn is 1 mile ahead on the left.

✳

J: *When you return to the inn after dinner at one of La Conner's many good restaurants, the Freys have* ☞ *a special treat waiting: big servings of warm, fresh-baked blackberry pie, ice cream, and hot coffee. Can you imagine the good conversation and friendships that are nourished when strangers gather over that?*

olive Metcalf

La Conner Country Inn
La Conner, Washington
98257

Innkeepers: Rick and Reinhild Thompson
Address/Telephone: Old Town; (206) 466–3101
Rooms: 28; all with private bath, fireplace, television.
Rates: $67 single to $90, double occupancy, including continental break-
   fast. Children 12 and under share room with parents at no charge.
Open: All year. Lunch, dinner, Sunday brunch, full bar.
Facilities and local attractions: Conference facilities. Walk, explore La
   Conner Historic District, galleries, shops, restaurants, waterfront;
   biking, boating, fishing; Swinomish Indian Village.

La Conner just has to face the music—it's too 🖝 picturesque
to escape its destiny of becoming the perfect getaway weekend
place, and only an hour and a half from Seattle. One citizen,
unhappy with his town's increasing popularity, suggested in the
local paper that signs on I–5 be swapped with those of another
town. I could have told him that is an old ploy that merely adds a
maverick appeal to the town. Bolinas, California, has become
famous, not for swapping, but *removing* signs to their town.
   One main street of unique shops, restaurants, and commercial
buildings dating from the late 1800s runs along the Swinomish
Channel. This protected waterway is lively with commercial and

pleasure crafts, and tugboats with rafts of chained-together logs in tow. The bustle of lumbering and fishing and the pastoral beauty of the surrounding countryside are both part of daily life here. Artists Mark Tobey and Morris Graves, among others, have been attracted to this little fishing community in the fertile Skagit Valley, with nearby mountains visible on the horizon.

The La Conner Inn is in the heart of the town, just a few steps from the waterfront. It is a new inn with attractive, weathered cedar-wood rooms and fireplaces. Some antique appointments like brass beds are used, but modern comfort is the tone, with private baths, and with TVs hidden in pine armoires. A large common room called the library is where continental breakfast is served—juice, coffee, tea, and hot chocolate, and large cinnamon rolls.

The restaurant adjacent to the inn is good news. Its specialty is local seafood, of course. But it also takes advantage of the fresh local fruits and vegetables—and prepares them beautifully. Try the tortellini primavera, and the fresh raspberry tart. Another dessert specialty that guests come back for is called Queen Mother's Cake. It's a dense chocolate cake made with pulverized almonds instead of flour.

How to get there: Driving north from Seattle, leave I–5 at Conway; follow signs west to La Conner. From Whidbey Island, go east on Highway 20 to signs for La Conner.

❁

J: Check out a shop across the street called Chez La Zoom. It has some extraordinary handmade clothing.

Olive Metcalf

Haus Rohrbach Pension
Leavenworth, Washington
98826

Innkeepers: Kathryn and Bob Harrild
Address/Telephone: 12882 Ranger Road; (509) 548–7024
Rooms: 10; 6 with private bath, 4 share 2 baths. Air conditioning. Separate
   Chalet for 6 with kitchen and bath.
Rates: $50 for single to $98 for Chalet; $10 each additional person; rates
   include full breakfast. No smoking; children welcome.
Open: All year, except closed November until day after Thanksgiving.
Facilities and local attractions: Heated pool, hot tub, sledding, snowshoeing
   in front meadow. Explore Bavarian-style village of Leavenworth;
   spring Mai Fest, white-water rafting, winter skiing, tobogganing,
   year-round fishing, hiking. Two mountain bikes for rent.

Forget about the high price of getting to Europe and take
yourself to the country byways of central Washington's Eastern
Cascade Mountains. In the Swiss-looking Tumwater Valley, you'll
discover an entire town that has adopted the image of a ☛
Bavarian village. Believe it or not, it works.

Similar gimmicks imposed on a town by the local merchants
can sometimes have grotesque results, but in this instance, the
natural setting is so perfect that the effect is quite pleasing. There
are several streets of Alpine-decorated shops and restaurants, with
☛ hanging baskets of brilliant flowers in every doorway.

374

Haus Rohrbach is a country inn nestled among the foothills overlooking the entire valley. The three-story Chalet has wide balconies adjoining almost every room, overflowing flower boxes, and views of meadow and mountains, cows, geese, and gardens.

A comfortably furnished common room and an adjoining deck overlooking the valley are where guests gather. After a day of outdoor fun, it's inviting to relax around the fire for conversation.

The Harrilds are always improving their deservedly popular inn. A few years ago, they added the pool and hot tub; most recently, Bob has redone several of the bedrooms and baths. The feeling is rustic, or at least as rustic as you can feel with down comforters, good reading lights, and modern baths. These are appealing rooms with pine details and colorful cotton fabrics. Families will appreciate the several rooms with daybeds and trundles.

Kathryn serves breakfast on the balcony in good weather—sourdough pancakes, cinnamon rolls, and other delights she bakes while you watch. She'll pack you a picnic, too, for a day of exploring the beautiful countryside.

The Terrace Bistro is *the* place to go in town for fine dining. The Harrilds agree the chef is world-class, but I advise you to come back to the pensione for your "afters." Get into something with a stretchy waistband and cast your eyes over the variety of desserts available every night: old-fashioned sundaes and shakes; apple, peach, blueberry, and (oh, joy!) peanut butter pies; rhubarb crisps; a white chocolate mousse cake, and Schwarzwalder Kirsch Torte. Courage. Your bed is just up the steps.

How to get there: Going east on Highway 2 after Stevens Pass, turn left on Ski Hill Drive at entrance to Leavenworth. Go 1 mile; turn left on Ranger Road. You'll see the inn on the hillside.

❈

J: *If you can look at valley and mountains from the balcony here without attempting to sing an exuberant chorus of "The hills are alive with the sound of music . . . ," you've more restraint than I. The cows didn't seem to mind.*

olive Metcalf

Mountain Home Lodge
Leavenworth, Washington
98826

Innkeepers: Chris Clark and Charlie Brooks
Address/Telephone: Mountain Home Road (mailing address: Box 687); (509) 548–7077
Rooms: 8; all with private bath.
Rates: $68 to $88 per couple, summer rates, meals not included; $128 to $148 per couple, winter, all meals, complimentary wine included. No children; no pets.
Open: All year. Breakfast, lunch, dinner.
Facilities and local attractions: Pool, hot tub, hiking trails; winter snowmobiling, sledding, cross-country ski trails; nearby fishing, golf, horseback riding. Television, VCR lounge.

Mountain Home Lodge was an unexpected discovery while traveling through central Washington—and one of the most memorable. This outstanding full-service country inn in the Wanatchee Valley (apple country) combines the luxury facilities of a resort with the intimate atmosphere of an inn.

Although it's only 3 miles above Leavenworth, getting there is an adventure. As the innkeeper warns you over the phone, it is on a "primitive gravel road" that winds up the mountain. When you emerge into the meadow surrounding the inn, you'll feel intrepidly off the beaten track. During winter, the inn's heated snowcat picks you up at the bottom of the road.

The contemporary cedar and redwood house with a broad deck surveys a ☞ spectacular Cascade Mountain setting. The greeting is a warm one. These innkeepers spare nothing in seeing that you feel at home and have any service that you require. One of them—usually Charlie—is always there.

The common-room decor suits the spacious mountain feeling, like the massive ☞ Attila the Hun–style sofas in sheepskin and burled redwood. Not the thing for your condo, but they look terrific flanking the stone fireplace. Carpeted bedrooms have fine tiled bathrooms (with an abundance of thick towels), colorful bed linens, and good reading lights.

The outdoor pool and hot tub (with fabulous views) are open Memorial Day to Labor Day. There is a 1,700-foot toboggan run and ☞ miles of cross-country ski trails, right from the back door. Since this is not a designated ski area, you can enjoy the quiet beauty in rare solitude.

In the late afternoon, I sat on the deck with other guests, sipping wine and watching the sun set over the Cascades. Hunger finally brought us inside to an Italian feast beginning with melon and finger-size pizza for hors d'oeuvres, then on to homemade ravioli *and* lasagna. We sat in one end of the living room looking out at the panorama of sunset and mountains. Soft music played, and deer grazed in the meadow below. The only flaw was the thought of having to leave.

How to get there: From Highway 2 just east of Leavenworth, turn south on Duncan Road (by the Duncan Orchard); it becomes Mountain Home Road. Follow to the inn.

Olive Metcalf

MacKaye Harbor Inn
Lopez Island, Washington
98261

Innkeepers: Rick and Terri Hickox
Address/Telephone: Route 1; (mailing address: P.O. Box 1940); (206) 468–2253
Rooms: 5; 1 with private bath on first floor, 4 share 2 baths.
Rates: $59 to $75, including full breakfast. Children over 9 welcome. No smoking.
Open: All year. Dinner served 6 to 9 P.M. May through October.
Facilities and local attractions: MacKaye Harbor is your front yard. Beachcombing, rowing, fishing, kayaking, windsurfing. Excellent bicycling.

This is a great getaway, beginning with the adventure going to an island always holds. The hourlong ferry trip from Anacortes to the San Juans stops first at Lopez Island. Depending on the weather, it can be a misty surrealistic glide through the islands when you can turn up your raincoat collar and feel mysterious, or a stunning, too-brief voyage of picture postcard scenes of the snowcapped Cascades, forested islands, and water.

A 12-mile drive to the other end of the island brings you to MacKaye Harbor and the inn, the only one on the island. The restored Victorian, unpretentious but comfortable, ☞ sits right on the beach. A lobby sitting room has an ever-ready pot of coffee, sofa and easy chairs, a television, magazines, chess, and other games. There are five pleasant bedrooms, including the Captain's Suite on the first floor with a fireplace and roll-out bed for a third guest.

An intimate (probably seats thirty-five) dining room runs across the front of the inn looking out at the harbor. Rick has experience as a chef at an Alaskan lodge, so the variety of seasonal fresh fish available is a natural for his skills. He usually has six or seven entrees, fresh oysters and clams in season, and always a good steak. Fresh is the all-important word—even desserts and bread are homemade. In the words of one of the staff, "Nothing is hung over here!" There is a selection of wine and beer and a dinner price range between $10 and $14. Sound good? It is.

Across the road is the beach, ☞ a quiet, clean stretch of sand and rock, fun to play on or to simply sit and watch the activity all around—otters, seals, eagles, and deer. If you like, you can help yourself to an old 12-foot rowboat. The harbor is an especially good spot for windsurfing and kayaking.

Think about having a picnic lunch prepared and going exploring. A must is a walk to Agate Beach, where you can watch the activity around the boat docks and the salmon fleets, July through September. Lopez is a low-key kind of island, not chic, no quaint streets of boutiques, no tarted-up storefronts. It's about 17 miles from end to end and 7 miles at its widest, with a tiny village, a few shops, and a museum. If you spot a delicatessen called Gail's, stop in. It has a fresh perky atmosphere and food to match.

The island is a ☞ bicycling heaven. Even if you haven't ridden for years, you won't have any difficulties managing these flat roads and lanes. When I was there in late April, few people were around, but the tulips and azaleas were blooming in profusion.

How to get there: Leave the ferry and proceed south on Center Road about 10 miles to a T in the road. Turn left on Mud Bay Road to the fire station. If you pass a service station, you've gone too far. Turn right on MacKaye Harbor Road; proceed to the inn on your left.

Olive Metcalf

Orcas Hotel
Orcas Island, Washington
98280

Innkeepers: Barbara and John Jamieson

Address/Telephone: Orcas Ferry Landing (mailing address: Box 155); (206) 376–4300

Rooms: 12; 3 third-floor rooms have private toilets and sink and share showers, 9 rooms share baths.

Rates: $48 to $65 October through May 15; $48 to $75 May 16 through September; $10 less for single; $10 for rollaway; $7 for crib. Rates include continental breakfast. No pets.

Open: All year. Dining room open every day from 5:30 A.M., breakfast, lunch, dinner. Full bar.

Facilities and local attractions: All water sports including kayaking. Boat charters. Tours to Yellow Islands and outer islands, picnics arranged. Bicycle, moped rentals. Golfing, horseback riding, hiking trails. Moran State Park, Mt. Constitution. Parlor available for private parties, small seminars. Babysitters reserved.

When you leave the Orcas Island ferry and gaze up at the ornate white hotel perched on a rocky knoll, you're going to be awfully pleased if you have reservations. It is quite captivating. The three-story Victorian with flowers lining the steps up to the long front veranda looks the very 🐦 picture of a quaint old inn, which it is.

Built between 1900 and 1904, the Orcas Hotel has the requisite checkered past to legitimately be called "colorful." It is on the National Register of Historic Places and was extensively restored in 1985.

It was lunchtime when I went through the handsome front doors with their brass hardware and hand-painted glass panels. There was a cheerful buzz emanating from the cocktail lounge, and a steady parade of customers passed through the parlor to the dining room. The old-fashioned Victorian parlor is pretty, but some ☞ wonderful photographs of Orcas almost a hundred years ago and the hotel with the original owners were what made me linger.

It's a country, seaside atmosphere in the dining room. There is a big rock fireplace, and you have a view of the harbor from one side of the room. Some of the kitchen's recipes date from the early days of the hotel, but the beautiful salads and entrees I saw came from a thoroughly modern kitchen. Fresh fish from the island's waters are a specialty, of course.

The feeling in the twelve bedrooms is Victorian. There are antiques, new queen-sized beds with quilts custom-stitched by Orcas quilters, and wonderful water views of Harney Channel, Shaw Island, and Blind Bay with its sentinel rocks.

Orcas Island's 56 square miles and 125 miles of coastline are enormously popular with hikers, boaters, and nature lovers. Lots of Northwest families have been coming here for summer vacations for generations. If at all possible, avoid your discovery trip during the peak of summer. Spring and fall are lovely times here with sprays of colors and a slower pace. If you're a writer, misanthrope, Greta Garbo, or just hiding out, the winter months will give you a blue-and-green landscape, soft rains with an occasional drencher, and plenty of quiet.

How to get there: From Anacortes, take the San Juan Islands ferry to Orcas Island. You may leave your car in the ferry parking lot at Anacortes and buy a "walk-on" ticket if you don't want to bring your car with you. The inn is directly above the ferry landing. Fly-in: Eastsound Airport. Boat moorage free for Orcas Hotel guests.

olive Metcalf

Outlook Inn
Orcas Island, Washington
98245

Innkeeper: Bill Myer
Address/Telephone: P. O. Box 210, Eastsound; (206) 376–2581
Rooms: 29; 11 with private bath, 18 with sink in room share full baths and
   showers. Some televisions.
Rates: $35 single to $72, double occupancy. No meals included. No pets.
Open: All year. Breakfast, lunch, dinner; wine and beer bar.
Facilities and local attractions: Hiking, biking; fishing charters arranged.
   Small beach across street. Walk to shops, Eastsound Museum.

A glassed-in dining room facing the sound runs across the
front of the Outlook Inn. Over hot oatmeal one September
morning, I was looking at the mist still hanging over the water and
the fir trees beyond, when suddenly a salmon leaped up out of the
sound, arched, and returned to the water.

That kind of heart-stopping moment is more than sufficient
reason for going to poky, old island towns like Eastsound. There's
also a log cabin museum of Orcas Island's history, some shops
with handcrafts, a few restaurants, and miles of beach to walk and
explore.

The gray-shingled inn built in the 1800s is one of the oldest
buildings on the island. You'll find simple, comfortable rooms at

reasonable prices that ramble upstairs and down in the original building. They're small but clean and cheerful. A new wing has larger rooms with bay windows and fine views of the sound from upstairs.

Downstairs is a wine bar (the painting of the white cat from the movie *Five Easy Pieces* hangs over it) and a pleasant dining room serving three meals a day. There's no pretense of chic cuisine, but it is good, hearty fare. If you like fresh fish, you're in luck—it's the specialty. The salmon was beautiful during my visit. Homemade soups and the 🖝 dark, grainy bread made daily are particularly good.

The Outlook celebrates Christmas in a big way, and the staff spends weeks decorating with a theme, like flowers or teddy bears. Most of the tourists on the island are gone, and old friends, and often performers from Seattle, gather to celebrate the season and entertain one another.

The Outlook is operated by members of a philosophic service group, the Louis Foundation, named for a Western mystic, Louis Gittner, who is sometimes there. His message seems to be the importance of devotion to others as well as ourselves, and "if you can't share it . . . throw it away, it isn't worth keeping." Nothing terribly threatening there. At any rate, the organization never intrudes itself on guests.

How to get there: From Anacortes, take ferry to Orcas Island. From the landing, continue on main road 8 miles, following signs to Eastsound. Inn is on your left as you enter town.

J: *Eastsound is a wonderful 🖝 biking town—not too hilly, not much traffic, only an occasional pickup truck to dodge on the main street.*

Ollive Metcalf

Turtleback Farm
Orcas Island, Washington
98245

Innkeepers: Bill and Susan Fletcher
Address/Telephone: Crow Valley Road, Route 1 (mailing address: Box 650, Eastsound); (206) 376–4914
Rooms: 7; all with private bath, queen-sized or twin beds, and individual heat control.
Rates: $50 to $90; $55 to $95 June 15 through September 15. Rate includes full breakfast. No smoking; no pets. Children by special arrangement only.
Open: All year.
Facilities and local attractions: Explore the farm; pond stocked with trout. Hiking trails in Moran State Park. Bicycle, moped rentals. Swim, picnic at Lake Cascade. Fishing, kayaking, sailing available. Good restaurants.

Set back from a country road, Turtleback Farm looks like an attractive, well-kept old farmhouse, a big green two-story clapboard building. But it's been featured in numerous articles, and, despite a remote location, it is usually booked months in advance. This may well be 🐢 the gem lodging of Orcas Island.

The reasons are clear once you settle in. This is a first-rate, impeccably maintained inn. It delivers the quiet country charm that so captivates inngoers but with all the comforts you could ask for.

The inn was actually an abandoned hay barn and built new from the ground up. Now there are seven guest rooms, a parlor, dining room, and a tree-shaded deck that runs the length of the house. This is a wonderful place to sit on a warm day and enjoy looking out at acres of meadow with mountains beyond. We're talking ☞ idyllic, tranquil setting.

Even if the weather turns dismal, the comforts of this house will keep you charmed. The decor is tasteful and nonfussy, with muted colors and mellow wood walls, floors and open-bean ceilings. Each guest room has a modern bath appointed with antique fixtures, claw-footed tubs, pull-chain toilets, and wall showers. The pedestal sinks came from the Empress Hotel in Victoria. There's a cozy parlor where you can curl up and read before a fire. (The custom here is, "If you find a book you can't put down, take it with you and just return it when you finish.")

The dining room is still another place to enjoy the view and have a cup of tea or a glass of sherry. An outstanding breakfast is served here, course by course at individual tables on bone china. The menus change, but a typical morning would see juices, local berries, granola, an omelet with ham, and English muffin. Seconds are always offered.

What do you do on an eighty-acre farm if you're fresh from the city? If you're smart, you settle yourself on the deck with a blade of grass between your teeth, a big hat tipped down over your nose, and think things over—very, very slowly. Then there are the exhausting demands of critter watchin'. There are ducks and blue heron, sheep, chickens, a rambunctious brown ram named Oscar, and visiting Canada geese. You're welcome to fish the large pond by the main house—it's stocked with trout. If you're a picnic fan, the paths leading to private little spots will be irresistible. The Fletchers make every effort to acquaint you with all that the island offers. They'll make arrangements for you to charter a boat, rent a moped, play golf, or whatever sounds good to you.

How to get there: From Orcas Island ferry landing proceed straight ahead on Horseshoe Highway to first left turn; follow to Crow Valley Road. Turn right and continue to the inn, 6 miles from ferry landing. Fly-in: Eastsound Airport.

Olive Metcalf

Arcadia Country Inn
Port Townsend, Washington
98368

Innkeeper: Michael Neubauer; owners, The Flying Karamazov Brothers
Address/Telephone: 1891 South Jacob Miller Road; (206) 385–5245
Rooms: 5; all with private bath.
Rates: $44.50 summer mid-week; $50 to $70 weekends; lower winter
   rates. Generous continental breakfast included. Discounts for stays
   more than five days and for groups. Children welcome.
Open: All year.
Facilities and local attractions: Hot tub. On ☞ route of Port Townsend
   Marathon and bicycle-racing teams; pasture is site of Jefferson
   County Air Show ultralight airplane races. Tour town's Victorian
   homes, antique shops, Fort Worden State Park. Close to clam
   digging, scuba diving, sailing on Straits of Juan De Fuca and Puget
   Sound. Many summer music festivals. Wedding and meeting facili-
   ties.

What a shame people don't survive a wild youth looking as
good as the Arcadia Inn does. Nestled in a pastoral setting of
seventy acres of thick forest and meadows, the 1908 red-brick
house reveals nothing of its rowdy past. Quite the contrary. You
have to smile at its wholesome appeal as you wind down the
driveway and catch sight of the bright flower beds, the big swing
on the front porch, and the flagpole waving Old Glory.

During Prohibition, the city fathers, having vowed to rid the city of prostitution, decided that since Arcadia was already the local "speakeasy," why not make it the centralized location for vice. They made Arcadia an offer it couldn't refuse: In exchange for the public-service gesture of providing a home for the working girls, the city agreed to provide them a 2-mile-long private water line from the city water system. What could be neater? The town was made pure, and the inn had all the water it needed.

An occasional federal raid kept business from being completely peaceful, and "The Untouchables" eventually destroyed the still in the biggest law enforcement raid ever held on the Olympic Peninsula. So much for creative politics.

Since its renovation, the big house in its idyllic country setting is the essence of gentility and comfort A 40-foot living room has a beamed ceiling, easy seating before a fireplace, and an 1890s upright piano. One bedroom is on the first floor, and a stairway leads upstairs to the others. They're spacious, antique-filled rooms with views from all of them—rolling meadows, forests, and the Olympic Mountains. Guests breakfast together at a 10-foot-long table in the dining room where an all-you-can-eat continental breakfast is set out—many fresh fruits, a variety of muffins and breads, coffee, and teas.

The surrounding land is a country paradise. Besides all the meadow to run free in, there's an outfitted children's play yard. Trails through the woods lead to a stocked pond where you can take a dip or give someone a first fishing lesson in catch and release. A campfire area appeals to faint-hearted wood nymphs (like *moi*) who love the fire and songs but appreciate clean sheets and a private bath back at the inn.

How to get there: From downtown Port Townsend, follow the main street (Highway 20) south out of town to South Jacob Miller Road, 100 feet north of Johnson's Rentals. Turn right; continue to inn on the right.

※

J: *Nearby is a place to watch a dying skill—a school teaching some of the last wooden-boat building in the country. Visitors are welcome.*

olive Metcalf

James House
Port Townsend, Washington
98368

Innkeepers: Lowell and Barbara Bogart
Address/Telephone: 1238 Washington Street; (206) 385–1238
Rooms: 12; 4 with private bath, 8 share 4 baths.
Rates: $42 single, to $95 for Garden Suite sleeping 4. Continental
breakfast included. Children welcome in the Cottage and Garden
suite.
Open: All year.
Facilities and local attractions: Walk to downtown Port Townsend water-
front attractions, shopping, restaurants; tour Victorian homes. Mu-
seum in City Hall. Convenient base for touring Olympic Peninsula.

Francis Wilcox James was a man who evidently believed in
thinking big. During the 1890s, when a fine, large house could
easily be built for $4,000, he spent $10,000 building James House
for his retirement. The parquet floors are made of oak, walnut, and
cherry woods. The newel posts, spindles, and banisters are fash-
ioned from native wild cherry from Virginia. James had the logs
brought around Cape Horn, and the carving was done in the
house.

Well, why not? He was probably the richest man in Port
Townsend. In an 1890 *City Directory*, he lists himself simply as

"Capitalist." What a solid, reliable ring it has. Why didn't I major in that at college?

His splendid Queen Anne extravaganza sits on a bluff above the town's waterfront and business district. It's now on the National Register of Historic Places and is one of the town's premier inns—the first bed and breakfast in the northwest.

Most of the twelve spacious guest rooms are furnished with massive antique furniture—the kinds of pieces that look right only in huge, high-ceilinged rooms like these. The Gardener's Cottage and Garden suite have some fine wicker pieces. These rooms will sleep three and four people.

☞ The Bridal Suite is the most luxurious of the accommodations. It has parquet flooring, a small, elaborate, mirrored fireplace, a balcony, and an anteroom with a Victorian, cranberry-red fainting couch. The enormous antique bed is perfectly at home here. A wicker settee, coffee table, and rocker sit in a four-window bay looking out at Port Townsend's waterfront and the mountains, snow-capped most of the year.

On the main floor are two elegant parlors with fireplaces and a formal dining room. A continental breakfast, featuring Barbara's ☞ homemade scones and muffins, is served in the dining room and around the oak kitchen table next to the wood cookstove.

How to get there: Three ferries serve the area: from Mukilteo to Clinton; from Seattle to Winslow; from Edmonds to Kingston. The latter two both lead to Hood Canal Bridge. Proceed to junction with Highway 20; follow to Port Townsend. After the first stoplight, take Washington Street off to the left, past the Port Townsend Motel. Inn is at top of the hill on the left next to the post office.

J: *Summer visitors to the peninsula are often frustrated by the complexities of the ferries and the long lines to get on them. Summer travelers are well advised to take the ferry routes that allow* advance *reservations rather than just line up. Washington State Ferry information (within Washington only): 1–800–542–6400 (outside Washington, 206–464–6400).*

Olive Metcalf

Old Consulate Inn
Port Townsend, Washington
98368

Innkeepers: Joanne and Rob Jackson
Address/Telephone: 313 Walker Street; (206) 385–3553
Rooms: 7, including tower suite with private bath; private half-baths; shared showers; shared baths.
Rates: $45 to $75, including full breakfast; reduced rate from November to February. No pets; no smoking.
Open: All year.
Facilities and local attractions: Television available. Walk to town, ferry, marina, restaurants. Tennis courts across street; tour Victorian homes of Port Townsend.

Things have changed at the Old Consulate, starting with its name. You might have known this Queen Anne inn as Hastings House, but the story now is new owners, new construction, new decor, and a new atmosphere.

In a town of fine Victorians, this one is a premier survivor. Like all the really big houses in Port Townsend, it sits on a bluff high above the town with ☞ commanding views of water and mountains. Frank Hastings, the son of the town's founder, built it in 1889. The Jacksons believe that this was the first house in Port Townsend to have electricity. It was once a consulate, which is how its new name came about.

390

Some of the mansion's outstanding features are a front parlor with its original chandelier, formed in the shape of big, green bunches of grapes, and a fireplace framed with Italian tile that was ordered in a kit. It must have been one of the first. ☞ Newel posts on the stairway are quite remarkable: an iron nymph on the main floor, and upstairs a Tiffany design. Even the hinges on some of the doors are intricate pieces of art. A handsomely designed new stairway is well worth a trip to the third floor just for the view looking down.

Every bedroom is decorated with fresh, light fabrics and colors that contrast with the Jacksons' collections of antique dishes, dolls, and furniture. Unless you make reservations well ahead, you'll miss the Tower Room, but do take a look, at least. There's a padded, circular window seat in the tower, and, of course, the view of the harbor is splendid.

Joanne has opened a study on the main floor that will ease the frustrations of the many men who are talked into a Victorian B&B by their wives and can't find a single spot to relax and be comfortable. It has big overstuffed sofas, a television, and magazines. At my visit, Rob had almost completed a garden-level billiard and reading room.

Guests gather in the ornate dining room for breakfast, family style. Joanne does all her own baking. She's the kind of open-handed innkeeper that always keeps snacks around. There's never a "keep out" sign on this kitchen. The coffeepot is always on, and you help yourself. The Jackson motto is, "Your room is just a bedroom; the house is yours to enjoy."

How to get there: Driving into Port Townsend on Highway 20, take Washington Street exit to the left, just past signs for Worden State Park. Inn is at top of hill on the left corner.

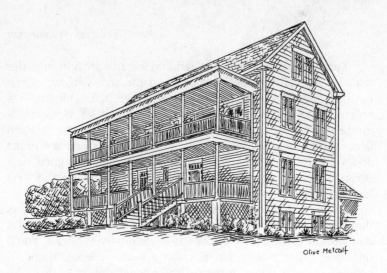

Olive Metcalf

Ravenscroft Inn
Port Townsend, Washington
98368

Innkeepers: Jack and Margaret Queen
Address/Telephone: 533 Quincy Street; (206) 385–2784
Rooms: 5; all with private bath, 1 with fireplace.
Rates: $63 to $78 including full breakfast. Children over 12 welcome. No
  smoking; no pets.
Open: All year.
Facilities and local attractions: Beautiful water views from a handsome
  house. Walk to many historical homes. Walk to waterfront, shops,
  galleries, restaurants.

A refreshing alternative to Victorian lodgings is now available
for visitors to Port Townsend. Ravenscroft Inn has elegant, contemporary comforts in a ☞ classic historical design that blends
gracefully into a neighborhood of nineteenth-century houses.

The Queens are long-time fans of colonial houses and researched plans carefully before choosing this design called a
Charleston Single. Their two-story house is authentically placed
on the lot as colonial houses were, facing the water. An ☞
upstairs deck (strictly speaking, a piazza) runs the length of the
house and offers wonderful views of the Olympic Mountains and
Mt. Baker. You can watch the waterfront activity, fóllow the Puget

Sound shipping lanes, and see the big white ferries gliding in and out.

When most people talk about a house they've built, they usually mean they *had* it built, or maybe did a little finishing work. But in the Northwest, I met people who meant it literally. "I've always loved homes," says Jack Queen, and he had plenty of experience building with the Army Corps of Engineers. But still, it gives you pause to walk through this splendid house and absorb the fact that he and Margaret actually built it all themselves.

The house has unusually large common rooms with beamed ceilings and an elegant open (and huge) kitchen. The white and colonial blue—maybe it's dapple gray—interior is uncluttered and light filled. In the sitting room a red oriental rug looks smart on gray carpeting. I was taken with a striking study with red walls on the main floor.

Five spacious guest rooms upstairs are well decorated with choice fabrics, queen-sized beds (one room for a family has a king-sized and twins) and wingback chairs. Three rooms have French doors opening to the piazza. If you're tired of inns with "authentic" bathrooms, these modern tile ones will look especially welcome.

Margaret is a gourmet cook, but as of this writing, you'll get to enjoy only her breakfasts. She bakes all the breads and has a repertoire of hot entrees. The coffee is ground fresh, of course.

Innkeeping is the latest in a number of fulfilling careers for the Queens. Jack says, "I've done a lot of things, and now I'm in search of a little excellence." Sounds like an innkeeper on the right track to me.

How to get there: Proceed along the waterfront to the end of Water Street at City Hall. Turn left up Monroe Street 2 blocks to Clay; turn left. Continue 2 blocks to Quincy Street. Inn is on the left.

J: *A colonial house going up in this town of Victorians was quite a curiosity. The Queens broke the ice by hanging a sign by the street reading, "Tours—5¢"*

Manor Farm Inn
Poulsbo, Washington
98370

Innkeepers: Jill and Robin Hughes
Address/Telephone: 26069 Big Valley Road N.E.; (206) 779–4628
Rooms: 6; all with private bath.
Rates: $65 to $140 (subject to change), including full breakfast, afternoon
   aperitifs. Not convenient for children or pets; no smoking.
Open: All year. Dinner by reservation.
Facilities and local attractions: Hot tub, fishing pond; walking the country-
   side.

Track down Poulsbo, Washington, on a map and you might
well wonder, "Why would I ever go to the interior of the Kitsap
Peninsula?" Don't say I didn't alert you. Here is merely everything
a country inn ought to be: a 🐾 tranquil, pastoral atmosphere,
completely insulated with fine decor and superior food and drink.

Jill and Robin Hughes are the young couple who have shaped
a clapboard turn-of-the-century farmhouse into a French-style
country inn. Robin is English and has skills as an architect,
horticulturist, environmentalist, farmer, veterinarian, and gourmet
chef. He and Jill exude enthusiasm for their 🐾 individual outlook
on innkeeping—a "hands-on environment" where people can
touch and experience country life while enjoying all the civilized

comforts. Dairy cows and sheep graze in the soft rolling country-side; there is Jacques the yak, exotic fowl, and even a pond stocked with clever trout to test your fishing skill.

The six luxurious bedrooms are painted white, with high, peaked ceilings and exposed supporting timbers. ☞ French country antiques—massive pine armoires, mellow pine writing desks—inviting beds with puffy eiderdowns, and a feeling of clean space are first impressions. Each room's welcoming extras include instant hot water for coffee or tea, homemade chocolates, fruit breads, and ☞ huge baskets of fresh flowers.

A morning knock on your door delivers fresh juice, hot scones, and jam, all to fuel you for the walk down the covered veranda to the dining room for a full breakfast. ☞ Dinner is a gourmet event, and Robin is head chef. First you join other guests in the drawing room for hot canapés and imported sherry. (It's a lovely room with raspberry-colored sofas and wingback chairs by a fireplace.) You're escorted to the dining room for a leisurely meal on snow-white linen with fresh flowers. A typical menu might include hot sole mousse, green salad with fresh fennel, poached oysters, scallops, shrimp in truffle sauce, rosemary roasted chicken, fettuccine with walnuts, a choice of sinful desserts (Jill's specialty), imported cheeses, fruit, port, and coffee in the drawing room.

How to get there: From Seattle, take Winslow Ferry; proceed on Highway 305 (about 10 miles) to Bond Road, and turn right. Go to Big Valley Road; turn left, and continue 4½ miles to inn on the left.

Olive Metcalf

Lake Quinault Lodge
Quinault, Washington
98575

Innkeeper: Rich Harrison, manager
Address/Telephone: South Shore Road (mailing address: Box 7); (206) 288–2571
Rooms: 56, including suites and fireplace cabins; 8 lakeside rooms have private bath, main lodge rooms have 1 bath between 2 units.
Rates: $68 to $85; special mid-week packages; EP. Children welcome; pets okay.
Open: All year. Breakfast, lunch, dinner, full bar.
Facilities and local attractions: Indoor swimming pool, Jacuzzi, saunas, exercise room, pool tables. Boating, fishing, hiking. Gift shop.

The Olympic Peninsula has a powerful attraction for nature lovers— 🖝 mysterious rain forests, towering stands of cedar and firs, rugged shores, peaceful beaches, and deep blue Lake Quinault.

The Lodge, situated on the lake shore, has spectacular views and a variety of accommodations. Add a good dining room (specializing in fresh local fish), a cocktail lounge, and 🖝 excellent indoor recreation facilities. You will be snug and well entertained here, even when the not-infrequent rains (this *is* a rain forest) might dampen your enthusiasm for the outdoors.

The imposing lodge was built in 1926 in the staggeringly short time of ten weeks. Lumber, brick, glass, and plumbing fixtures were hauled over fifty miles of dirt road, and craftsmen from all over the Northwest came to work on it. The large, rustic lobby and its fireplace are the heart of the lodge. It's filled with original wicker settees and chairs, Indian objects, and art of the Northwest, such as the stenciled designs on the beamed ceilings. There are cozy corners for reading, chess and checkers, and for electronic game tables.

Downstairs are a swimming pool, sauna, Jacuzzis, and a recreation room with pool and Ping-Pong tables. Outdoors, all the water sports are available. Some of the ☞ finest steelhead fishing in the world is found between Quinault and the Hoh River.

Bedrooms range from simple and rustic to modern suites with gas fireplace. The decor is not designer league, but the rooms are comfortable and clean.

But the real story here is the ☞ beautiful sight of Lake Quinault surrounded with timbered hills. Everything at the lodge is poised to enjoy the view: The broad deck and lawn behind the lobby, the dining room and lounge, even the downstairs recreation room, all look out at the lake.

How to get there: From Highway 101, 40 miles north of Aberdeen-Hoquiam, take Lake Quinault South Shore Recreation Area exit. Follow road 2 miles to the lodge.

❋

J: *Driving through the Olympic National Forest, not another car in sight, I passed a cluster of six buildings, preceded by a State Highway sign reading, SLOW, CONGESTED AREA; 45 MPH. I call that wooded tranquility.*

Clive Metcalf

San Juan Inn
San Juan Island, Washington
98250-0776

Innkeepers: Joan and Norm Schwinge
Address/Telephone: Friday Harbor (mailing address: P.O. Box 776); (206) 378–2070
Rooms: 10 share 3 baths.
Rates: $55.90 single, to $75.25 (tax included) for 4 people, summer rates. Rollaway beds available. Lower winter rates. Continental breakfast included.
Open: All year.
Facilities and local attractions: Walk to ferry landing; bike and moped rentals; Friday Harbor shops, restaurants. Explore American Camp, English Camp. Whale Museum.

San Juan Island is the second largest in this cluster of 172 islands. Still, it's a rather unlikely place to have once been considered an international tinderbox. The "Pig War" of 1859 is now part of the romantic history of the islands, but at the time it was a full-fledged confrontation between Great Britain and the United States. It started when an American potato farmer shot a pig running through his potato patch. The unfortunate pig belonged to an Englishman, and the incident was the spark that ignited the long-simmering dispute between the two nations. The

United States actually had cannons poised, and the British had five warships ready for action when an agreement was reached that eventually made San Juan an American possession.

Historic buildings of both the American and English camps survive, with exhibits and picnic areas. Both historic sites are within easy bicycling distance from the San Juan Inn, which also offers the more contemporary diversions of Friday Harbor's unique shops and restaurants.

The inn has been around since 1873, but the Schwinges have wisely rewired, replumbed, and restored it for comfort. (Mindful that a pig almost started a war, who knows what damage an obstreperous toilet might cause?)

As the inn is only a block from the waterfront, breakfast in the parlor is especially entertaining, with a view of the big white ferries pulling in and out of the harbor and dislodging hikers, bikers, and cars. Rigors of the morning watch are sustained with coffee and tea, juice, and hot blueberry and honey-bran muffins. This room is pleasant at night, too, with its old iron stove and big chairs from which to watch the harbor lights reflected in the water.

Bedrooms are named after local islands and ferries. They are small and clean, with a Victorian feeling in flowered wallpaper, and wicker headboards and chairs. Some rooms have brass beds and pine washstands. A few rooms have harbor or garden views.

A tiny brick patio garden—a cozy spot to sun and watch the ferries or perhaps read up on the Pig War—is adjacent to some interesting craft shops.

How to get there: From Anacortes, take the ferry to Friday Harbor. Inn is one-half block from landing on your right. Fly-in: Friday Harbor and Roche Harbor airstrips. Marine facilities.

❋

J: *This is not major information, but the calico cats used as doorstops are awfully cute.*

Ollue Metcalf

The Shelburne Inn
Seaview, Washington
98644

Innkeepers: David Campiche and Laurie Anderson
Address/Telephone: Pacific Highway (mailing address: Box 250); (206) 642–2442
Rooms: 16; 2 3-room suites share baths, all other rooms with private bath.
Rates: $67 for shared baths, $85 to $125 for private baths, $6 less for singles. Full breakfast included. Well-supervised children welcome.
Open: All year. Lunch, dinner, Sunday brunch, full bar.
Facilities and local attractions: Handicapped access to dining room and 2 guest rooms. Beach walks, walk to North Head Lighthouse, charter fishing, clamming. Visit historic Oysterville; drive "World's Longest Beach Drive."

Around the Shelburne breakfast table one recent morning, a poll of home towns revealed that all the guests except one were within 75 miles of home. Even people living close by come to stay here because the Shelburne is a rarity in southwest Washington—a Victorian inn with authentic period atmosphere *and* an excellent restaurant.

It was built in 1896 as a boarding house, and later joined to another building with a covered passageway. The present owners kept the original design in mind as they expanded and refurbished.

Their most outstanding addition is a treasure from Morcambe, England. Art Nouveau stained-glass windows dating from the late 1800s were rescued from an old church that was being demolished there. These floral-patterned beauties are now in the restaurant wing and pub, looking as though they've been there for the past one hundred years.

The wood-paneled common room is a cozy setting, with a stone fireplace, and with coffee, current magazines, and newspapers at hand. The innkeepers' country breakfast is served family style at a large table here. Fresh herbs from their garden flavor the egg entrees, the sausage is homemade, and pastries are freshly baked. Pretty civilized fare to find on this wild stretch of seacoast. A sun deck and the Blue Heron and Beaver Pub are recent additions.

The creaky-floored bedrooms are cheerful with fresh flowers, antique furniture, and bright quilts that set the color scheme. My fancy for "extras" was well satisfied when I was welcomed with a basket of Crabtree and Evelyn toiletries and a generous sampling of designer chocolates in my room.

The restaurant has many fresh fish specialties prepared with skill and sophistication. No batter-fried fish plates here. Salmon in season always heads the list of favorites, but the availability of fresh local oysters and mussels provides wonderful eating. My filet of rockfish was moist and sauced with capers, olives, and fresh tomatoes and accompanied by wild rice with raisins and nuts. The "house salad dressing" is a standout. It involves a sour cream base with Dijon mustard. Homemade desserts, an extensive wine list, and thoughtful service made for a thoroughly pleasant meal.

How to get there: From Seattle, take I–5 through Olympia to Highway 8, then to 101 South. Avoid major detours in Aberdeen by taking Highway 107 or Montesano cutoff before Aberdeen to meet Highway 101. Follow south to Seaview and flashing yellow light. Turn right onto Highway 103; the inn is five blocks ahead on the left.

*

J: *Don't think of leaving without a walk to the beach. It's a particularly secluded stretch.*

Olive Metcalf

The Moore House
South Cle Elum, Washington
98943

Innkeepers: Connie and Monty Moore
Address/Telephone: 526 Marie Avenue (mailing address: P.O. Box 2861);
  (509) 674–5939
Rooms: 10; 4 with private bath, 6 share 2 large compartmentalized baths.
Rates: $30 to $79, including full breakfast. Ask about family rates.
  Children welcome.
Open: All year.
Facilities and local attractions: Hot tub. Winter cross-country skiing from
  back door, sleigh rides. Paddock facilities. Summer trail rides, river
  rafting, floating, hiking, fishing, apple picking. Nearby old towns to
  explore. Facilities for weddings, small meetings. Special events as
  planned by innkeepers. Additional meals by pre-arrangement.

Connie and Monty Moore have salvaged a bit of 🚂 railroad
history in quiet little South Cle Elum. They've turned a 1913,
L-shaped building originally used as a crew house for the Chicago,
Milwaukee, St. Paul and Pacific Railroad into a homespun country
inn. It's an inn that will delight railroad buffs and give visitors a
taste of once-thriving railroad days.

What were thirty-two bare-essential rooms for a group of
rugged men have been turned into ten cheerful guest rooms, many

with brass beds, quilts, and antique wardrobes. Each one has a small brass plaque on the door bearing the name of one of the men who actually worked the Milwaukee and stayed at the crew house. Outside the two-story colonial-blue building are several working railroad breaker signals, and inside is a steadily growing collection of that era's memorabilia.

But the railroad theme goes beyond a mere decorating ploy. Both the Moores have researched that time period and their building. Connie has traced some of the men on the crews, some of whom became interested and involved in the restoration. Many have contributed ☞ wonderful photographs of their railroad days, now displayed on the inn's walls. The Moores also have letters, a conductor's uniform, even china from the dining car.

You'll find an unpretentious, relaxed atmosphere in the dining room and sitting area that opens through French doors to a deck and hot tub. It's a house furnished for casual comfort, conversation, and children. (The Moores have two young daughters.) There is an upright piano, games, books, and a large wooden train that younger children love to ride. While I visited, children played games on the big dining room table, enjoyed the hot tub, and downed platters of Monty's blueberry pancakes.

The Moores are a brainstorming duo of innkeeping ideas that always keep them busy. They host parties, meetings, covered-wagon trail rides, and have barbecues in the yard. Monty (I believe he could persuade Eskimos they need more snow) has instigated the nation's first Volksport-sanctioned, long-distance round walk, persuading twelve fellow innkeepers to participate by checking in participants and just incidentally, introducing walkers to some remote Washington inns. His mystery weekends sound like the funniest I've encountered, and there's a caboose sitting in the backyard just waiting to be turned into a private guest room . . . when he has some spare time.

How to get there: From Seattle on I–90, take first Cle Elum exit. Turn right at sign for South Cle Elum and follow the Moore House signs.

J: *Try a "why don'tcha" idea on Monty and watch him go. These innkeepers are always ready to spend time with their guests and are always ready for fun.*

Olive Metcalf

The Captain Whidbey Inn
Whidbey Island, Washington
98239

Innkeeper: John Colby Stone
Address/Telephone: 2072 West Captain Whidbey Road, Coupeville; (206)
   678–4097
Rooms: 30, including waterfront cottages and duplex; 13 rooms in main
   building share 2 baths, newer lagoon rooms with private bath.
Rates: $60 to $105, including continental breakfast. Children okay; pets in
   cottages only.
Open: All year. Breakfast, lunch, dinner, full bar.
Facilities and local attractions: Explore Coupeville, Victorian homes, mu-
   seum, waterfront shops, restaurants. Fort Casey State Park; Deception
   Pass. Near Keystone Ferry to Port Townsend. Boat rental. Golf and
   tennis nearby.

A funny thing happened to me at The Captain Whidbey. I
blame it on the gray, drizzling weather the day I discovered it. I
momentarily forgot that I'm a sunshine-loving, white wine–
quaffing, nouvelle cuisine–eating Californian, and I had an overwhelming urge to have double Old Fashioneds from the bar, toast
my toes at the stone fireplace, and order steak—rare—with fries!
In spite of Mr. Stone's dismay ("We don't have fries and haven't
for the twenty-five years my family has owned the inn!"), it *still*
feels like that kind of place to me.

The 🖝 ambience at this funky, offbeat inn has been marinating since 1907, when it was an ideal hideaway for guests from Seattle. On this dreary day, the wood-smoke smell from the fire, the creaky floors, and the warmth of the madrona log interior were cheering. The sense of being very remote, but in friendly hands, added to its charm.

The first floor of the inn is as it's always been: a comfortable sitting room and fireplace, with a cozy bar and dining room overlooking Penn Cove. The food reflects the Northwest abundance of fresh salmon, oysters, crab, and 🖝 Penn Cove mussels, as well as steaks.

Up the stairway at the large landing is a 🖝 library with such appealingly jammed shelves it almost forces you to browse. There are well-worn upholstered sofas and chairs to sink into, and funny old floor lamps. Continuing down the hall to the bedrooms will take some time. The walls are covered with family mementos—everything from John's father's grammar school diploma to his great-grandfather's naval uniform from the 1800s.

The thirteen bedrooms are small (or cozy, depending on how you look at these things), with low log ceilings and furnished with antiques. Some have sinks in the room, but everybody in this original building goes down the hall to use the bathrooms and showers. You can have private baths and fireplaces in the waterfront cottages. Newest accommodations are the twelve lagoon rooms with verandas and lovely views.

How to get there: From the Mukilteo Ferry landing at the south end of Whidbey Island, take Highway 525, to Highway 20, and go 3 miles past Coupeville. Look for sign on right for the inn; take next right (Madrona), and go approximately ¾ mile. From the north, cross Deception Pass Bridge, one of the most scenic spots in the Northwest.

J: *I confess a fervent bias for Coupeville. One of the oldest towns in the state . . . a waterfront setting . . . Victorian homes—it's enchanting.*

Olive Metcalf

Saratoga Inn
Whidbey Island, Washington
98260

Innkeepers: Debbie and Ted Jones
Address/Telephone: 4850 South Coles Road, Langley; (206) 221–7526
Rooms: 5; all with private bath.
Rates: $70 to $85, double occupancy, including generous continental
    breakfast. No children; no smoking; no pets.
Open: All year, except for 2 weeks over Christmas.
Facilities and local attractions: Croquet. Walk to Langley shops, restaurants,
    theater. Tennis. Beachcombing.

An inn has already won me over if it's a shingled, rambling
Cape Cod on an island, if it sits on a hill overlooking a sound, and
if it has a romantic English garden. Everything about the appearance of the Saratoga Inn, including the 🐾 views of meadows,
forests, the Saratoga Passage, and the Cascades, is captivating.

Debbie and Ted Jones bought twenty-five acres on the
southern portion of Whidbey Island and built this beauty of an inn
on the property in 1982. They made it traditional in style, but
spacious and open. Light floods in through the beveled-glass
windows onto gleaming woods and an enviable collection of
English antiques and beautiful objects.

The 🐾 common rooms are decorated in understated good

taste and are invitingly warm. There's a large fireplace, books, taped music, and a fine view past the patio and garden to the sound. Some of the ☞ Chippendale and Queen Anne pieces are outstanding, but there is also cushy comfortable furniture.

Each of the five bedrooms is distinct and is decorated so engagingly that I couldn't choose one over another. One has a cozy Franklin fireplace and a good spot for watching storms and ships; another has a white linen chaise, and another a bent-willow bed and rocker. Linens, pillow shams, comforters, and wallpapers are all of fine quality. Each room has a sitting area, ☞ good reading lights, and those extras so pleasant to find—English toiletries and freshly cut flowers.

Breakfast is as first-class as the surroundings. There are freshly ground coffee, teas, freshly squeezed orange juice, seasonal fresh fruit, and then homemade muffins or coffee cake and jams.

The integration of setting and gardens, house and decor gives a feeling of serenity—everything seems so right. You don't build and decorate a home as beautiful as this one without the skills of a lot of people, and the Joneses remember them in a graceful way. Framed and hanging in the entryway are the names of all those who contributed their work and talents.

How to get there: From Seattle, drive north to Whidbey Island-Mukilteo Ferry exit 189. Take 15-minute ferry ride to Clinton, Whidbey Island. Proceed on 525 south to Langley. Inn signs are on the right as you enter Langley city limits. Fly-in: South Whidbey's Porter Field.

J: ☞ *Langley's restaurants and shops are a delight to explore. Think of a mini-Sausalito . . . with elbow room.*

Olive Metcalf

Whidbey Inn
Whidbey Island, Washington
98260

Innkeepers: Shannon and Richard Francisco
Address/Telephone: 106 First Street (mailing address: Box 156), Langley;
  (206) 221–7115
Rooms: 3 rooms and 3 suites with fireplace; all with private bath.
Rates: $70 double occupancy. Continental breakfast included.
Open: All year.
Facilities and local attractions: Beachcombing, bicycling, hiking the island.
  Langley's shops and restaurants. Ferry to Seattle.

Here's a romantic, intimate waterfront inn on Whidbey
Island. Open a picket gate, walk down a few steps, and you come
to a freshly painted ☞ white deck hanging right over Puget
Sound. Stretching the entire length of the building, the sun deck
has lounge chairs, is decorated with colorful planter boxes spilling
over with flowers, and has an entrance to each room.

Quaint lodgings tucked into vine-covered small places are
terribly appealing, but once you're in them, it's especially winning
when they open up to give you elbow room. That's the case at
Whidbey Inn—cozy but not cramped, and ☞ very private. ☞
Dramatic views from the deck are a major attraction here: the
Saratoga Passage, Camano Island, and the North Cascade Mountains beyond.

I fell in love with Langley, the largest town on the island. It's an enchanting "village by the sea," as it bills itself. There are no traffic lights, but plenty of historic charm and good restaurants, and the inn is tucked into the very heart of the town. The village motif is somewhat turn-of-the-century Western. Antique shops, crafts, and homemade clothing were notches above the usual. The treasures in Silk Road, an attractive shop beside the inn, for a time easily managed to divert my attention away from the scenic beauty of the sound.

Back at the inn after walking Langley, your room is a tranquil retreat. Shannon has furnished them with just the kinds of country antiques, fabrics, and wall coverings that she'd choose for her own home. Provincial pastel linens, puffy comforters, clean, polished hardwood floors, and lots of fresh flowers give them a country French feeling.

A continental breakfast is brought to your room in a basket to enjoy there or out on the deck: freshly ground coffee or tea, fresh orange juice, and homemade muffins.

This is a quiet, romantic inn with the kind of special touches that persuade you to slow down and enjoy—a glass of sherry, scented bath gels and shampoo, fresh fruit, and chocolates on your pillow at night.

How to get there: From Seattle, go north to Whidbey Island-Mukilteo Ferry exit 189. Take 15-minute ferry ride to Clinton, Whidbey Island. Proceed on Highway 25 south to Langley. Inn is on the water side at the town's center.

❧

J: *Overnight or temporary boat moorage is available one block away at the Langley Marina.*

olive Metcalf

Inn of the White Salmon
White Salmon, Washington
98672

Innkeepers: Bill and Loretta Hopper
Address/Telephone: 172 Jewett (mailing address: Box 1446); (509) 493–2335
Rooms: 20; all with private bath, television, telephone.
Rates: $68 to $98, including enormous full breakfast. No children under 10.
Open: All year.
Facilities and local attractions: Hot tub. Columbia Gorge fishing, hiking, rafting. Maryhill Museum; skiing at Mount Hood.

About Loretta's now-famous country breakfast, my heartfelt advice is to pace yourself. One guest, rationalizing his third trip to the sweet-laden buffet table, kept insisting that it was very European: "Why it's common practice there to have desserts before a meal and afterwards too!" I simply faced the fact squarely that I was taking ten years off the useful life of my arteries and took comfort in dispatching them happily.

European or just good Ohio cook, Loretta's ☞ display of *forty or more* freshly baked pastries is stunning. It is heavenly fare like Pears Frangipane (wine-poached pears in an almond crust with custard), strudels, fruit tarts, tortes, breads, and buttery morsels like Hungarian "Love Letters." I assumed I was looking at breakfast when I saw the astonishing table that morning along with its array of fresh fruit, but *noooooo*.

Loretta or one of her helpers, in lace blouse and long skirt, pours coffee from silver pots into china cups and recites an extraordinary choice of hot dishes. Many have an ethnic flair: Chili Rellenos, Hungarian sausages, several quiches, artichoke frittata, and more. I saw no other sensible course but to spend the morning there eating and chatting with Loretta and Bill. After all, it *was* raining outside.

Although their building's exterior is undistinguished, the Hoppers have added a public view point in front of the inn overlooking the National Scenic Area of the Columbia Gorge with a full view of Mt. Hood. Through the beveled-glass doorway is an attractive lobby. The bedrooms have a Victorian look with brass beds and antique dressers. Some of the second-floor rooms have ☞ good views of the Columbia River and Mount Hood.

Bill is a former airline pilot. He sometimes tells Loretta that the work involved in her breakfast "experience" is getting out of hand. But she compares it to his landing a plane and putting the center wheel down on the line precisely. "That breakfast," she says "is my center line. I want it to be perfect."

How to get there: Follow I–84 east from Portland to Hood River; exit to 64 North. Cross Columbia River; follow 141 to White Salmon; continue through town. Inn is last large building on the right.

❋

J: *Don't miss a little-known museum a few miles away at Maryhill. Can you believe that it houses Queen Marie of Romania's throne and coronation robes and a collection of Rodin, and that there is a replica of Stonehenge nearby? It's all here, above the mighty Columbia.*

Indexes

Alphabetical Index to Inns

Inns with Restaurants or That Serve Dinner by Special Arrangement

Romantic Inns and Wedding Sites

Especially Elegant Inns

Rustic and Rural Inns

Architectural Treasures

Inns with Historic or Colorful Pasts

Inns with Fabulous Views

Inns Near Water

Inns with Swimming Pools

Inns with Skiing Nearby

Outstanding Inns for Fishing

Mountain Retreats

Lively Inns

Peaceful, Quiet Inns

City Inns

Children Welcome

Inns with Small Conference Facilities

Handicap Accessible

About Reservation Services

Most innkeepers in an area network with one another. If their inn is full, they're usually happy to refer prospective guests to other available accommodations. In addition, the following non-fee agencies give referrals and will make reservations for you.

Bed and Breakfast International
1181-B Solano Avenue
Albany, CA 94706
(415) 525–4569

Napa Valley's Finest Lodging
1834 First Street
Napa, CA 94559
(707) 257–1051

American Family Inn/Bed and Breakfast San Francisco
P. O. Box 349
San Francisco, CA 94101
(415) 931–3083

Seattle Bed and Breakfast Inn Association
Box 95835
Seattle, WA 98145
(206) 547–1020

Bed & Breakfast of Los Angeles
32074 Waterside Lane
Westlake Village, CA 91361
(818) 889–8870 or 888–7325

About the Author

Juilanne Belote claims she writes about country inns because it gets her out of the house and because she loves breakfasts that someone else fixes. A love affair with the West Coast and a husband's penchant for back roads began her discovery of inns more than twenty years ago, when there were few such havens. Now she drives to hundreds from the Mexican border to the San Juan Islands.

Her reviewing standards are subjective and firmly flexible. She's in favor of good beds, crisp sheets, reading lights, and freshly ground coffee beans but admits to being beguiled by innkeepers who may fall short here and there but lavish guests with warm hospitality. Solid comfort and a bit of charm are what she's tracking; and given her usual strategy of arriving at an innkeeper's doorstep without advance notice, she says it's easy to see how deep the charm goes.

Julianne has written three other books, including one about Colonial housewives, and she writes frequent magazine articles —when not getting her own breakfast.